THE ENVIRONMENTAL KNOWLEDGE COMMONS

Our natural environment constitutes a complex and dynamic global ecosystem that provides essential resources for well-being and survival. Yet the environment is also subject to unprecedented threats from human activities, such as climate change, pollution, habitat loss, biodiversity decline, and the overexploitation of natural resources. This volume argues that such complex, multidimensional challenges demand equally complex, multidimensional solutions and calls for coordinated multistakeholder action at all scales, including governments, civil society, the private sector, and individuals. To meet the moment effectively, such interventions require both scientific knowledge about how the environment functions and social and institutional knowledge about the actors involved in environmental governance and management. Chapters include case studies of environmental knowledge collection, management, and sharing to explore how data and knowledge sharing can inform effective multistakeholder action to combat global threats to our environment. This title is also available as Open Access on Cambridge Core.

Anjanette (Angie) Raymond is Director of the Program on Data Management and Information Governance at the Ostrom Workshop, a professor in the Department of Business Law and Ethics at the Kelley School of Business, Indiana University, and an adjunct professor of law at Maurer Law School (Indiana). She has written widely in the areas of online dispute resolution, data governance, artificial intelligence governance, privacy, international finance, and commercial dispute resolution.

Scott J. Shackelford serves on the faculty of Indiana University where he is Cybersecurity Program Chair along with being Executive Director of the Ostrom Workshop. He is also an affiliated scholar at both the Harvard Kennedy School's Belfer Center for Science and International Affairs and Stanford's Center for Internet and Society, as well as a senior fellow at the Center for Applied Cybersecurity Research. His previous books include *The Internet of Things: What Everyone Needs to Know* (2020), *Governing New Frontiers in the Information Age: Toward Cyber Peace* (2020), and *Managing Cyber Attacks in International Law, Business, and Relations: In Search of Cyber Peace* (2014).

Jessica Steinberg is Director of the Program on Environment and Natural Resource Governance at the Ostrom Workshop, Associate Professor and Chair in the Department of International Studies at the Hamilton Lugar School of Global and International Studies, Indiana University, and an adjunct professor of political science. Her research focuses on the political economy of development, local politics of natural resource extraction, information politics, and violent conflict. Her first book, *Mines, Communities, and States: The Local Politics of Natural Resource Extraction in Africa* (2019), was awarded the 2020 Sprout Award for the best book in environmental politics by the International Studies Association.

Michael Mattioli is a former Sun Microsystems microchip designer turned award-winning professor of law at the Maurer School of Law, Indiana University. Mattioli's scholarship on law and technology has been published in leading law reviews. He is also the co-editor of *Big Data Is Not a Monolith* (2016).

CAMBRIDGE STUDIES ON GOVERNING KNOWLEDGE COMMONS

The mission of the series is to provide an authoritative space for high quality scholarship on the governance of knowledge commons. Following the path pioneered by Elinor Ostrom, recipient of the Nobel Prize in Economics for her work on institutional analysis of commons regimes in the natural environment, and the editors' work in *Governing Knowledge Commons*, this series uses a similar framework to systematically study knowledge commons in various sectors. Readers seeking more information on knowledge commons and this series can visit http://knowledge-commons.net, a repository for scholarship produced by an international, interdisciplinary group of knowledge commons researchers.

Series Editors
Katherine J. Strandburg
Brett M. Frischmann
Michael J. Madison

Other Books in the Series
Madelyn Rose Sanfilippo and Melissa G. Ocepek, *Governing Misinformation in Everyday Knowledge Commons*
Brett M. Frischmann, Michael J. Madison and Madelyn Rose Sanfilippo, *Governing Smart Cities as Knowledge Commons*
Erwin Dekker and Pavel Kuchar, *Governing Markets as Knowledge Commons*
Madelyn Rose Sanfilippo, Brett M. Frischmann and Katherine J. Strandburg, *Governing Privacy in Knowledge Commons*
Katherine J. Strandburg, Brett M. Frischmann and Michael J. Madison, *Governing Medical Knowledge Commons*

The Environmental Knowledge Commons

CASES AND LESSONS FOR KNOWLEDGE SHARING

Edited by

ANJANETTE RAYMOND
Indiana University, Bloomington

SCOTT J. SHACKELFORD
Indiana University, Bloomington

JESSICA STEINBERG
Indiana University, Bloomington

MICHAEL MATTIOLI
Indiana University, Bloomington

CAMBRIDGE
UNIVERSITY PRESS

CAMBRIDGE
UNIVERSITY PRESS

Shaftesbury Road, Cambridge CB2 8EA, United Kingdom

One Liberty Plaza, 20th Floor, New York, NY 10006, USA

477 Williamstown Road, Port Melbourne, VIC 3207, Australia

314–321, 3rd Floor, Plot 3, Splendor Forum, Jasola District Centre, New Delhi – 110025, India

Cambridge University Press is part of Cambridge University Press & Assessment, a department of the University of Cambridge.

We share the University's mission to contribute to society through the pursuit of education, learning and research at the highest international levels of excellence.

www.cambridge.org
Information on this title: www.cambridge.org/9781009482141
DOI: 10.1017/9781009482134

When citing this work, please include a reference to the DOI 10.1017/9781009482134

First published 2026

Cover image: wildart / iStock / Getty Images Plus

A catalogue record for this publication is available from the British Library

A Cataloging-in-Publication data record for this book is available from the Library of Congress

ISBN 978-1-009-48216-5 Hardback
ISBN 978-1-009-48214-1 Paperback

This volume is dedicated to our families for their ongoing support and encouragement, as well as to all those working for peace and environmental sustainability, both online and offline.

Contents

Figures

Tables

Contributors

Todd Aagaard joined the Villanova Law School faculty in 2008. He served as Vice Dean of the Law School from 2015 to 2019. His scholarship focuses on environmental law, energy law, and administrative law. His publications include "Energy-Environment Policy Alignments," 90 *Wash. L. Rev.* 1517 (2015); "Environmental Law Outside the Canon," 89 *Ind. L.J.* 1239 (2014); "Environmental Harms, Use Conflicts, and Neutral Baselines in Environmental Law," 60 *Duke L.J.* 1505 (2011); "Environmental Law as a Legal Field: An Inquiry in Legal Taxonomy," 95 *Cornell L. Rev.* 221 (2010); and "Factual Premises of Statutory Interpretation in Agency Review Cases," 77 *Geo. Wash. L. Rev.* (2009). In addition, he is a coauthor of *Practicing Environmental Law*, a practice-based environmental law casebook published in 2017 by Foundation Press. Aagaard received his BA with honors from Pomona College, his MS from the University of Michigan School of Natural Resources and the Environment, and his JD magna cum laude from the University of Michigan Law School. While at Michigan, he was the editor-in-chief of the *Michigan Law Review* and an executive editor of the *Michigan Journal of Race & Law*. Following completion of his JD and MS degrees, he clerked for Second Circuit Judge Guido Calabresi before joining the Environment and Natural Resources Division of the US Department of Justice as an attorney in the Appellate Section. At the Justice Department, he briefed and argued civil and criminal cases in federal courts of appeals in the areas of environmental law, natural resources law, Indian law, and administrative law.

Wa'ed Alshoubaki is an associate professor of public policy at Prairie View A&M University, Texas, and is also affiliated with the University of Jordan, Amman. Her expertise lies in public policy and governance, with ongoing research on immigration and refugee resettlement in the Middle East, Europe, and the US. Dr. Alshoubaki has extensively published on forced migration, governance, climate change, social policy, crisis management, and public procurement. Her peer-reviewed articles, book chapters, and notable monograph on the resettlement of forced migrants in the US significantly contribute to the field. Her research has been expanded to address urgent issues, including climate change policy innovation, loss and damage assessment in Jordan, climate-induced displacement, and sustainable livelihoods. She has received numerous awards and research grants, such as the Fulbright Scholar Research Award, an outreach lecture fund, and the King Abdullah II Centre for Excellence grant. As the principal investigator, she leads the Jordan team on a Swiss Network of International Studies grant focusing on urban forced migrants, collaborating with Swiss and Moldovan scholars on this multidisciplinary project. Her professional experience includes consulting for the UNDP on governance and local development, curriculum development, and advising the Jordanian government on decentralization and public sector reforms.

Greg Bloom is Senior Director of Strategy and Partnerships at Inform USA. He founded and leads the Open Referral Initiative, which promotes open access to information about the health, human, and social services available to people in need. He is also a strategic advisor on community resources and engagement for the Gravity Project and a visiting scholar at Indiana University's Ostrom Workshop on the Commons. Previously, Greg managed communications for Bread for the City in Washington, DC. He is a cooperative developer and community organizer. He has published in *The Cambridge Handbook of Commons Research Innovations* (2021), *In These Times*, *Civic Quarterly*, and Code for America's *Beyond Transparency*.

Laetitia Cesari is a consultant at the United Nations Institute for Disarmament Research (UNIDIR). Her research interests focus on space law and policy, focusing on security and safety aspects, space traffic management, and space situational awareness, as well as the nexus between space and cybersecurity. Prior to joining UNIDIR, she worked in the space industry, specifically telecommunications. Before that, she had the opportunity to support the work of national governments on defense and space. Laetitia holds a doctorate in law focused on the legal aspects of cybersecurity of space systems from the University of Luxembourg and has been a visiting scholar at the International Institute of Air and Space Law at Leiden University and at the University of New South Wales, UNSW Canberra – Space. She also holds a certificate from the Hague Academy of International Law, a master's degree in space law and telecommunications from the University of Luxembourg, a master's degree in aeronautics law from the University Toulouse 1 Capitole and a master's degree in business law from the University Paris 1 Panthéon-Sorbonne. Laetitia speaks French, English, and Italian.

Jorge L. Contreras is the James T. Jensen Endowed Professor for Transactional Law and the Director of the Program on Intellectual Property and Technology Law at the University of Utah S.J. Quinney College of Law. He has previously served as a visiting fellow at the London School of Economics and Political Science and Tilburg University in the Netherlands and a visiting professor at the University of Minnesota School of Law. Professor Contreras's research focuses on intellectual property, antitrust law, technical standardization and science policy. Prior to entering academia, Professor Contreras was a partner at an international law firm where he practiced transactional law in Boston, Washington, DC, and London. He has published more than 150 academic articles and chapters and has written or edited fourteen books, including *The Genome Defense: Inside the Epic Legal Battle to Determine Who Owns Your DNA* (2021), which was recognized by the *New York Times* as one of the top nonfiction books of the season and has received praise from news outlets ranging from the *Wall Street Journal* to *Nature*. Professor Contreras's scholarship has received numerous awards and recognition, including the Patent & Trademark Office Society's 2021 Rossman Memorial Award and the University of Utah's 2020 Distinguished Research Award, and he is a three-time winner of the IPKat blog's award for Best Patent Law Book of the Year. He is an elected member of the American Law Institute and the former cochair of the National Conference of Lawyers and Scientists. He has testified before committees of the US Senate and House of Representatives, the Federal Trade Commission, and the European Commission, and has served as an expert witness in complex intellectual property cases in the US, Canada, Germany, the UK, India, Taiwan, and Brazil. He received his JD from Harvard Law School, earned his BSEE and BA in English at Rice University, and clerked for Chief Justice Thomas R. Philips of the Texas Supreme Court.

Patrick J. Doran joined The Nature Conservancy (TNC) in 2005 and currently serves as the Director of Strategy, Measures and Science for TNC's five-state Midwest Division in the US. In this role, Patrick leads a team that demonstrates excellence in the areas of strategic planning, measures, evaluation and learning, and evidence-based science, and promotes a consistent approach to implementing the tenets of TNC's Conservation by Design approach. Patrick earned his PhD in ecology from Dartmouth College, where he studied forest bird populations at the Hubbard Brook Experimental Forest in the White Mountains of New Hampshire. Patrick also holds degrees from Indiana University (MS/MA) and Villanova University (BA). He has published over fifty peer-reviewed papers on a wide variety of conservation topics.

Chris Draper is a technologist whose career has focused on reducing human errors using novel technologies in safety critical environments. He has held roles from computational modeler in the aerospace industry to C-suite positions in the renewable fuels industry and supported entrepreneurial and intrapreneurial efforts at companies ranging from startups to Fortune 500 companies in industries including real estate to automotive to education. In the legaltech space, he has been a longtime contributor and leader to problems of data security, confidentiality, and equitable information use for applications ranging from dispute resolution to access to justice. He is a visiting scholar at the Indiana University Ostrom Workshop focusing on blockchain governance and intangible valuation and a fellow of the National Center for Technology in Dispute Resolution.

Brett M. Frischmann is the Charles Widger Endowed University Professor in Law, Business and Economics at Villanova, an affiliated scholar of the Center for Internet and Society at Stanford Law School, an affiliated faculty member of the Vincent and Elinor Ostrom Workshop in Political Theory and Policy Analysis at Indiana University, and a trustee for the Nexa Center for Internet & Society, Polytechnic University of Turin. Frischmann also served as the Microsoft Visiting Professor of Information and Technology Policy at Princeton University's Center for Information and Technology Policy. Frischmann is an expert on intellectual property, privacy, cyber/internet, and other areas of technology law as well as the intersection of these areas of law with other disciplines, including economics, computer science, political science, science and technology studies, and engineering. His research spans these disciplines, often involving collaborations with experts outside of law and often leading to publications in disciplinary (nonlegal) peer review journals. His ongoing interdisciplinary research on the relationships between infrastructural resources, governance, commons, and spillovers includes a series of foundational books and articles. His book *Re-Engineering Humanity* (coauthored with philosopher Evan Selinger, 2018) thoroughly examines various mechanisms for techno-social engineering of humans, including algorithmic amplification, as well as the normative conflict between a commitment to pluralism and engineered optimality. Recent interdisciplinary work explores and advocates for different forms of friction-in-design as a means for counteracting dominant efficiency logics and consequently safeguarding human capabilities and values. Representative examples include better digital contracts, demonstrably informed consent, and age gating.

Christian Glupker is a senior clinical professor of economics at Grand Valley State University's Seidman College of Business. His research centers on applied regional economics, emphasizing the measurement and modeling of economic impacts associated with universities, cultural institutions, and community events. He has coauthored numerous studies quantifying the fiscal and employment contributions of nonprofit and public organizations. Glupker holds a master's from Western Michigan University and a Bachelor of Business Administration from Grand Valley State University, following a decade of professional experience in corporate banking and small-business consulting.

Sam Haapaniemi is a project manager at The Nature Conservancy, where he helps teams in the Midwest US track progress, measure impact, and apply adaptive management practices to their conservation strategies. Previously, he worked in the Healthy Cities program, where he participated in a variety of activities in service of building the case for green stormwater infrastructure and supporting nature in Detroit, Michigan. Sam holds an MPA from the University of Washington and a BA in Political Theory and Constitutional Democracy from Michigan State University.

Andrea J. Harrington currently serves as the Institute of Air and Space Law Co-Director and Associate Professor at the McGill Faculty of Law. She also teaches in the Space Resources Program for the Colorado School of Mines. Professor Harrington previously served as Dean of Space Education and Full Professor at Air University for the United States Space Force. She served as Associate Director of the University of Mississippi Air and Space Law programs and has taught for the International Space University's Space Studies Program. She holds a DCL and LLM from McGill, a JD from the University of Connecticut, an MSc in European Politics and Governance from the London School of Economics, and a BA from Boston University. Her research is focused on public international space law. Among notable publications, her book *Space Insurance and the Law* (2021) was awarded the 2022 British Insurance Law Association Annual Book Prize.

Elaine Isely joined West Michigan Environmental Action Council to lead its Water Programs in 2012. She is a veteran of the West Michigan legal and environmental communities and has served as a research associate and assistant for the Robert B. Annis Water Resources Institute at Grand Valley State University, as Project Manager for the West Michigan Strategic Alliance's Green Infrastructure Initiative, and Sea Grant Fellow with the Great Lakes Commission. Elaine was also previously a litigation attorney working on behalf of social justice causes in West Michigan, serving as a staff attorney for Michigan Migrant Legal Assistance Project, Inc. (Migrant Legal Aid) and Legal Aid of West Michigan in Grand Rapids. Elaine holds a BS in finance from the University of Maryland, a JD from Wayne State University, and an MS in biology/natural resources management from Grand Valley State University. She is appointed to the City of Grand Rapids' Stormwater Oversight Commission, the Wolverine Worldwide Tannery Community Advisory Group, and the Michigan State Waterways Commission. She has published several academic and technical papers on environmental and collaborative management topics, and currently serves as an advisor to Grand Valley State University Natural Resources Management Department and to the Michigan Water School led by Michigan State Extension and Michigan Sea Grant. She works on many initiatives to strengthen collaboration between community groups and other project partners.

Paul Isely is the Associate Dean and Professor of Economics for the Seidman College of Business at Grand Valley State University, which he joined in 1995 after earning his PhD in economics from Purdue University. He also holds an MS in economics from Purdue University and a dual BS in physics and economics from the University of Wisconsin-Madison. Dr. Isely's research interests have led to many local articles and reports. These articles have explored West Michigan's economy including forecasts of growth, the state of entrepreneurship, healthcare costs, environmental clean-up values, economic impacts of various activities, and the costs and benefits of wind power. He has been interviewed extensively by TV, radio, and newspapers on the West Michigan economy and its relationship to the national and state economies.

Yu Kojima has over twenty years of international experience in the area of gender, migration, and development through program management/gender research for public policy and planning and advocacy in Asia and the Pacific region. Yu offers expertise drawn from combination of experience in both academic and policy research, while she brings in development planning experience earned through working with several United Nations (UN) agencies, including the UN Development Programme, the UN Development Fund for Women, UNICEF-Innocenti Research Centre, and the UN University Institute on Globalization, Culture and Mobility. In recent years, Yu has expanded her scope of expertise by engaging with environment and development policy, climate justice, and methodologies for monitoring, evaluation, and learning for climate adaptation in the capacity of Co-Director, The Climate Panel Pennsylvania USA – an initiative which aims to energize the international development mechanism by transforming data into actionable insights to enhance the resilience of the global food system. Yu is also a member of the Regional Gender Specialist Group hosted by UNICEF in Asia and a member of the Gender Specialist Roster, the Consultative Group for International Agricultural Research, based in Rome, Italy.

Mathew Kurian is an international expert with over twenty years of global experience in climate justice, adaptive monitoring, evaluation, and learning. He served as Co-Director of The Climate Panel in Pennsylvania and is a former fellow at the Institute of Science, Technology, and Public Policy at Texas A&M University.

As Consortium Lead for the Belmont Forum's cyber-enabled disaster resilience initiative, Dr. Kurian facilitated the development of the Theory of Change Observatory at Penn State, supported by agencies including NSF, São Paulo Research Foundation, and UK Research and Innovation. His scholarly work, spanning institutions such as the Tata Energy Research Institute, the World Bank, UNESCO-IHE, and United Nations University, has significantly influenced policies and curricula related to governance, environmental monitoring, and climate justice.

He played a pivotal role in launching the Nexus Observatory, a cutting-edge big data analytics platform for environmental modeling, and founded the Africa Points of Excellence consortium focused on drought risk monitoring. His expertise has also informed monitoring and evaluation strategies for the Green Climate Fund and CGIAR. Dr. Kurian's prolific publication record includes influential books and peer-reviewed articles on water governance, the Water–Energy–Food Nexus, urbanization, and sustainable development policy.

Michael J. Madison is Professor of Law and Faculty Director of the Future Law Project at the University of Pittsburgh School of Law, Pennsylvania. He is a senior scholar with the University of Pittsburgh Institute for Cyber Law, Policy, and

Security, Faculty Director of the Future Law Project, and a John E. Murray Faculty Scholar. He is a co-Principal Investigator of the Workshop on Governing Knowledge Commons global research collaborative, a series editor of the Cambridge University Press Studies in Governing Knowledge Commons series, and the co-editor of *Governing Knowledge Commons* (2014); *Governing Medical Knowledge Commons* (2017); and *Governing Smart Cities as Knowledge Commons* (2023).

Michael Mattioli joined the Indiana University Maurer School of Law faculty in 2012. His research examines cooperative challenges concerning technology and public policy. Mattioli's scholarship asks how information-sharing can make society healthier, safer, and more prosperous. Through this lens, Mattioli has examined the pooling of cancer research data, the costs and benefits of patent pools for digital media, and how public policy is shaping "Big Data" technologies that relate to health and public infrastructure. Mattioli shows that law and policy – from intellectual property, to antitrust, to privacy – can lead such endeavors to success or failure. Mattioli has coedited a book on Big Data (*Big Data Is Not a Monolith*, 2016), he has authored numerous academic articles and essays in leading law reviews, and he has written book chapters that examine patent pools and the promise and perils of data sharing. In 2018, Indiana University honored Mattioli with a Trustees Teaching Award. Mattioli is affiliated with Indiana Law's Center for IP Research, the Ostrom Workshop in Political Theory and Policy Analysis at Indiana University. A graduate of the University of Pennsylvania Law School and Tufts University, Mattioli has held fellowship appointments at Berkeley Law and Michigan Law. Before attending law school, he worked as a microchip designer.

Erik Nordman is an environmental social scientist, climate resilience consultant, and adjunct professor of natural resources management at Grand Valley State University in Michigan, US. His work focuses on the social dimensions of natural resources, including energy, nature-based solutions, and commons. Nordman served as a Fulbright visiting professor at Kenyatta University in Nairobi and a visiting scholar at Indiana University-Bloomington's Ostrom Workshop. He holds master's and doctoral degrees from the State University of New York – College of Environmental Science and Forestry in Syracuse.

Anjanette Raymond is the Director of the Program on Data Management and Information Governance at the Ostrom Workshop, is a professor in the Department of Business Law and Ethics, at the Kelley School of Business, Indiana University, and an adjunct professor of law at Maurer Law School (Indiana). She completed her PhD at the Centre for Commercial Law Studies, Queen Mary, University of London, where she researched the creation of policy to assist in managing bias, partiality, and dependence in online justice environments. Angie has written widely in the areas of online dispute resolution, data governance, artificial intelligence governance, privacy, international finance, and commercial dispute resolution in such publications as the *Harvard Negotiation Law Review, Cardozo Journal of Conflict Resolution, Journal of Dispute Resolution, Wisconsin Law Review, Northwestern Journal of Technology and Intellectual Property*, and the *American Review of International Arbitration*. Angie is currently one of the US National Consultants to the United Nations (UN) Commission on International Trade Law, reporting on electronic commerce related issues and has previously attended the UN Commission on International Trade Law Online Dispute Resolution (ODR) Working Group. She is an identified expert in ODR at the Asia-Pacific Economic Cooperation, where she is one of the academic leads in the Collaborative Framework project on cross-border ODR.

V. Ratna Reddy is an economist by training with experience in the fields of environmental economics and natural resource management, environmental impact assessment, climate change, livelihoods, and institutions. He is an Alexander von Humboldt fellow at South Asian Institute, Germany, a visiting fellow at the Institute of Development Studies, Sussex, UK, the University of Leeds, UK, and the UN-University, Dresden, Germany. He has served as consultant to organizations such as the World Bank and Independent Evaluation Group, the World Bank, Washington and India, ADB, ADBI, UNDP, DFID, EC, WWF, IWMI, ICRISAT, UNU, OPM, and IFDC. He has also served as a working group member in the preparation of the Eleventh and Twelfth Plans for the Government of India. He has published fifteen books and more than two hundred research papers in international and national peer-reviewed journals.

Scott J. Shackelford is the Provost Professor of Business Law and Ethics at the Indiana University Kelley School of Business. He serves as the Executive Director of the Ostrom Workshop and the Center for Applied Cybersecurity Research. He is also an affiliated scholar at both the Harvard Kennedy School's Belfer Center for Science and International Affairs and Stanford's Center for Internet and Society. Professor Shackelford has written more than 100 articles, book chapters, essays, and op-eds for diverse publications. Similarly, Professor Shackelford's research has been covered by an array of outlets, including *Politico, NPR, CNN, Forbes, Time*, the *Washington Post*, and the *LA Times*. He is the author of *Forks in the Digital Road: Key Decisions in the History of the Internet* (2024), *The Internet of Things: What Everyone Needs to Know* (2020), *Governing New Frontiers in the Information Age: Toward Cyber Peace* (2020), and *Managing Cyber Attacks in International Law, Business, and Relations: In Search of Cyber Peace* (2014). He is also the lead editor of the first volume dedicated to cyber peace entitled *Cyber Peace: Charting a Path Toward a Sustainable, Stable, and Secure Cyberspace* (2022). Both Professor Shackelford's academic work and teaching have been recognized with numerous awards, including a Harvard University Research Fellowship, a Stanford University Hoover Institution National Fellowship, a Notre Dame Institute for Advanced Study Distinguished Fellowship, the 2014 Indiana University Outstanding Junior Faculty

Award, the 2015 Elinor Ostrom Award, and the 2022 *Poets & Quants* Best 40-Under-40 MBA Professors Award.

Jessica Steinberg is Associate Professor in the International Studies Department at the Hamilton Lugar School of Global and International Studies at Indiana University, in Bloomington, Indiana. She is also Director of the Environment and Natural Resource Governance Program at the Ostrom Workshop. Her research focuses on the political economy of development, local politics of natural resource extraction, state capacity, and violent conflict. Her work has been published in the *American Political Science Review, Annual Review of Political Science, Journal of Theoretical Politics, Journal of Conflict Resolution*, and *Political Geography*. She employs a mixed-methods approach, including game theory, comparative case analysis, and statistical methods, and she has conducted fieldwork in Congo-Brazzaville, Zambia, the Democratic Republic of Congo, Senegal, and Mozambique.

Valerie Strassberg serves as the Director of Urban Water Infrastructure for The Nature Conservancy's Brightstorm program, where she leads public partnerships and advances projects at the intersection of public policy, design, community engagement, and integrated water resource management. She provides technical, policy, and regulatory support for stormwater management and climate-resilient freshwater protection initiatives across North America and globally. With twenty years of experience, Valerie has led transformative projects, including Detroit's first Post-Construction Stormwater Ordinance and Ann Arbor's pioneering Green Streets Policy, and supported the development of the State of Michigan's Low Impact Development Manual and the City of Ann Arbor's Climate Action Plan. As the past Director of Detroit's Healthy Cities Program, she spearheaded the integration of nature-based green stormwater infrastructure into city policies, programs, and tools, benefiting public and private properties. A founding member of Engineers Without Borders USA and former Environmental Commissioner for Ann Arbor, she has also codirected nonprofit initiatives and served on multiple academic and advisory boards, including Wayne State University's Civil and Environmental Engineering Department and Detroit Future City. Valerie holds a BA in Geological Engineering from the Colorado School of Mines, with a Professional Engineering license in Water Resources.

Simon Sun is an assistant professor at National Yang Ming Chiao Tung University School of Law. He specializes in internet intermediary liability, privacy, cybersecurity, artificial intelligence, blockchain governance, and space technology. His research also explores the application of Elinor Ostrom's Commons theory and polycentric governance in digital society. Simon holds an SJD from Indiana University, an LLM from Duke Law School, and an LLB from National Chung Cheng University.

Sekela Twisa is a senior environmental officer currently employed at Water Resource Centre of Excellence (WRCoE) under the Ministry of Water, United

Republic of Tanzania. She coordinates research projects on water resource-related issues and the effects of climate change, land use/cover changes, and emerging concerns about drought and flood disasters. Prior to joining WRCoE, she held various positions at the Water Institute, where she worked on creating curricula for innovation trainings, knowledge transfer, consultancy, and water resources research. Additionally, she serves as a research assistant for the Tanzania-based EU-Drought Early Warning and Forecasting to Strengthen Preparedness and Adaptation to Drought in Africa. She has over ten years of experience in hydrology, environmental science, water resources, drought and flood management, including risk reduction, Remote Sensing and Geographic Information System. Ms. Twisa's current focus is on sustainable development, with a particular focus on the climate change related impacts on water resources ecosystem services, water supply, and sanitation. Her ultimate goal is to provide knowledge on water sector disaster risk reduction in evidence-based decision-making at various scales.

Shanyn Viars is an economist specializing in sustainable urban planning, currently working at American Rivers. Passionate about fostering an equitable clean water future, Shanyn explores the intersection of climate resiliency and development to encourage community-led investments in healthy watershed management. Shanyn collaborates with municipal leaders and community organizations to restore urban rivers, mitigate climate threats through natural infrastructure, and develop alternative funding mechanisms for sustainable water management. Shanyn holds both an MS and BS in economics from the Belk College of Business at the University of North Carolina-Charlotte. Currently in the Great Lakes region, Shanyn previously served as an adjunct professor in economics at Grand Valley State University and participates in various regional environmental committees as Great Lakes Senior Environmental Leadership Fellow.

Acknowledgments

This volume is like an iceberg: What you see reflects only a small part of the enormous efforts that lie below the surface.

The book authors and editors would like to thank Katherine J. Strandburg, Brett M. Frischmann, Michael J. Madison, and Madelyn Sanfilippo for their leadership in creating a wonderful, collaborative group of scholars and researchers within the field of the Knowledge Commons. Their willingness to provide feedback, structure, and guidance throughout the process has been invaluable.

This book would not have been nearly as good without the funding support from the National Science Foundation, General Knowledge Commons, Research Coordination Network grant, which also allowed us (and many others) to publish this book in an open-source format.

The editors would like to acknowledge the contributions made by the phalanx of graduate students from Indiana University involved in copy editing the chapter drafts, including Simon Sun, Yash Dutt Sharma, Madelyn Darlene Gamble, Max Fang, and Anirudh Diwakar.

Finally, our thanks go out to Matt Galloway, Jadyn Fauconier-Herry, and the team at Cambridge University Press for this editorial and production assistance. For additional funding and support, thanks go to Indiana University and the Ostrom Workshop, which support all of the editors in so many, immeasurable ways.

Introduction

The natural environment constitutes a complex and dynamic global ecosystem that provides essential resources for societal well-being and survival. However, the environment is also subject to unprecedented threats from human activities, such as climate change, pollution, habitat loss, biodiversity decline, and the overexploitation of scarce natural resources including rare-Earth metals that are vital to driving the transition to cleaner technologies but also risk further habitat destruction. To address these challenges, there is an imperative need for coordinated polycentric action by multiple stakeholders at various governance scales, including governments, civil society, the private sector, academia, self-organized communities, and individuals. Such interventions require not only scientific knowledge and data about the state and functioning of the environment, but also social and institutional knowledge and data about the values, preferences, norms, and behaviors of the actors involved in environmental governance and management to build trust, and ultimately community.

Yet environmental knowledge and data are often dispersed, heterogeneous, incomplete, inaccessible, or contested, making it difficult to share, integrate, and apply these data for the common good. Moreover, environmental knowledge and data are not static or neutral, but rather are often dynamic and value-laden, reflecting the interests, perspectives, and power relations of different knowledge producers and users. Therefore, finding ways to govern shared environmental knowledge commons that can serve the needs and goals of diverse and sometimes conflicting stakeholders is a formidable challenge that requires careful design and governance.

There are numerous examples underscoring the stakes of information sharing in the environmental context. Consider the global processes undergirding the Intergovernmental Panel on Climate Change, which involves more than 750 scientists from around the world exploring the physical science of climate change as well as studies involving adaptation and mitigation (IPCC n.d.). Similar issues are playing out in near-Earth orbital space with growing constellations of satellites competing for scarce slots while avoiding crashing into each other, or the estimated 34,000 other objects that clutter the cosmos (Bongers and Torres 2024; Pultarova 2024). Absent concerted, multistakeholder information sharing, cascading accidents, translation errors, and associated governance gaps can worsen global collective action challenges.

In this book, *The Environmental Knowledge Commons: Cases and Lessons for Knowledge Sharing*, we examine this challenge through the lens of the environmental knowledge commons itself, which is a concept that draws on the literature on knowledge commons and the literature associated with the Ostrom Workshop including the commons itself (Agrawal et al. 2023, which defines "commons" as "resources used or governed by groups of heterogeneous users through agreed-upon institutional arrangements"), polycentricity, the Institutional Analysis and Development (IAD) framework, and the Governing Knowledge Commons (GKC) framework. The first efforts to extend the IAD framework to knowledge sharing occurred in 2006 with Elinor Ostrom and Charlotte Hess (Hess and Ostrom 2007), which laid the groundwork for later efforts to create the GKC framework, which "is an institutional approach to governing the management or production of knowledge commons" (Ostrom Workshop n.d.). "Knowledge commons" in this context refers to "information, science, knowledge, data and other types of intellectual and cultural resources" (Ostrom Workshop n.d.). The GKC, then, is a framework to study the institutionalized community governance of the sharing and, in some cases, creation, integration, and preservation of information, science, knowledge, data, and other types of intellectual and cultural resources (Frischmann et al. 2014). "Environmental commons" are systems that allow communities of users to devise and enforce rules on how to sustainably manage and use biophysical resources that are essential for their livelihoods and well-being (Poteete et al. 2010).

We contend that the environmental knowledge commons can be seen as a special type of knowledge commons that focuses on the collection, management, and sharing of knowledge and data related to the natural environment and its governance. We further assert that the environmental knowledge commons can benefit from applying the GKC framework, which enables us to identify and analyze the key components and variables that shape the performance and outcomes of the environmental knowledge commons, such as the characteristics of the knowledge resources, the actors and their interactions, the rules and norms that govern the commons, the external factors that influence the commons, and the evaluation criteria that measure the success of the commons. The GKC framework also allows us to compare different cases of environmental knowledge commons across various domains, contexts, and scales, and to derive generalizable insights and lessons for knowledge sharing and governance.

The network of universities, organizations, governments, scientists, and private citizens working to address environmental challenges is decentralized and polycentric in nature. Given the recognition of the natural environment as a system of interconnected ecosystems and socioecological contexts, there is a growing demand for understanding about the best ways to collect, manage, and share environmental data. The framework of GKC provides a useful starting point to address this demand and answer the following question: *What makes a successful environmental knowledge commons?* Building on an emerging field of knowledge commons study in which a growing knowledge commons community has worked to enhance the GKC framework, this edited volume addresses challenges particular to managing a successful environmental knowledge commons.[1] The GKC approach capitalizes upon the parallels between the institutional analysis initially developed by Ostrom and continued through the GKC framework and the contextual integrity framework, allowing new questions, surrounding data and information, to be included in diverse analyses, such as questions about legitimacy, power imbalances, regime effectiveness, and equity.

The main objective of this book is to showcase the application and usefulness of the GKC framework for the study of the environmental knowledge commons, by presenting a diverse and rich set of case studies that illustrate the challenges and opportunities of creating and governing environmental knowledge and data for the common good. The case studies cover various topics, such as climate change, forestry management, space, and green tech that span different geographical regions, levels of analysis, and types of actors and institutions. The case studies are based on original empirical research conducted by the contributors, who come from different disciplinary backgrounds and perspectives. The case studies also demonstrate the policy relevance and implications of the environmental knowledge commons, by showing how they can inform and support decision-making and action for environmental sustainability and justice. For instance, some of the case studies extend the scope of the environmental knowledge commons to the space domain, by examining how knowledge and data about the Earth's orbit and the outer space can be shared and governed for the benefit of humanity and the environment.

The book is structured in four parts, focusing on environmental knowledge commons. Part I is composed of Chapters 1–3. Chapter 1, "The Value of Having Values: Artifacts of Normative Knowledge as Instruments of Collective Self-Governance for Data Flows," by Greg Bloom, focuses on boundaries around data resources

[1] See Brett M. Frischmann, Michael J. Madison, and Katherine J. Strandburg (eds.), *Governing Knowledge Commons* (New York: Oxford University Press, 2014); Katherine J. Strandburg, Brett M. Frischmann, and Michael J. Madison (eds.), *Governing Medical Knowledge Commons* (Cambridge: Cambridge University Press, 2017); Erwin Dekker and Pavel Kuchař (eds.), *Governing Markets as Knowledge Commons* (Cambridge: Cambridge University Press, 2021); Madelyn Rose Sanfilippo, Brett M. Frischmann, and Katherine J. Strandburg (eds.), *Governing Privacy in Knowledge Commons* (Cambridge: Cambridge University Press, 2021); Brett M. Frischmann, Michael J. Madison, and Madelyn Rose Sanfilippo (eds.), *Governing Smart Cities as Knowledge Commons* (Cambridge: Cambridge University Press, 2023); Madelyn Rose Sanfilippo and Melissa G. Ocepek (eds.), *Governing Misinformation in Everyday Knowledge Commons* (Cambridge: Cambridge University Press, 2025).

that can be drawn through the intentional development and application of values statements. Chapter 2, "Inexorably Entangled Environmental and Knowledge Commons," by Todd Aagaard and Brett M. Fischmann, analyzes the interrelationship between environmental and knowledge commons that weave together different strands of commons research and practice. Chapter 3, "RACs: Truth as a Shared Resource within the ESG Knowledge Commons," by Chris Draper and Simon Sun, examines the role of Human Impact Units and Regenerative Authentication Credits (RACs) in transforming Environmental, Social, and Governance (ESG) governance into a more transparent and equitable knowledge commons.

Part II comprises Chapters 4 and 5. Chapter 4, "Linking Physical and Knowledge Commons in a Green Stormwater Infrastructure Program," by Erik Nordman, Patrick J. Doran, Christian Glupker, Sam Haapaniemi, Elaine Isely, Paul Isely, Valerie Strassberg, and Shanyn Viars, investigates the ecological paradigm in stormwater management that mimics natural hydrology by diverting stormwater into well-designed green stormwater infrastructure practices. Chapter 5, "Co-Curating Institutional Data on Climate Change-Induced Loss and Damage via Expert Panels: Implications for the Environmental Knowledge Commons," by Mathew Kurian, Yu Kojima, Wa'ed Alshoubaki, Sekela Twisa, and V. Ratna Reddy, focuses on analysis of five cases of common pool resources management combined with an expert panel review of climate loss and damage in Jordan to examine their implications for the knowledge commons framework.

Part III focuses on environmental knowledge commons in the space context. Specifically, Chapter 6, "Building A Sustainable Space Knowledge Commons," by Laetitia Cesari and Simon Sun, examines the extent to which the Space Data Association has become an effective stop valve for gaps in prevailing multilateral space governance instruments. Chapter 7, "Terrestrial Environmental Data Obtained from Space," by Andrea J. Harrington, examines the institutional barriers surrounding the sharing of environmental data from Earth-orbiting satellites and associated infrastructure with stakeholders around the world.

Finally, Part IV, comprising Chapters 8 and 9, begins with Jorge L. Contreras' chapter, "The Prospects for Green Patent Commons," which considers whether, and under what conditions, private firms can productively combine existing patent assets to support the dissemination and use of green technology. Chapter 9, "The IPCC as Expert Knowledge Commons," by Michael J. Madison, uses the IPCC's governance of that shared knowledge to motivate and illustrate a model of expert knowledge commons. At the end, we provide a brief summary and couch these findings within the growing literature on GKC, along with providing a research agenda to help highlight unanswered questions on the road ahead.

In this effort, we are building on previous successes and applying the framework to systematically study scientific data issues within knowledge commons, including the ways that sharing, cooperation, hubs, and trusts aid or act as governance and how questions of collaboration and cooperation are raised relative to governance when examining data sharing, specifically in scientific communities. As we have recognized from the beginning, the GKC framework requires an iterative case study process, to both improve the framework and support identification of patterns across studies. To do so effectively, we continue to try to attract other scholars to this collaborative research project. We will continue to solicit interdisciplinary contributions to develop a rich set of case studies. We are also now able to draw on both the network we have developed in studying knowledge commons and the interdisciplinary environmental studies, with which we work. Our hope is for this book to be among the first, but certainly not the last, to tackle the thorny topics associated with governing the environmental knowledge commons.

PART I

1

The Value of Having Values

Artifacts of Normative Knowledge as Instruments of Collective Self-Governance for Data Flows

*Greg Bloom**

1.1 INTRODUCTION: AVERTING TRAGEDY BEGINS WITH UNDERSTANDING DILEMMAS

The concept of "data" carries implicit promises of potential value: information, knowledge, and wisdom. Digital data's attributes as a resource – nonrivalry, inexhaustibility, instantaneous transmission – lend themselves to assumptions that reinforce such promise: of generative, if latent, energy. This promise is expressed quite literally in the cliché that "data is the new oil," which posits data as an opportunity for propulsive intelligence, bringing forth a new industrial revolution, this one on purportedly cleaner terms than the last, as if the "exhaust" of data systems is not pollution but rather recursive resource streams to be reprocessed into cybernetic meta-intelligence.

This promise has expressed itself in various formulations – open data, big data, blockchained data, and most recently large language models and other trappings of "artificial intelligence" – which have tended to swell, crest, and crash like waves through elite discourse and the marketing strategies of technology companies and consulting firms. Across these episodic cycles, a theme is apparent: In the shadows between promise and reality, there lurk dilemmas. Many of these dilemmas are by now quite predictable: often economic, occasionally technical, and to a certain extent even material, but above all social. Such dilemmas have confounded many efforts to use data as a resource, perhaps especially well-intentioned aspirations that instead tend to fizzle out or even result in undesirable outcomes that run counterproductive to the original purpose. By now it is almost equally clichéd to observe that, very much like oil, industrialized data systems yield toxic externalities that corrode societal trust and institutional integrity.

* The author is very grateful to Jessica Steinberg, Brett M. Frischmann, Elizabeth Barry, and Luis Villa for their valuable feedback in the development of this chapter. The Ostrom Workshop at Indiana University has provided invaluable support through its visiting scholarship program, especially under the leadership of Angie Raymond.

To the extent that there are common patterns in these effects, we can seek to understand them – and strive to perhaps overcome them. Following Elinor Ostrom (2007), we can ask: Under what circumstances can collective efforts *avoid failure* when producing and using data for some social purpose, despite the myriad dilemmas that they may inexorably face?

1.2 WHAT ARE BOUNDARIES IN DIGITAL RESOURCES?

Ostrom's framework might at first glance seem like an awkward fit for digital resources, because of conceptual disjunction with the first principle articulated in governing the commons: *clearly defined boundaries.*

Governing a resource begins with agreement upon *what is the governed resource.* In the context of natural resource systems, the most significant dimensions of this principle are spatial and material: The governed resources are physical things that exist in a place. Digital resources, however, seem to invert important attributes of natural resource systems: They can be accessed anywhere, by anyone with capable equipment and connectivity, simultaneously and inexhaustibly. Furthermore, the potential value of data resources tends to *increase* in scale with use, as the types of use for which such data can be leveraged tend to increase over time.

In conventional institutional settings – of a private firm or public organization – boundaries around digital resources are established through the means of authority and hierarchy. The potential benefits of knowledge that is public, or at least *shared,* however, hinge to a significant degree on transcending such institutional boundaries.

1.3 WHAT KINDS OF BOUNDARIES ARE RELEVANT TO INSTITUTIONAL DESIGN OF KNOWLEDGE-SHARING SYSTEMS?

There are at least a couple of obvious answers to the question of what kind of boundaries can be drawn around knowledge commons. First and foremost, there is the boundary of *scope*, which specifies the kinds of information that are managed within. Any information that falls out of scope should be, presumably, excluded. Boundaries can also be literally drawn in data flow diagrams that describe the entities and relationships in an information system; through such technical documents, designers can specify the various users, structures, and data flows that are involved in the production, management, and use of data over time.

Scope and *system* boundaries, however, are insufficient to describe the breadth of potential uses and users associated with digital resources, which can expand in number and kind far beyond that which was initially envisioned by a system's architects, especially in open systems. In Levin and Beckwith's framework (2015) of a "datashed," the flows of data are conceived as if through a natural ecosystem, like the water cycle – but one that is easily dissociated from place and local context. This ecosystemic understanding of digital resources reveals collective action problems that are different in kind from those of natural resources – not owing to subtractability and exclusivity of the resources themselves, but rather the social and institutional relationships from which they are extracted and in which they are used. Indeed, just a few years after the dawn of the modern internet, communities of environmental planners already recognized that the rapid expansion of data-sharing capacities posed not just opportunity but also significant risks, as the "permeability of boundaries threatens to inhibit the ability for groups of people to sustain the trust needed for effective cooperation" (Van House et al. 1998, 341).

What kinds of boundaries, then, can delineate not just *what* and *where* a knowledge resource *is*, but who (among potentially overlapping sets of data contributors, data subjects, and/or data consumers) ought to have what privileges in it, toward what ends?

1.4 KNOWLEDGE COMMONS ARE CONCEPTUALLY BOUNDED BY THE VALUES ASSOCIATED WITH THEIR PROVISION

This chapter argues that a key principle of institutional design for provision of knowledge resources is the explicit articulation and deliberative application of value statements.

Knowledge is inherently structured in accordance with certain values – that is, *what is good? What are our purposes? What are the positive qualities that we expect as a result?* What kinds of outcomes are, in turn, considered undesirable and even unacceptable?

Different parties are likely to have different answers to these questions. (Some impacted parties might never be directly involved with the knowledge production and sharing process – and likely will never have the privilege of being asked in a meaningful way.) Many of these answers can conceptually align in harmony with each other; some, however, might conflict.

In this context, value statements, then, function as a kind of boundary object, in that they enable groups of people with different perspectives to collaboratively share meaning (Star and Griesemer 1989; Carlile 2002) – in this case, by creating a normative conceptual space within which different parties' interests can be aligned. As such, these boundary objects are of a constitutional nature: They establish the terms under which communities can make an array of subsequent collective-choice decisions pertaining to the design, promotion, evolution, and protection of knowledge resources.

1.5 THE GOVERNING KNOWLEDGE COMMONS FRAMEWORK ADAPTED OSTROM'S INSTITUTIONAL ANALYSIS AND DEVELOPMENT (IAD) FRAMEWORK TO THE ANALYSIS OF INFORMATIONAL RESOURCES

This claim may have been implicitly assumed by Frischmann et al. (2014) as they adapted Ostrom's IAD framework for application to the domain of informational resources. Their Governing Knowledge Commons (GKC) project was introduced with a set of research questions that can guide the empirical analysis of knowledge-sharing initiatives. One of the first questions in the GKC research framework is: "What normative values are relevant for this community?"

The GKC authors carefully noted that their own work is empirical in nature, rather than normative, "focused primarily on community goals and objectives rather than on values from higher-level social contexts or foundational ethical and moral principles" (Madison et al. 2022, 18). For the purposes of research and analysis, this position is logical. However, as a practitioner with decades of experience in building (and defending) community-based capacities for knowledge sharing, I want to uphold a particular pragmatic principle: A community should explicitly state its core principles. There is value in the collective declaration of shared values.

In practice, these constitutional artifacts can be instrumental in the practice of institutional design and governance for collaborators who may lack technical knowledge of such processes. Likewise in research, such artifacts can guide analysis of the relationships among a community's normative claims, collective choices, and operational processes. By naming value statements as the tools with which communities can draw normative boundaries, we make it easier to apply the Ostromian theory of institutional analysis and design to the practice of sustainable knowledge sharing.

1.6 WHAT ARE VALUE STATEMENTS?

Value statements are part of a family of artifacts that are often – but not always – found across organizational contexts, sometimes described (especially in the nonprofit sector) with the shorthand of "MVV" – which stands for Mission, Vision, and Values.

A *vision* statement describes a project's idealized future, the utopian destination that is pointed toward by a *mission* statement, which describes a project's work. Such statements are similar to statements of *purpose* or *scope* – which specify what kind of *result* a project intends to achieve, and what *product* it produces toward that end.

Value statements tend to further qualify the attributes of a project's purpose and vision: They make normative claims about the positive qualities that animate a project – such as *sustainability*, *accountability*, *accessibility*, and so on. Conversely, these statements imply a set of qualities which should be avoided, discouraged, or even refused – qualities which presumably describe the status quo or the result of failure.

Principle statements may be considered distinct from and complementary to value statements. In my own practice, I posit that principles describe procedural attributes, that is, the ways a group agrees to do work. If value statements articulate the reasons "why" a group does work, principle statements articulate "how" the work ought to be done. Principles underlie working agreements and decision-making processes – specifying collective expectations such as "rough consensus and running code" (associated with early web standards initiatives such as the Internet Engineering Task Force) (Russell 2006; see also Lessig 1999, 4) or "We begin by listening" (Allied Media Projects n.d.).

For the purposes of this chapter, I will refer broadly to value statements as the primary example of this broader family of normative artifacts – making distinctions when relevant, but otherwise assuming that statements of purpose, vision, values, and principles perform boundary-drawing roles that are similar enough to be considered together.

1.7 ARE THE VALUES TYPICALLY ASSOCIATED WITH KNOWLEDGE-SHARING INITIATIVES CLEAR AND SUFFICIENT?

So far, so obvious. A reader might understandably consider value statements to be mundane, tactically ornamental rather than strategically instrumental.

And yet fully articulated value statements are not ubiquitous either. Indeed, many knowledge-sharing initiatives simply declare a value in their name – such as "Open" this and "Smart" that – without any further specification.

Close examination of these common, nominal claims reveals various problems that arise from ambiguity in and underspecification of such value statements.

1.8 "OPENNESS" IMPLIES THAT DATA CAN BE ACCESSIBLE TO ANYONE FOR ANY NUMBER OF USES

"Open," for instance, has been waved as a banner of progress by advocates, consultancies, and information technology contractors alike. On President Barack Obama's very first day in office, he signed two executive orders (out of a total of three) issuing "open government" directives. Four years later, McKinsey published a widely cited report on "open data" which estimated its total potential economic benefit across sectors as amounting to more than $3 trillion.

Among just these two examples we find a diverse array of value claims: The Obama administration's open government directives called for "transparency, participation, and collaboration" (Coglianese 2009) while McKinsey focused on "efficiency" and "optimization." The former implies purposes of public accountability and "democratization" that redistributes political agency among citizenry; the latter implies market-shaping infrastructure that can foster competition and innovation. As a signifier, *open* is open to all of these interpretations; sometimes, they might comfortably coexist. But such harmony cannot be taken for granted.

The hypothetical promise of *democratization through openness* is tested by the actual qualities of our existing political economy. While, hypothetically, anyone *could* use and benefit from open data, the actors who are *most likely* to actually use open data are not those who previously lacked access to such data. Rather, the actors who are most likely to directly benefit from open data are those who already had the means and motivation to use public knowledge to private ends. The late Michael Gurstein was a champion of the field of "community informatics," yet when considering the value of *access* to open data, he observed that it is in and of itself "sufficient only to … provide additional resources to the Sheriff of Nottingham rather than to Robin Hood" (Gurstein 2011).

Indeed, some of the most prominent large-scale open data initiatives have resulted in – for instance – transfers of property rights from low-income communities, or public lands, to corporate interests (McKenzie 2017).

1.9 "SMARTNESS" IMPLIES THAT DATA CAN BE PROCESSED INTO INTELLIGENCE – LIKE FUEL FOR AN ENGINE

"Smart," like *open*, is a similarly common value statement, with similarly problematic ambiguity. Most commonly associated with the "smart cities" meme, *smart* in such contexts presumably refers to intelligence that can emerge from cybernetic flows of massive data about the activities of people and things. "Smartness" seems inherently beneficial, and the word "city" implies collectivity – yet the phrase itself does not specify who, exactly, gets to be smart and attain the benefits of *smartness* (Beckwith et al. 2019).

Indeed, the objects of *smart city* discourse tend to be large-scale surveillance endeavors, established through processes that are often opaque and undemocratic (Scassa 2020). As Frischmann et al. observe in the first chapter of *Governing Knowledge Commons* (2014):

> The "smart" character of the smart city elides the fact that resident identities and behaviors are necessarily abstracted in smart city processes in the conversion from their material origins to their digital representations. That makes these digital representations controllable, shareable, and analyzable in ways that living humans being often are not. It also makes it easier to keep the collection and manipulation of the data hidden from the people that the data represent.

Observing this trend in which "smartness" is often used as justification for efforts that enclose knowledge about communities, and privatize decision-making apparatuses about surveillance and data use, Beckwith et al. propose "stewardship" as a protective value through which communities can reassert control over their own informational resources and, in turn, preserve collective autonomy and personal dignity.

1.10 ARTICULATING THE VALUES AND PRINCIPLES OF DIGITAL INFRASTRUCTURE FOR THE COMMON GOOD

In a current working paper about "digital public infrastructure" – a concept that is implicitly posited as a corrective to the ambiguous framing of "smart cities" and "open data" – Eaves and Mazzucato (2024) assert that the concept of "public value" must be carefully specified in order to ensure that information systems that serve the public are created and governed for the "common good."

Toward this end, they make a distinction between two frames for understanding the values imbued in sociotechnical systems: the frame of "attributes" that describe the technical design of such systems, and the frame of "functions" that describe their societal purpose and benefits.

As an example of this distinction, consider the complementary difference between the FAIR Principles and the CARE Principles.

1.11 THE FAIR PRINCIPLES: SETTING BOUNDARIES AROUND THE TECHNICAL ATTRIBUTES OF "OPENNESS"

The FAIR Principles (Findable, Accessible, Interoperable, and Reusable) describe specific attributes that qualify the "openness" of data (Wilkinson et al. 2016). Each such attribute is further defined in substatements with principles by which open data can be made useful at scale – such as metadata with relevant attributes, unique and persistent identifiers, and detailed provenance.

These principles are technical and tactical – offering standardized criteria for production of data that is *useful*. This concretizes the meaning of "open data" as that which is specifically designed to be shared and used across many technologies and contexts.

Despite its name, however, the FAIR statement makes no normative claims about the purposes for which open data might be used – fairly or otherwise. The boundaries of openness are drawn around a set of objective questions pertaining to data formatting, publication, and licensing.

1.12 THE CARE PRINCIPLES: SETTING BOUNDARIES AROUND THE NORMATIVE DIMENSIONS OF DATA PRACTICES

The CARE Principles, by contrast, describe the positive functions of shared data: CARE – which stands for "collective benefit, authority to control, responsibility, and ethics" – describes the circumstances in which environmental, communal, and personal data can be collected and used for beneficent purposes (Carroll et al. 2020).

As such, these principles draw a standardized set of normative boundaries around the purposes of data sharing, especially that which involves Indigenous people and/or the environmental resources that they steward. In Eaves and Mazzucato's terms, these are functional values that complement the FAIR Principles' technical attributes.

1.13 "DIVERSITY, EQUITY, AND INCLUSION": ATTRIBUTES OF PLURALISM

Similar analysis can be applied to the common triad of "diversity, equity, and inclusion" (DEI) value statements. Democracy presumes equality among citizens – but in a world in which the boundaries and terms of citizenship are compromised in various ways by racism and wealth inequality, the attributes of democracy must be further qualified. The values of DEI are commonly posited in recognition of the otherwise-invisible power structures within and around institutions, as a declaration of commitment to strive to avoid the default states of hegemonic whiteness and capitalist disenfranchisement of those who do not have such claims to hegemonic power.

As with *openness* and *smartness*, however, DEI does not fully describe the functions to which these attributes are applied. Does inclusion of individual people of color in an organization's board – and, in turn, equitable remuneration of those persons – in and of itself mean that the organization serves a broader democratizing function in a diverse society? Perhaps not. Without further qualification, we can expect the interests of capital to be served often in ways that conflict with the interests of people and the public.

Functional values would specify *the ends* to which DEI serves democratic purposes. By answering the question *what are the results that we value?* a community can qualify what it would look like to achieve diverse, equitable, and inclusive results.

1.14 EXAMPLES OF VALUE STATEMENTS IN ACTION

For digital infrastructure processes that are committed to the maximization of the common good, Eaves and Mazzucato (2024, 18) assert that "a combined functional and attribute perspective is desired." They acknowledge, of course, that such common good will not be maximized simply through the act of articulating these values of functional purpose and technical attributes. Instead, this synthesis must be enacted through governance.

With just a brief glance at some examples, we can see what it looks like to apply values as boundaries in practice. These examples display a range of conditions on access to data – from partially open, to conditionally shareable, to entirely closed – that reflect values which have been intentionally prioritized over "openness" and "smartness."

1.15 THE INTERNATIONAL UNION FOR CONSERVATION OF NATURE RED LIST: WEIGHING OPENNESS AGAINST CONSERVATION

The International Union for Conservation of Nature (IUCN), for instance, is a global authority on ecosystem science. The IUCN's Red List compiles granular data about the location and concentration of plant and animal species. This data is essential for conservation efforts, and the IUCN's purpose is for public education – so an abstracted level of the data is intended to be "open" (in the sense of the FAIR principles) as a public knowledge resource. However, this data can also be useful for poaching efforts that target specific species. This is to say that there are tensions between the values upheld by the IUCN's mission.

As a result, the more granular levels of data in the IUCN's Red List are only available on request, under a licensing agreement that requires adherence to a stated function of conservation. The value of *conservation* is first established as a norm, reinforced by trust-building processes and, ultimately, rules. None of these steps can entirely prevent bad actors from conceivably repurposing this data for poaching purposes, but they can mitigate such risks – and establish the necessary preconditions for remediation.

1.16 TE MANA RARAUNGA'S CONSENT-BASED LICENSE

Te Hiku Media is a cultural initiative that has recorded and annotated hundreds of hours of spoken Māori language. This data is an essential input for the development of technologies that could serve iwi communities such as speech-to-text tools. Before sharing this cultural data trove on the internet, however, Te Hiku Media first designed and assigned a special license, the Kaitiakitanga License. This license is not premised on openness, but rather consent. The license requires that any project which uses the data must directly benefit the Māori people, subject to their approval.

In describing the rationale for this license, Te Hiku Media cites Te Mana Raraunga (n.d.), a network of Māori technologists that advocates for tribal *sovereignty* in matters pertaining to digital information about Māori people, language, culture, resources, and environments. Their statement of principles specifies *Authority*, *Relationships*, *Obligations*, *Collective benefit*, *Reciprocity*, and *Guardianship* (as translated from Māori language).

Accordingly, this license reinforces these boundaries around local knowledge, in defense of autonomy against more powerful private interests that might otherwise use open geographic, linguistic, and cultural data to facilitate a new wave of tribal dispossession.

1.17 MAPPING PALESTINIAN JERUSALEM: WEIGHING OPENNESS AGAINST JUSTICE

In another example, Public Lab worked with Palestinian communities to produce a participatory map of the urban environmental attributes of their neighborhoods in Jerusalem. Public Lab's mission specified the production of shared outputs – by which they typically meant open hardware, open-source software (such as MapKnitter, the tool used in this project), and open data – but this project's output was never published online in any format. This decision was made in order to protect the communities involved in its production. As Public Lab's leadership codesigned this project with Palestinian community leaders, they articulated values for the project that included "justice" and "sovereignty," which participants noted were directly in tension with "openness" in this context.

"Maps are so political," says Public Lab co-founder Liz Barry, reflecting on this project years afterward. "They are objects of power at the same time as they are objects of science. Open data isn't a universal good when its subjects are vulnerable. They may be producing data about themselves so that they can have more agency to determine their own fate, but that same data in other hands could enable outsiders to gain power and dominate them" (personal correspondence; see also Rambaldi et al. 2006).

1.18 WHY THIS MATTERS: WISHFUL WORDS OR DESIGN PARAMETERS?

Just as a natural resource system does not resemble the simplistic "commons" of Garrett Hardin's thought experiment (just a field, barren of any social context), a knowledge commons is more than just a dataset (Hardin 1968). Knowledge commons include systems of collective choice-making about what kinds of data will be collected, what kinds of data are considered useful, how data is made available. We make these choices in accordance with our values.

Of course, we know that any given institution's declared value statements will not necessarily inscribe all of the values that drive the collective choices of a community, much less the actions of the individuals within it – as with Ostrom's distinction between rules-in-form and rules-in-use, what is written down does not necessarily correspond with what actually happens (Ostrom 2005).

And yet value statements can serve as the cornerstones of institutional design – shaping a conceptual container from which new norms can emerge, and with which collective choice-making processes can be steered toward congruency in rules and equitability in outcomes.

1.19 COMMON OBJECTIONS TO THE ARTICULATION OF VALUES

Yet I often come across projects that seem to lack any such statements, or that have never bothered to apply or update them after their initial formative stages. In my experience, proposals to draft value statements, or revise them, tend to meet with resistance.

This resistance typically takes the form of some combination of the following reasons:

First, different people may have different values, so communities might be reluctant to exclude any particular group.

Second, value statements can be interpreted in different ways by different people, which leads some to conclude that such statements are useless or, even worse, may foment uncertainty and friction.

Third, value statements are in and of themselves unenforceable – and therefore are considered performative artifice rather than instrumental artifact.

Finally, value statements are assumed to be difficult to articulate in a democratic process.

The rest of this chapter will address each of these concerns. In order, I will observe that value statements can help to establish a community's identity, and subsequently apply this identity to the process of coping with dilemmas that naturally emerge among members with diverse interests; as such, value statements are *instrumental in even if insufficient for* good governance; and, finally, these statements are quite practical to draft without getting mired in endless procedural contention. I will conclude by offering pragmatic guidance for developing and applying value statements in open knowledge communities.

1.20 VALUES CAN SHAPE A GROUP'S IDENTITY: EXCLUDING BEHAVIORS, IF NOT PEOPLE

Different people have different values, and sometimes these values can be in tension with each other. So the concern is that a given set of values might exclude some people from a resource that is meant to be universally shared. This, however, is precisely a reason to articulate values: By specifying those values that are of presumably universal benefit and appeal, a community can delineate between those interests of its members that are held in common, and, conversely, those that may not be served.

As boundary objects, these artifacts create the space in which collective goals can emerge. Practically speaking, this can facilitate the formation and growth of a knowledge-sharing community by signaling trustworthiness to prospective contributors. By clearly articulating the good qualities associated with a knowledge-sharing initiative, the initiative can more easily attract participants and provide them a shared sense of identity.

In my own experience, this process can even shift the dynamics of competition in markets that otherwise risk failure. By articulating a shared purpose, and involving market actors who might feel accountable to that shared purpose (given its alignment with their brand, mission statement, etc.), value statements can imply the threat of a reputation cost to those who might not participate, because such nonparticipation may signal a rejection of these values.[1]

1.21 VALUE STATEMENTS ENABLE THE GENERATION OF "NORMATIVE KNOWLEDGE" FOR COPING WITH DILEMMAS

While shared data is the basis of "descriptive knowledge" produced by an informational commons, shared values are the basis of "normative knowledge" – about the purposes of such information, and the prospective risks that may be associated

[1] In the context of international relations, this is known as the power for otherwise nonbinding treaties to "tie hands" among actors who might otherwise act competitively, but wish to avoid the costs to reputation of noncompliance (Fearon 1997).

with it. Of course it is true that the same statement can be interpreted differently by different people (each of whom might have different secondary values, as acknowledged earlier) (Voida et al. 2014). This diversity of meanings, however, can itself be a strength rather than a liability for a community, in that it cultivates a rich collective understanding of its own dilemmas.

As Friedman et al. wrote (2006) about Value-Sensitive Design: "Generally, the more concretely (act-based) one conceptualizes a value, the more one will be led to recognizing cultural variation; conversely, the more abstractly one conceptualizes a value, the more one will be led to recognizing universals. Value Sensitive Design seeks to work both levels, the concrete and abstract, depending on the design problem at hand." This normative knowledge can facilitate the emergence of new kinds of norms – and, eventually, rules – by creating a shared framework for discourse and, in turn, deliberative institutional design. By establishing a rubric for articulation of trade-offs posed by dilemmas emerging from conflicts among stakeholders – including situations where different shared values are in tension with each other – communities can engage in a kind of "value-sensitive institutional design."

With this logic, communities can more effectively coordinate activities that might constrain some individual interests in order to promote those that are shared. As such, value statements enable the emergence of other logical and ethical boundaries not just around scope but also around contributors, data subjects, uses, and outcomes. By equipping a knowledge-sharing community to describe both the common good and individual benefit using the same terms, we can translate Ostrom's second principle – "Rules regarding the appropriation and provision of common resources that are adapted to local conditions" – from a primarily spatial orientation to a social context.

1.22 VALUE STATEMENTS ARE NOT DIRECTLY ENFORCEABLE, BUT THEY ARE USEFUL FOR PRIORITIZATION

In and of themselves, value statements may not be enforceable as rules. They express aspirations. Even if a norm is essentially universally recognized, there is not any consensus as to what consequences should result from its violation.

Value statements, however, can entail attendant logics about what *kinds of use* are intended, and what *kinds of outcomes* are expected. In turn, uses and outcomes that are considered inappropriate and unsanctioned can be disincentivized, if not prohibited (Sanfilippo and Frischmann 2023).

Despite the limitless potential inherent in the promise of openness, there are always constraints of time and energy that require some kinds of data, and some kinds of uses, to be prioritized over others. In this way, value statements can help overcome the conceptual limitations of "open" or "smart" initiatives by specifying additional parameters for successful outcomes. Certain kinds of values such as *trust* and *safety* are essentially subtractable resources: They can be depleted by inappropriate actions. Such undesirable actions might not be entirely preventable by a given community – given the nature of the knowledge and/or the other kinds of values in a community – but the community can decide to establish processes and structures that can mitigate these risks.

1.23 VALUES HELP US KNOW WHAT WE WANT TO KNOW: HOW TO MONITOR, WHAT TO EVALUATE

Values also clarify the kinds of curation and feedback that are desirable – making explicit the kinds of user inputs that are considered positive or negative. This, in turn, may have significant implications on design decisions pertaining to monitoring and evaluation of data quality. Without such normative knowledge, many knowledge-sharing projects might default to monitoring that which is easily quantifiable – number of entries, rate of growth, and so on – which does not necessarily accord with the most important aspects of the health of the knowledge ecosystem and its community of users.

How do we observe what is happening with the resource? Do we have processes for reflecting on this analysis, and acting accordingly in affirmation of our values?

Parmiggiani and Grisot (2020) observe that these questions are not just asked by designers, but also through the distributed activities of administrators and users in a knowledge-sharing commons, as they engage in "situated resolution" of various kinds of problems encountered as they engage in *achieving data quality, filtering the relevant data, and ensuring data protection.*

"[T]he practices for assessing data quality are emergent and contextual, as well as involve stakeholders with different interests and training in data management and who actively participate in producing the data and ensuring their quality by means of several informal heuristics. Generating good quality data is thus open to interpretation and context dependent." Parmiggiani and Grisot (2020, 22) describe examples, for instance, in which satellite monitoring includes cranes in a dataset about urban trees – a kind of error that is more likely to be caught by local knowledge that can distinguish among signals such as height. "Often, these contributions remain visible to other workers on the same research site but invisible to managerial levels in the organization where data governance decisions are formally made" (Parmiggiani and Grisot 2020, 28). By explicitly stating values, a knowledge-sharing community can promote distributed data governance decisions as close as possible to the context in which data is gathered, verified, and used.

1.24 DEMOCRATIC WRITING WITHOUT GRIDLOCK: THE ADVICE PROCESS

Useful value statements reflect a variety of perspectives, and as such the process of crafting them tends to benefit from a degree of democratic input (Allen 2014). As per

Ostrom's principle of "collective choice arrangements," truly valuable value statements are those that reflect (and can be changed in accordance with) the perspectives of the various members of a community that contributes to and uses a resource.

Effective "democratic writing," however, does not need to be conducted by committee. Responsibility for drafting value statements on behalf of a community can be distributed through a method such as the Advice Process (Bakke 2013; see also the Equal Experts' Advice Process Playbook n.d.). Through such a process, authorial power is delegated to an individual, or small group of people, with requirements to engage all interested parties in iterative cycles of review, feedback, and revision.

Before further considering these means, I should briefly address the ends: *True consensus is not strictly necessary for effective democratic writing.* A middle path between majority vote or unanimous agreement is *concordance and consent*: The result should reflect the broadest possible agreement that can be reached without strong objection. In other words, everyone does not have to totally agree with everything, as long as all are willing to live with it. This process – delegation, feedback, and consent – can enable a group to account for differences without getting bogged down by disagreement.

1.25 IDENTIFYING AND ENGAGING STAKEHOLDERS

Assuming there is already an articulated purpose for a given project, the next step is to identify the different sets of stakeholders who are impacted by this purpose. This might include the public at large, but also should include specific groups of direct participants and indirectly impacted parties – data contributors, data subjects, and so on. With the purpose statement front and center, invite representatives of each group to share their reactions. This can be done in many one-on-one dialogues, though group discussions can generate invaluable energy and, in turn, insights. Write down what they say (and make sure to review with them to affirm you have got it right).

1.26 ARTICULATION AND SYNTHESIS

As this process iterates, different stakeholders will likely use different vocabularies. This is OK; patterns will emerge. Look for similar statements that can be coherently grouped together under a single word or phrase: These are your contenders. Polling can help identify those which resonate the most across groups.[2] This process may benefit from cycles of expansion and convergence: generation of all possible

[2] The CARE principles hold that, while each group might perceive different benefits and risks, those who are most directly impacted (such as data subjects and/or those whose livelihoods might be directly affected by data use) should typically receive deference in this process. This principle, however, may merit exceptions in cases of public interest such as disease tracing and water quality assessment.

value statements, followed by clustering, synthesis, and naming the smallest possible set of unique themes.

My personal preference for formatting value statements takes a pyramidal approach: Values ought to be expressible as a single word or phrase, and from there can be elaborated. A single word or phrase ought to be definable in a single sentence. And this single phrase with its one-sentence definition can then be elaborated in a longer paragraph that addresses the various permutations of that value across significant contexts. Such a nesting structure enables the artifact as a whole to be adapted for multiple purposes – from thumbnails to essays.

There is no rule about this, but I suggest looking for a number of value statements that can be counted on one hand. Any larger and it is hard to keep track; anyway, I would bet that among six or more potential statements, at least two will be similar in intent and can be merged.[3]

1.27 FORGE A BALANCING INSTRUMENT

An appropriate set of values should work together as a system – like primary colors, elemental attributes, or cardinal directions. One value on its own might be insufficient and conflict with others if prioritized exclusively; together, they can form a kind of normative compass. (For instance, a value of *sustainability* might entail revenue-generation strategies, but these might conflict with values of *equitability* or *accessibility*; there may not necessarily be one right way to resolve these tensions, yet by naming them communities can begin to cope with them.)

The value statements should be political, in the sense that they offer a positive vision of how the world should work, though noncontroversial, in that they should be universally appealing (at least among the identified stakeholder groups).

With these values in hand, a community can continue this practice of dialogic inquiry throughout its lifecycle: In any given context, ask how a given value can be best realized, how a given set of values can best be brought into balance.

1.28 IN CONCLUSION: A WAY TO BEGIN, AND MEANS TO ENDURE

In reviewing my outline for this piece, I spoke with one organizer who expressed that they had once relented in the face of resistance to this process – "There was a sense that we didn't have time, that just doing the work was more important" – only to eventually regret it when conflicts later emerged. "Spending time to agree on these principles and values enables you to be flexible and adaptive later. It enables different people working on different things to feel committed to each other, because they share this common language."

[3] Odd-numbered sets seem to be somewhat more satisfying and easier to remember than those with even numbers, for reasons that I find hard to explain.

Through this process of elaboration, a community can both set the parameters for more complex forms of collective choice-making and engage in collective learning about the process thereof, in order to clear pathways through what might otherwise seem to be intractable dilemmas.

Value statements are of course not sufficient – not inherently binding in and of themselves, and subject to interpretation by different stakeholders with different logics that may be in tension with each other and result in conflict. For effective and sustainable collective action to steward digital resources, however, value statements may be considered practically essential – critical inputs to ongoing, iterative processes of evaluation and collective choice-making.[4]

This foundation of normative knowledge can give leaders, members, and subjects alike a common framework for communication about their motivations, and about the rationale for decisions, as they navigate and negotiate across contexts. By explicitly stating its values, a community establishes an agenda for education of its members as cocreators of a shared world.

4 To borrow Lee Vinsel's provocative formulation (2023): Value statements equip us with the compass we need to be better reactionaries.

2

Inexorably Entangled Environmental and Knowledge Commons

Todd Aagaard and Brett M. Frischmann

For people to effectively share an environment, they usually also must effectively share knowledge about that environment. While seemingly obvious and intuitive, this insight is often overlooked in literature about governing resources as commons.[1] Focusing on the knowledge commons associated with an environmental commons helps to illuminate a host of complex governance dilemmas. This chapter examines the interrelationship between environmental and knowledge commons, weaving together different strands of commons research and practice.

Every environmental commons has a corresponding knowledge commons that provides an essential foundation for managing the shared environmental resources.[2] We can improve our understanding of an environmental commons by investigating its associated knowledge commons.[3] In addition, our prescriptions for environmental commons governance should account for the relationship between an environmental commons and its associated knowledge commons and for the challenges of creating and maintaining an associated knowledge commons.

1 "'[X] commons' … refers to an approach (commons) to governing the management and/or production of a particular type of resource ([X]). Commons refers to a form of community management or governance. It applies to resources, and involves a group or community of people, but commons does not denote the resources, the community, a place, or a thing. Commons is the institutional arrangement of these elements…. Critically, commons governance is used by a wide variety of communities to manage many different types of resources. Commons governance confronts various obstacles to sustainable sharing and cooperation. Some of those obstacles derive from the nature of the resources and others derive from other factors, such as the nature of the community or external influences." (Frischmann et al. 2014, 2).

2 Although we begin with examples that involve natural resources commons, the term "environmental commons" – and the framework we offer here – applies equally to built environments such as road traffic and the internet. Later in the chapter we offer some examples of built environments and their associated knowledge commons.

3 For ease of exposition, we generally refer to the environmental commons–knowledge commons relationship as if it were one-to-one, with a single environmental commons for each knowledge commons, and vice versa. The reality is often more complex, with multiple domains of knowledge relevant to multiple environments. These domains may overlap, nest, or relate to each other, such that identifying and defining a single environmental commons or knowledge commons as if it were a distinct and discrete phenomenon oversimplifies a web of relationships.

The knowledge commons associated with an environmental commons includes a diversity of knowledge relevant to the environmental commons. At a minimum, the knowledge commons includes the knowledge necessary for a relevant community to delineate and understand the shared environmental resources, their collective relationships with those resources, and the social demand for institutionalized governance. In addition to this *descriptive baseline knowledge*, the knowledge commons includes *managerial knowledge* – that is, descriptive knowledge about the community's relationship to the shared resources that enables the community to make ongoing decisions about how to manage the resources. This may include, for example, knowledge about how one use of the shared environmental resources affects other uses. It also may include knowledge about how to operationalize rules-in-use. At a minimum, the knowledge commons provides the type of descriptive account of the environmental commons that community members might provide first hand or that one might encounter in a conventional Ostrom-inspired case study of a commons.

Effective management requires more than just descriptive knowledge of the environmental commons. In addition, the community must make certain normative judgments about the environmental commons that are in some sense constitutive of the community itself. The community must, for example, define whose interests in the environmental commons count and who will have a voice in managing the environmental commons. And the community will have to determine other normative judgments that will guide its management decisions, such as whether the community will adhere to an egalitarian ethic or give some uses or users of the environmental commons priority over others. An understanding of these normative judgments among the community will be crucial to the ability of the community to manage the environmental commons. Indeed, to the extent that the community lacks a shared understanding of the environmental commons or of its normative priorities, this is likely to significantly impede the community's ability to effectively manage the environmental commons. Normative disagreements about the environmental commons are likely to induce disagreements about even the descriptive knowledge in the knowledge commons. The knowledge commons thus plays an important role as a venue for communicating, contesting, and negotiating normative judgments and governance decisions about the environmental commons. Because the knowledge commons is crucial to managing the environmental commons, conflicts about managing the environmental commons will often manifest themselves in conflicts in the knowledge commons.

As Figure 2.1 illustrates, the relationship between an environmental commons and its associated knowledge commons is bidirectional. The physical, social, and political characteristics of the environmental commons generate the knowledge that constitutes the associated knowledge commons. In this sense, the knowledge commons depends deeply on the environmental commons. But humans understand the environmental commons through the lens of the knowledge commons, and governance

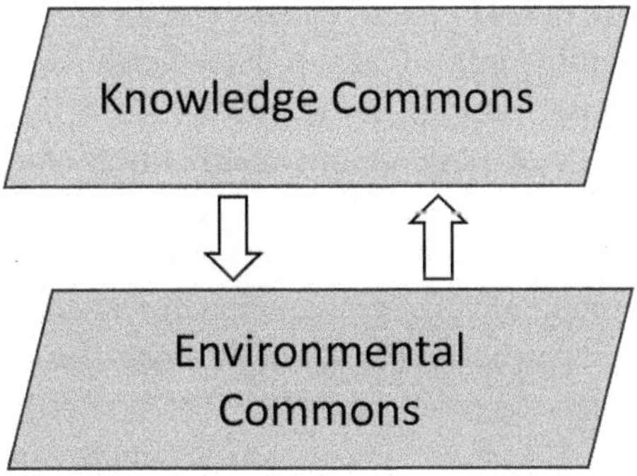

FIGURE 2.1 The knowledge commons–environmental commons relationship.

of the environmental commons therefore requires the knowledge commons to inform decision making about the environmental commons. The bidirectional relationship creates an interdependency between environmental commons governance and knowledge commons governance. Controversies in environmental commons governance are likely to cause controversy over the knowledge commons, and vice versa.[4]

Recognizing the existence of knowledge commons associated with environmental commons, and the role of knowledge commons in managing environmental commons, yields at least three important insights. First, to understand environmental commons, we often will have to study their associated knowledge commons.[5] Second, because normative judgments are embedded in the knowledge commons, understanding the relevance of knowledge commons to environmental commons also highlights the role of normative judgments in what otherwise may be assumed to be objective information about the environmental commons. Understanding knowledge commons as commons means recognizing that the knowledge in a knowledge commons is itself a socially determined product of governance decisions, not merely "the facts." Third, as shared resources and potential loci of stakeholder conflict, knowledge commons present distinct social dilemmas that demand governance institutions. Ostrom's design principles for commons, as well as the Governing Knowledge Commons (GKC), Institutional

4 Not all information about an environmental commons is necessarily in the knowledge commons. Some information may be treated as proprietary – for example, the location of resources in the environmental commons. Many people who search for mushrooms or berries on public lands keep information about their choice locations secret – that is, out of the knowledge commons regarding the lands. Archeologists often keep confidential the location of sites to prevent looting.

5 This insight runs both ways. As we have explored in the GKC tradition, understanding knowledge commons requires paying careful attention to background contexts, including natural, material, and technosocial environments, and these often involve environmental commons. In this chapter, we do not mean to prioritize environmental commons and cast knowledge commons as adjuncts. We recognize, and have elsewhere written about, the complex interdependencies among resource systems, polycentric governance, and other such complications.

Analysis and Development (IAD), and Social-Ecological Systems frameworks, can be useful for understanding and managing knowledge commons associated with environmental commons.[6]

Section 2.1 illustrates our basic points about the environmental commons–knowledge commons relationship with a simple example, the well-trodden allegory of a pasture shared by a community of herders. We extend the descriptive account of the environmental commons to show the necessary existence of a corresponding knowledge commons. Then, we illustrate the additional functions of the knowledge commons.

Section 2.2 takes the shared grazing pasture example and expands it in three deliberate steps, by adding stylized variations in the types of grazing animals and corresponding effects. Each step complicates the scenario in ways that present different governance challenges and depend upon different knowledge. The final two extensions present distinct types of normative complications that present additional demands on knowledge institutions. One involves interaction effects that force a normative choice about priorities among uses of the shared resource, and the second involves external effects that extend beyond the community and shared resource system itself; these are like an extraterritorial effect. Whether or not, and to what extent, a community cares about such effects is a sociopolitical consideration about priorities.

The highly stylized examples in Section 2.1 and Section 2.2 are merely illustrative. In lieu of a pasture, we could present similar stylized examples and variations using a different shared natural resource, such as a lake or woodland, or even a built environment, such as a road system, computer server, or living room. By illustrating different types of social dilemmas and governance challenges, we hope to provide a bridge between the environmental commons and knowledge commons. Essentially, we show how governance of the environmental commons depends upon the knowledge commons, and how, as the scale, scope, and heterogeneity of the environmental commons increase, the complexity of the knowledge commons increases as well.

Section 2.3 applies the insights developed in Sections 2.1 and 2.2 to a series of examples. We open with an example of a natural environment (forest management) and then turn to two examples of built environments (road systems and living rooms).

Section 2.4 builds on the insights from these examples to begin to address questions of how attributes of environmental resource commons affect their associated

6 As GKC scholars have discussed extensively, neither Ostrom's design principles nor the IAD framework maps perfectly onto knowledge commons because of fundamental differences in the underlying resources systems and corresponding social dilemmas and governance challenges. See Frischmann et al. 2014: 12–21 (providing explanation and developing GKC framework as an adaptation of IAD framework).

knowledge commons, and how to govern knowledge commons so that they can support better governance of environmental commons.

In conclusion, we propose additional research both to retrospectively mine past case studies of environmental commons to highlight the often-hidden knowledge commons at work and additional case studies of more complex commons that may raise more complicated and nuanced issues with respect to the environmental commons–knowledge commons relationship. Overall, this is an area rich with opportunity for additional theoretical and empirical inquiry.

2.1 A STYLIZED EXPLORATION OF A CLASSIC ENVIRONMENTAL COMMONS AND CORRESPONDING KNOWLEDGE COMMONS: HERDING SHEEP ON A SHARED PASTURE

Assume an environmental resource, such as a meadow (natural) or highway (built), that is shared freely without restriction. That is, assume the resource is presumptively open to all-comers and there is no mechanism for coordinating the actions of resource users. Consumption may initially be nonrivalrous, if, for example, the population is small relative to the capacity of the resource, but it may turn rivalrous over time.[7] The resource may be depleted and even destroyed entirely, as individuals rationally decide to use the resource at a rate and in a manner that maximizes private gains but disregards the effects that such use has on other users or more generally on the sustainability of the resource. Here is how Hardin (1968, 1244) famously explained it:

> Picture a pasture open to all. It is to be expected that each herdsman will try to keep as many cattle as possible on the commons…
>
> As a rational being, each herdsman seeks to maximize his gain. Explicitly or implicitly, more or less consciously, he asks, "What is the utility to me of adding one more animal to my herd?" This utility has one negative and one positive component.
>
> 1) The positive component is a function of the increment of one animal. Since the herdsman receives all the proceeds from the sale of the additional animal, the positive utility is nearly +1.
>
> 2) The negative component is a function of the additional overgrazing created by one more animal. Since, however, the effects of overgrazing are shared by all the herdsmen, the negative utility for any particular decision-making herdsman is only a fraction of −1.
>
> Adding together the component partial utilities, the rational herdsman concludes that the only sensible course for him to pursue is to add another animal to his herd. And another; and another.… But this is the conclusion reached by each and every rational herdsman sharing a commons. Therein is the tragedy. Each man

7 Nonrivalrous means that one user's consumption of the resource does not impact the resource capacity (i.e., supply) available to satisfy the demands of other users.

> is locked into a system that compels him to increase his herd without limit – in a world that is limited. Ruin is the destination toward which all men rush, each pursuing his own best interest in a society that believes in the freedom of the commons. Freedom in a commons brings ruin to all.

Hardin recognized two potential solutions to this type of social dilemma: government regulation and privatization. Both rely on collective action through governmental institutions to introduce constraints on resource consumption. Government can constrain consumption by directly managing or regulating use of the shared resource, limiting consumption to sustainable levels. Alternatively, government can create a system of private property rights delineating ownership of the resource, which supports incentives for conservation by internalizing the externalities of resource use. The approaches differ substantially in terms of the manner in which ongoing (month-to-month, day-to-day) resource allocation decisions are made. Both effectively eliminate the commons and replace it with a different governance regime.[8] Notably, although not explicitly described in most accounts of commons, including Hardin's, both governance approaches require a body of knowledge about the resource that is accessible to those managing the resource, whether government officials or private owners.[9] This knowledge includes an understanding of the resource itself, but also an understanding of the relationships between users and the resource and of the normative judgments underlying management of the resource.

Elinor Ostrom challenged Hardin's frame by asking two foundational sets of questions: First, how well does the tragedy of the commons allegory describe reality? Does the allegory accurately predict real-world behavior of individuals sharing common-pool resources? Second, does the allegory provide a useful basis for choosing or designing management solutions? Are the governance options limited to government command-and-control regulation and private property-enabled markets? (Frischmann 2013).

As to the first set of questions, Ostrom posited that reality is much more complicated and nuanced than Hardin's simple allegory suggests, in ways that are important to managing resources. Ostrom (2007; 1990) identified many ways in which Hardin's allegory was overly reductionist and distorting, so much so that it could "lead the analyst to miss what is most important and focus on what is least relevant" (Frischmann 2013, 390). In other words, Hardin's allegory itself presented a knowledge dilemma.

8 This is a strong statement based on the idea that primary authority over how to govern the resources no longer rests with the community as such. Instead, authority is vested in government actors (e.g., regulators) or market actors (e.g., property owners), and those authorities may serve other interests besides those of the community. Of course, these authorities ultimately may create and depend upon different commons embedded in and structured by regulatory or market regimes.

9 This observation could easily open a complex can of worms. One strand to consider in the comparative evaluation of government and market processes for generating, curating, sharing, and acting upon such knowledge. There is a rich literature on this topic.

Hardin conflated resource and governance by referring to the shared pasture that was openly accessible to all-comers as the commons, which then, on certain strict assumptions, was doomed to tragedy. But the resource (e.g., pasture) is distinct from the governance regime (e.g., open access, commons, government regulation, private property enabled market) that manages it. The term "commons" describes a form of governance, not a type of resource. Furthermore, a resource managed as a commons is not necessarily subject to open access. Commons involve "institutionalized sharing of resources among members of a community," but not necessarily with nonmembers or the general public (Madison et al. 2010, 841).

As to the second set of questions, Ostrom argued that effective cooperative management is theoretically and practically feasible. Natural resource commons can be effectively managed as commons and therefore are not doomed to suffer tragedy and need not be eliminated. Community management, social norms, and other related institutions can and often do outperform government regulation and privatized market arrangements.[10]

How to effectively govern shared resources as commons has been a core interdisciplinary research question for decades. The provisional answer is that effective commons governance depends on the context and community. It also depends, we argue, on shared knowledge.[11] Based on extensive fieldwork, Ostrom proposed the following design principles:

1. Define clear boundaries for the community and shared resources.
2. Tailor appropriation and provision rules to local needs and conditions.
3. Enable those affected by operational rules to participate in modifying the rules.
4. Ensure monitors are accountable to (or are) the appropriators.
5. Use graduated sanctions for rule violators.
6. Provide accessible, low-cost means for resolving conflicts.
7. Make sure external authorities recognize and respect the rule-making authority of community members.
8. When part of larger resource systems, build responsibility for governing the common resource in nested tiers.

These offer useful, albeit broad, guidance. Notably for our purposes, each principle relies substantially on shared knowledge – for example, how different rules would affect use of a resource, or whether different possible sanctions might

[10] In reality, these are not wholly independent. Government regulation, for example, often builds on existing social norms, and government regulation can influence the development of social norms. The evolution of social norms and laws regarding alcohol-impaired driving provide an apt example.

[11] While this seems intuitively obvious and thus not an argument that needs to be made, the role(s) of shared community knowledge in enabling effective governance of shared environmental resources is *underrepresented* in case studies and other scholarship on environmental commons. Consequently, the governance challenges associated with generating, curating, sharing, and maintaining such knowledge is understudied.

deter potential rule violators. The design principles promote effective governance because they help individuals understand their capacity to cooperate in self-governance, which in turn depends on a shared base of knowledge about the resource and the community. Ostrom recognized this, albeit sometimes only implicitly and indirectly. Ostrom explained how the credibility of the design principles as an explanation of persistent, and thus effective, commons governance depended on showing that the design principles affected incentives of community members and perpetuated across generations. Both of these impacts – incentivization and perpetuation – require internalization and transmission of knowledge.[12]

To illustrate how environmental commons are inexorably linked to knowledge commons, let us return to Hardin's stylized allegory of a pasture shared by a group of sheepherders. For the herders to manage the pasture as a commons, they need to share some knowledge about the pasture and about themselves as a community. For our sheepherders, that knowledge may be as simple as understanding that other sheepherders are using the pasture to graze their sheep and that the pasture's capacity to sustainably support grazing is limited. Conceivably that knowledge alone could be enough to lead the herders to limit their use of the pasture for their common benefit.

More sophisticated management of the pasture may require more knowledge. The herders would benefit from recognizing themselves as the group of individuals that is mutually dependent on the pasture. It also would be helpful if they have a technical understanding of the pasture and the effects of grazing on the pasture. Beyond such technical knowledge, the herders have certain normative understandings of themselves as a community – for example, whether their access to the pasture is presumptively equal or whether some herders have priority over others, or whether the pasture should be managed for short-term benefit or long-term benefit, and whether anyone else other than the herders should have a say in managing the pasture. If there are any rules governing use of the pasture, the herders need to know them. Perhaps the herders should consider whether the pasture should be used for grazing or instead for other uses, such as cropland, hunting, or natural preserve. It is also helpful, albeit not necessarily essential, if the herders communicate with each other about these areas of knowledge and share a common understanding.[13] In short, to relate this discussion to the IAD and GKC

[12] For example, Ostrom explained how knowledge about boundaries and rules-in-use shape expectations and actions of community members. Participation in monitoring, for example, generates useful information and reduces uncertainty about how rules-in-use might be applied. Overall, the design principles promote governance because they help individuals understand their capacity to cooperate in self-governance, which in turn depends on a shared base of knowledge about the resource and the community.

[13] Customs can evolve without planning and explicit communication. For example, if a few individual users of a shared warming hut individually decide to replenish the firewood before they leave, then a

frameworks, the herders must have some shared understanding about the action arena within which they operate, and this requires shared knowledge about the biophysical characteristics, attributes of the community, and rules-in-use.

To be clear, this common knowledge need not be perfect, in the sense of being comprehensive, fully accurate, or universally agreed upon. The herders may disagree about the carrying capacity of the pasture, about whether grazing rights should be allocated equally among herders, or about who has the right to graze on the pasture. Differences of opinion regarding management of the pasture may well manifest in differences of opinion as to the relevant knowledge about the pasture. The more accurate and agreed upon the knowledge is, however, the better the knowledge can motivate and support cooperation via community governance. Given an opportunity to communicate (and not artificially forced into a one-shot prisoner's dilemma), the herders may be able to develop, share, and act upon such common knowledge.[14]

Despite the centrality of knowledge to commons governance, we, as analysts or storytellers about environmental commons, tend to presume that a knowledge commons functions effectively in the background but generally do not focus on the knowledge commons as a subject of our analysis or story.

Suppose our group of sheepherders agrees about the collective need to constrain use of the pasture according to a set of agreed-upon rules. The pasture, they realize, can become overcrowded with sheep, causing deterioration. Assume each sheepherder uses the pasture similarly and that the sheep graze similarly. The social dilemma they face is thus what economists call an "anonymous crowding" (congestion) problem because using the pasture in this scenario entails homogeneous uses (Cornes and Sandler 1996, 355). The attributes of individual users (herders, sheep) do not matter for the purpose of making the rules for the pasture. What matters is the overall capacity of the pasture, the overall number of sheep grazing in the pasture, and the rate (intensity) at which the sheep are consuming the pasture grass. It follows that effective governance in this situation requires some knowledge about each of these parameters. Such knowledge informs the primary governance decision about allocation rules for the pasture, which may boil down to simple rationing – that is, how many sheep can each herder graze, and for how long.[15]

custom of replenishing the firewood could develop without any explicit planning or communication. On commonsensical social norms, see Frischmann (2021).

14 To highlight the importance of shared knowledge to governance of the environmental commons, imagine strangers who lack the (pre)requisite common knowledge – for example, a new herder who, ignorant of the scarce capacity in the pasture or the existence of other herders using the pasture, brings new sheep onto the pasture and thereby unintentionally causes severe damage to its ability to support grazing.

15 Other means for addressing anonymous crowding include capacity expansion and congestion- or usage-sensitive pricing (Frischmann 2012, 141–149).

Game theory models and common knowledge. The tragedy of the commons has been modeled in game theory as a prisoner's dilemma. While the model predictably leads to defection and tragedy, Ostrom emphasized how real-world scenarios rarely fit the model (Frischmann 2013, 390–392; Ostrom 2007, 15183). Once communication among players and/or repeated interactions among players is allowed (rather than assumed away), cooperation is much more likely. Notably, to talk meaningfully about available moves, strategies, and consequences – i.e., the "payoff structure" in game theoretic terms – requires some base level of shared understanding, which in turn implies the existence of knowledge commons.

If the sheepherders are committed to governing their shared pasture as a commons, rather than resorting to other governance regimes such as government command-and-control or privatization, then a corresponding knowledge commons dilemma also arises.[16] Essentially, the community of herders must generate and share the knowledge needed to govern its environmental commons. The herders may need, for example, to develop an understanding of consumption patterns and long-term impacts. Understanding the need for such information, the herders may create the knowledge commons intentionally through planning and study. Alternatively, the knowledge commons may arise informally and unintentionally as individual herders debating governance options share their experiences with the pasture and what they have observed about the effects of grazing.

The relevant information in the knowledge commons may develop through consensus, or it may be hotly contested among stakeholders. Conflicts may arise over how to frame risks, resolve uncertainty, or deal with contested knowledge. Heuristics, biases, and other psychological and sociological phenomena may challenge the commonality of the knowledge commons. Or, by contrast, the herders may govern the knowledge commons in ways that reduce conflict and build consensus about how to manage the pasture. They may, for example, agree to defer to the judgment of an appointed person – someone known and trusted by the community, or an outside expert – as to the carrying capacity of the pasture.

Regardless, our point is simply that even the most basic environmental commons requires joint effort toward the generation, curation, and sharing of knowledge about the environmental commons. This is implicit in Ostrom's first three design principles, which focus on defining the resource and the community, finding rules that reflect local needs and conditions, and enabling participation to change rules.

16 In fact, knowledge commons dilemmas lurk behind most governance decisions, regardless of whether a commons resource is involved. Government regulation as a general matter depends on knowledge commons, involving different sets of stakeholders, governance institutions, and so on. Frankly, the same can be said in the context of privatization and markets (Dekker and Kuchař 2021). Nonetheless, our focus here is on collective governance of resources managed as commons.

Ostrom's other design principles also depend upon developing and communicating shared knowledge – among community members, with outsiders, and as integral parts of governance institutions (e.g., sanctions, dispute resolution). Suppose, for example, that our community of sheepherders agrees on a system for allocating grazing rights among themselves. Effective governance will require monitoring and tracking compliance with these rules-in-use.[17]

The quality of an environmental commons – its value to the community – depends on the effectiveness of the community's governance. Like an environmental commons, a knowledge commons also may need active management to serve its function of informing decisions about the environmental commons. Left unmanaged, problems of inaccurate knowledge and lack of access to knowledge may dominate the knowledge commons. The absence of definitive information about transmission of the COVID-19 virus, for example, deprived public health experts of a consensus of information on which to build norms of mutual protection. Because effective environmental commons governance requires a well-functioning knowledge commons, effective environmental commons governance therefore will require an effective strategy for governing the associated knowledge commons.

So far, we have described the environmental resource as if it only generates outputs – here, grazing areas for the herders' sheep. This view implicitly presumes the pasture is natural.[18] Of course, it is not. The pasture itself is a social construction, involving a reshaping of the natural environment through particular human activities. Rather than a pasture, it could be many other things.[19] Further, consider how the community contributes inputs that affect the environmental resource as well as complementary goods that affect how community members interact with the resource and each other. Herders may, for example, create trails in the pasture, construct a fence around the pasture, or build a place to sit while the sheep graze. The benefits of these inputs and complementary goods inure to the herders who invest in them, but also to all other herders as well. This creates a potential problem. Users of shared resources may be disinclined to invest in contributions that would add value to the resource system without any confidence that they, as opposed to other users, will be able to enjoy the fruits of their efforts. A herder may

17 Some knowledge resources for these purposes may be simple, such as tracking the number of sheep each herder brings to the pasture to graze. Still, deciding who collects, records, curates, and has access to such information raises distinct governance concerns. Should herders be relied upon to self-report, or will some designated person keep track? Some information may be more complicated and difficult to obtain, such as data on actual consumption rates and corresponding impacts on resource capacity. Such data can help to reduce uncertainty, resolve conflicts, and revise rules. But herders who oppose limits on pasture use may attempt to hinder gathering of reliable information about pasture use and its effects.

18 It also can lead to the mistaken impression that the pasture is passive and static, like a mine yielding ore, when in fact it is dynamic and full of life.

19 Designating the land a pasture and deciding it should be used for herding animals is a significant use restriction as it may preclude a wide range of other uses, such as recreation, cropland, or leaving it fallow. We revisit this point in the context of interaction effects. See Section 2.2.

not bother to build a place to sit, for example, even though other herders would also enjoy sitting there and benefit from the first herder's efforts.

Similar issues arise for knowledge resources, which often function as inputs and complementary goods and face incentive issues rooted in concerns about free riding. Take, for example, information about areas of the pasture that are especially good for grazing. A herder with knowledge of the best grazing areas may be disinclined to share that information with other herders because sharing the information will not benefit, and may in fact disadvantage, the first herder. Similarly, a user may be disinclined to invest in contributing potentially valuable information to the knowledge base because other users will take advantage of the information, without benefit (and potentially with detriment) to the first user. For example, a herder may be disinclined to invest the time to survey the precise boundaries of the pasture because the cost of surveying the pasture outweighs the benefits to the herder, not taking account that the survey would be valuable to other users as well.

Yet in some cases, unlike a conventional environmental resource, information will be *more* advantageous to the user if other users have access to it. For example, if the pasture is generally believed to support only grazing by 200 sheep, but one herder who would like to have more sheep has information (or an innovation) supporting the idea that the pasture actually can sustainably support grazing by 300 sheep, it is in that herder's interest first to invest in contributing that information to the communal knowledge base and second to make that information accessible to the other herders. Thus, here the incentives have reversed. The presence of other herders gives the herder more, rather than less, incentive to invest in contributing the information to the communal knowledge base and to make the information accessible to others. Managing a knowledge commons effectively requires taking into consideration the different incentives that members of the community will have to contribute to, or hinder, the accumulation and distribution of information about the environmental commons.

2.2 EXTENDING THE STYLIZED EXPLORATION OF CLASSIC ENVIRONMENTAL COMMONS AND CORRESPONDING KNOWLEDGE COMMONS: HERDING SHEEP AND OTHER ANIMALS ON A SHARED PASTURE

We now build from the sheepherding example and expand it in three deliberate steps, by adding stylized variations in the types of grazing animals and corresponding effects. At each stage, varying the facts has implications both for the environmental commons and the associated knowledge commons.[20]

[20] This section draws from the "Managing Congestion" chapter of Frischmann (2012), which developed these stylized examples to illustrate different governance dilemmas and solutions. Frischmann did not, however, elaborate on the corresponding knowledge commons.

Even prior to undertaking the challenge of managing the pasture as a commons, the community must make certain foundational decisions. The herders and perhaps others must decide, either individually or collectively, that they want to use the land as a pasture rather than for other purposes, such as homesites, a forest for harvesting timber, cropland, or recreational uses. This decision presents a governance dilemma, which requires both descriptive and normative knowledge for the community to address. Descriptively, the community must understand the land in question as a potential pasture site. Ideally but not necessarily, the community also will have some knowledge about other potential uses for the land, and the relative advantages and disadvantages of each alternative use. Normatively, the community must define who may participate in the decision about how to use the land and the process for making that decision, as well as the criteria the community will apply in deciding among alternatives. Like the use of the land itself, contributions of information to the knowledge commons are likely to occur strategically. A proponent of using the land as cropland, for example, may publicize the benefits of cropland and the disadvantages of other potential uses. How the community creates and manages the knowledge commons may effectively decide how it decides to use the land, such as if the community envisions land use as a matter of tradition and the land has traditionally been used as a pasture. Or the knowledge commons may play a supporting but not defining role in managing the environmental commons. The ability of the community to decide the best use of the land will depend in significant part on whether it is able to generate a robust and diverse knowledge commons on which to base its decisions about the land.

Turning to management of the land as a pasture, in the first scenario, described in Section 2.1, a community of sheepherders shared a pasture and governed it (and themselves) as a commons. Grazing sheep on the pasture gave rise to a potential social dilemma that can be framed as an anonymous crowding congestion problem. Managing congestion and avoiding tragedy required the community to determine rules-in-use regarding grazing and to monitor compliance with and to enforce the rules. The management decisions that created and implemented the rules depended on the existence of a shared body of knowledge, with both descriptive and normative components, about the pasture and the herders' relationship to the pasture and to each other. Thus, this natural resource commons is accompanied by an associated knowledge commons. We also highlighted potential social dilemmas concerning incentives to invest in public goods (whether inputs or complementary goods) that contribute to the environmental and knowledge commons.

2.2.1 *Herding Sheep and Goats on a Shared Pasture: Knowledge Concerning Heterogeneous Uses*

Now suppose our community of herders share the same pasture but some fraction herd sheep and the rest herd goats. Thus, we are shifting from homogeneous use to heterogeneous uses, albeit still within a rather narrow scope (herding livestock). Assume that the only relevant difference between sheep and goats for purposes of managing the shared pasture is the rate at which the grazing animals consume the resource.[21] On these stylized facts, the addition of goats presents a complication for rules-in-use concerning allocation and tracking.[22] The herders will have to decide whether and how to factor the differences between sheep and goats into the rules-in-use.

The additional complication for rules-in-use for grazing creates complications for the associated knowledge commons as well. The herders will have to understand the different rates of consumption and will have to track sheep and goats separately. They also will have to communicate with each other about whether and how the differences between sheep and goats should influence the allocation rules. Yet the move from the base scenario in Section 2.1 to this variation does not necessarily present a substantial challenge, either for governing the pasture or for developing the underlying requisite knowledge commons, so long as the only difference between sheep and goats is in the rates of consumption.

There could be complications, and even conflict, in distinguishing animal types and measuring consumption rates, and dealing with such complications could put pressure on the knowledge commons institutions. Herders may engage in strategic behavior to game rules-in-use by, for example, selectively highlighting information favorable to their interests in discussions over management of the pasture. Nonetheless, if the only difference between sheep and goats is their rate of consumption, the information challenges for the shift from sheep to sheep and goats primarily concern descriptive and managerial knowledge similar to the initial sheep-only scenario.[23]

We can extend this scenario along similar lines, for example, from 2 → 3 → … → n different types of animals, which would complicate matters mostly in terms of accounting. Creating and maintaining a knowledge commons is costly to the community. As the number of types of grazing animals increases, the cost of creating and maintaining a knowledge commons sufficient to support management of the pasture increases as well. If these costs (a form of transaction costs for governing the pasture) increase enough, then they may constrain governance choices.[24] If, for

[21] This is a stylized fact. There are both quantitative and qualitative differences in how sheep, goats, and other livestock consume pasture resources.

[22] Allocation may include pricing if a usage-based fee is implemented.

[23] Note that the stylized assumption does a lot of work. If we relax the assumption and, for example, recognize that community members may have preferences for one animal over another, for historical, cultural, or other reasons unrelated to the rate of consumption, then additional information challenges arise that implicate normative knowledge in addition to descriptive and managerial knowledge. We return to this extension in Section 2.2.

[24] As Frischmann (2012, 150–151) explains:

> Heterogeneity introduces variance in the capacity consumption of different uses. E-mail and video conferencing consume bandwidth at different rates. Grazing sheep on a meadow imposes

example, ten different breeds of goats graze on the pasture, each with a somewhat different rate of consumption, the cost of understanding the differences between the breeds at some point may exceed the benefits of differentiating among the breeds, leading the herders to treat all goats alike even if they are not.

2.2.2 *Herding Sheep, Goats, and Donkeys on a Shared Pasture: Knowledge Concerning Interaction Effects*

Heterogeneity also can introduce potential interdependencies among uses, referred to as interaction effects. Some interaction effects can be positive, as when uses are complementary (mutually beneficial). Some can be negative, as in the case of interuse congestion, also referred to as cross-crowding. Various uses may interact with each other in a manner that goes beyond competition for scarce capacity. Rivalrousness may arise because a certain use raises the marginal costs for another use, reducing consumption opportunities for that use, even if the capacity of the underlying resource is not scarce. To illustrate, consider once more our shared pasture.

Suppose our community of herders share the same pasture, and they herd sheep, goats, and donkeys. Again, assume the only relevant difference in resource consumption between sheep, goats, and donkeys is quantitative (rate, intensity). This presents the same issues raised in Section 2.2.1. Now assume the following stylized fact: Donkeys and sheep don't get along and tend to fight with each other.[25] Herding both types of animals on a common pasture would then give rise to negative interaction effects and rivalry, even if the capacity of the pasture is more than enough to support both flocks.

Interaction effects can give rise to another type of externality; individuals choosing which and how many animals to add to their flock may not account for the interaction effects and consequential impacts on other herders in the community. Again, as with the previous scenarios, this presents a social dilemma, and thus creates demand for governance, in both the natural resource commons and corresponding knowledge commons. The community must be able to describe, understand, and address the challenge of interaction effects.

a different burden than grazing goats or buffalo, much less flying a kite. Driving an SUV on the highway imposes a different burden than driving a Honda Civic or a Mack truck, much less a motorcycle or a bicycle. Some uses may be particularly intense, whereas others are not. Some uses may be particularly sporadic or bursty in their utilization rates, while others may be more uniform. Such variations among uses of the shared resource can complicate congestion management, including provisioning of capacity, membership size, and pricing.

25 Alternatively, assume that for cultural/historical reasons, most community members have a strong preference for herding sheep over any other animals. Or instead, assume sheepherders have traditionally come from higher socioeconomic classes than goatherders. We could go on inventing variations on the theme of interdependencies among uses that give rise to interaction effects.

Cross-crowding complicates conventional approaches to managing congestion. A sizable capacity cushion does not necessarily eliminate cross-crowding; nor does restricting total membership size of the user community; nor does congestion pricing. Interaction effects arise because of interdependencies among uses that are unrelated to scarce capacity. As a result, where interaction effects are significant, some other manner of coordination may be necessary. In particular, managing cross-crowding may entail managing the membership size of subsets of users based on the identity of their use. In the context of our stylized scenario, this would mean the community might choose to restrict (or even prohibit) sheep or donkeys.

Heterogeneity thus introduces another choice in governance, which is the scope of uses – whether to allow all types of animals or limit the range. In other words, the community may decide to (de)prioritize some uses. Importantly, this type of decision can push beyond managerial in the descriptive and technical sense and have a sociopolitical, normative dimension, much like the constitutive community decision to designate the shared natural resource a pasture rather than a recreational field, wildlife preserve, or something else.

Where two uses are interdependent in a fashion that gives rise to interuse congestion, both uses cause the congestion (Coase 1960).[26] Cross-crowding is not attributable exclusively to one use or the other. Interuse congestion would not arise unless both uses were present. For example, interaction effects between industrial pollution and swimming in a lake are attributable to both uses, and not, as is often assumed, to the industrial use alone. Eliminating interaction effects between these uses can be accomplished by eliminating either of the two uses, or in some cases, by restricting the intensity, timing, or some other characteristic of one use or the other.

Deciding how to coordinate interdependent uses, and which use(s) to restrict, are difficult questions that must be evaluated in context. This contextual evaluation depends heavily on shared knowledge. Some of this knowledge is descriptive and similar to the type of knowledge necessary to manage the pasture for its carrying capacity, as in the first scenario. For example, it may be that sheep and donkeys only bother each other when they are in close proximity, and that problems can be avoided if they are kept apart. But other knowledge necessary for managing a pasture with sheep, goats, and donkeys is more constitutive. For example, do some grazing animals have normative priority over others? Perhaps sheep have long-standing cultural resonance in the community, and therefore the community, in managing the pasture, will give sheep preference over donkeys. This type of knowledge may be subject to debate within the community. There may be questions, for example, regarding who may speak to the community's normative preferences.

The basic point of this subsection is to show how interaction effects can force (de)prioritization and thus trigger (additional) normative, even constitutive, decisions. In prior scenarios without interaction effects, the community did not need to

[26] This paragraph draws directly from Frischmann (2012, 153).

choose among types of grazing animals. Of course, choosing to designate the land as a pasture for grazing animals is itself a normative decision, constitutive of the community. It is worth noting that such a decision also deals with potential interaction effects, not among types of grazing animals (uses of the pasture) but rather among land uses (pasture, cropland, recreational park, etc.).

2.2.3 *Herding Sheep, Goats, and Cows on a Shared Pasture: Knowledge Concerning External Effects to Outsiders*

Now suppose our herders share the same pasture, and they herd sheep, goats, and cows; let's leave the antagonistic donkeys aside. Again, assume the only relevant difference in resource consumption between the animals is quantitative (rate, intensity). This presents the same issues raised in Section 2.1. However, now assume that grazing sheep, goats, and cows causes soil erosion that deposits sediment in the river that runs by the pasture. The sediment pollutes the river, which downstream communities use for drinking water. The sediment in the river is thus a byproduct of grazing animals in the pasture.

Some byproducts of grazing animals, such as wool and milk, are private goods that yield benefits captured by the herders, whether directly through their own use of those goods or through market transactions in which they sell those goods. The sediment byproduct of grazing animals, however, is a public bad – bad because the water pollution is harmful rather than beneficial, and public in the sense that the water pollution it causes is nonexcludable and nonrivalrous. This is a type of negative externality, yet it is a different type of negative externality than the one posited by Hardin. Hardin described a negative externality among community members, where each herder made a decision that generated unaccounted-for harm to other herders sharing the pasture. In this stylized scenario, each herder's animals may generate both the Hardin-style externality associated with overconsumption of the shared pasture and a productive-use-style externality involving unaccounted-for harm to outsiders, meaning people who are not community members.[27]

The sediment (productive use externality) scenario raises three distinct knowledge dilemmas for which knowledge commons could play a critical role. First, the community must be able to understand the new environmental problem. The

[27] Consider alternatively a scenario in which grazing cows generate substantial amounts of methane that contributes to global warming. This scenario introduces two additional complications not present in the sediment scenario. First, whereas the sediment affected only outsiders (downstream communities), the methane contributes to global warming that affects both the herders and outsiders. Second, whereas it might be relatively easy to trace the effect of grazing the pasture on downstream water quality, the effect of one pasture of grazing cows on global warming would be extremely difficult to determine, especially in the context of a world in which an extreme variety and number of carbon emissions are cumulatively exacerbating global warming. This complexity makes the environmental resource – the atmosphere – much more difficult to govern than a small river, which nevertheless does present its complexities.

harms associated with the sediment byproduct are quite different and more complex than what we have encountered so far. It can be difficult to know that the downstream effects exist, to appreciate how the harms come about, and to attribute them to individual decisions about herding animals on the pasture.[28] This additional knowledge may implicate new sources of information and new expertise.

Second, the community must recognize (or choose to ignore) the need for community governance regarding the sediment byproduct, and this entails deciding whether and to what degree the consequences to outsiders *matter* to the community. The political economy of such a decision depends on shared knowledge, for example, about who the outsiders are and where and when they may suffer the harms. It also depends on existing relations with other communities and whether there are intercommunity norms and governance institutions that mediate these types of relationships. A community may decide wholly on its own that it cares about the impacts on outsiders, or it may be pressured (forced) to internalize the externalities by outsiders.

Third, community governance of sediment production (river pollution) presents a different environmental commons dilemma in the sense that rationing pasture use based on resource consumption does not address the productive use externality problem. Other governance mechanisms are needed. A tax on animals, for example, could reflect the marginal external cost and lead herders to internalize the external effects of their decisions. We leave aside a more detailed comparative analysis of options, and instead note that these will generate the same types of demands for ongoing descriptive and managerial knowledge described previously.

The first and third types of knowledge dilemmas are similar to those raised in Sections 2.1 and 2.2, with the added difficulties of generating and sharing descriptive and managerial knowledge about more complex and attenuated phenomena. But the second dilemma implicates specific normative values of the community – namely, whether, to what degree, and how to care about outsiders. This dilemma is constitutive of the community's identity – what type of community it is and wants to be, how the community regards outsiders, and so on. Of course, all normative considerations are to some extent constitutive of community identity. For example, how community members treat each other is similarly constitutive. Even treating the land as a pasture rather than a nature preserve is constitutive of community identity.[29] Our point is to highlight how knowledge commons support the social processes communities undertake to deal with these types of issues.

[28] In this scenario, for brevity, we have assumed the herded animals contribute to soil erosion homogeneously. Relaxing that assumption complicates the analysis in a similar fashion as the discussion of heterogeneous uses in Section 2.1.

[29] Indeed, how we see ourselves affects our understanding of even the most basic descriptive and managerial knowledge. Herders who do not want to see themselves as polluters will tend to interpret information so that they do not seem like polluters.

The stylized scenarios in this section illustrate how governance of an environmental commons depends on the associated knowledge commons, and vice versa. Moreover, as the scale, scope, and heterogeneity of the knowledge commons increase, its dynamic, constitutive functions in the associated environmental commons become both more important and more challenging. Conscious consideration of the environmental commons–knowledge commons relationship therefore can facilitate more effective governance of the environmental commons and the knowledge commons. The same combined environmental commons–knowledge commons analysis can apply to many other shared resource settings, such as traffic on roads involving cars, trucks, bicyclists, and pedestrians; uses of the internet involving streaming video, gaming apps, and social media; or even the atmosphere, involving numerous uses including aesthetics, air travel, supply of life-sustaining gases, water vapor storage and transport, pollution dumping, and heat traps.

2.2.4 *Summary*

In the preceding scenarios, we have shown how each governance dilemma in the environmental commons is associated with a corresponding body of information in the knowledge commons. The ability of the community to address a governance dilemma in the environmental commons will thus depend in part on the community's ability to manage the associated knowledge commons effectively, and how the community manages the knowledge commons will influence how it governs the environmental commons. In Table 2.1, we summarize the types of knowledge necessary for effective resource governance in each scenario.[30] As the resource governance dilemmas increase in complexity, the requisite knowledge that must be available to the community increases in complexity as well. At every stage, the requisite knowledge includes both descriptive components and normative components and includes the knowledge required for prior scenarios. Thus, for example, when the herders confront the problem of congestion among sheep, they must reach a common understanding of who participates, what criteria to apply, and what process by which to decide how to limit sheep on the pasture.

Although the different scenarios outlined in the table are analytically discrete, in practice the classification of a commons may be fluid and depend on judgments made within the community. For example, before the pasture can be managed for homogeneous congestion in Scenario 1, the community must decide – perhaps explicitly, perhaps implicitly – that all sheep are to be treated equally.

[30] As GKC studies have documented, different knowledge requirements may involve different social dilemmas and generate social (community) demand for different governance institutions. For example, descriptive knowledge may implicate issues of standardization and coordination, whereas normative knowledge requirements may implicate conflicting values and fairness concerns. Different knowledge dilemmas may, in turn, call for different institutional responses. For brevity, we did not include another column that listed corresponding knowledge commons dilemmas and institutions.

TABLE 2.1 *Requisite knowledge for environmental commons dilemmas*

Scenario	EC Dilemma	Requisite Knowledge Descriptive	Requisite Knowledge Normative
0	Choice of land use (e.g., pasture, preserve, recreation)	Possible uses Consequences of uses	Who participates What criteria What process
1	Homogeneous congestion (potential externalities among community members)	Capacity of pasture Number of sheep grazing Rate of consumption Rules-in-use Monitoring/tracking use	Same as for Scenario 0 How to govern (e.g., government, market, or community)
2	Heterogeneous congestion (potential externalities among community members)	Same as for Scenario 1, but more complex	Same as for Scenario 1, but more complex
3	Interaction effects (potential externalities among community members)	Interdependency effects among uses (e.g., conflict between different species) Rules-in-use Monitoring/tracking use	(De)prioritization of uses Same as for Scenario 1
4	Productive use externalities (potential external effects on noncommunity members)	External effects, who is impacted, to what extent, and how Mechanisms can be complex	Who matters and how much Same as for Scenario 1, but complicated by external governance structures and relations

This decision requires both descriptive knowledge about the sheep (how different are they, and in what ways) and normative knowledge about the community's priorities (whether it wants to overlook any differences). As another example, the community may decide for normative reasons or for ease of administration to treat sheep and goats as if they were the same, even though they are not – essentially, to treat a Scenario 2 situation as a Scenario 1 situation. Similarly, if the community chooses to ignore effects outside the community, it might treat a Scenario 4 situation as if it were another type of scenario, but such a community decision is normative and could, and we suggest should, be based upon knowledge about external effects. Of course, in reality, incomplete knowledge about external effects is a persistent governance challenge.

To some extent, the interrelated environmental commons and knowledge commons resemble the interrelated governance functions that Michael McGinnis has described in his work on networks of adjacent actions (McGinnis 2011, 52). McGinnis argued that, whereas scholarship under the IAD framework often focuses on a single regulatory function, in reality, commons governance entails multiple interrelated functions, each of which "constitutes an action situation in its own right." Complex policy settings, especially those characterized by polycentric governance, can thus be framed as networks of mutually dependent adjacent action situations, with each governance function entailing its own action situation.

Interdependent environmental commons–knowledge commons relationships, like McGinnis's networks of adjacent action situations, highlight related commons. In some sense, environmental commons–knowledge commons relationships could be viewed as a specific type of networks of adjacent action situations. But environmental commons–knowledge commons relationships also have their own distinctive attributes. First, using the GKC framework incorporates insights from the knowledge commons literature. The GKC framework builds from the IAD framework but with substantial adaptations that account for many differences in the underlying resources, governance dilemmas, and dynamic and often constitutive relationships among resources and communities. Second, the environmental commons–knowledge commons relationship generally operates at a broader level than the network of interdependent governance functions that McGinnis describes. The information, knowledge, and beliefs that comprise the knowledge commons underlie every governance decision for the knowledge commons, and the knowledge commons itself includes numerous governance decisions and functions. The environmental commons and the knowledge commons thus each encompass their own networks of adjacent governance functions, and the environmental commons–knowledge commons relationship involves a web of relationships among specific environmental commons functions and knowledge commons functions.

2.3 ADDITIONAL EXAMPLES

The stylized pasture hypothetical described in Section 2.2 offers just one example of the environmental commons–knowledge commons relationship. This section describes additional examples drawn from both natural and built physical environments.

2.3.1 *Natural Environmental Example: Forest Management*

Forests are a well-known example of an environmental commons subject to potential management issues of congestion, conflicts among uses, and externalities (e.g., Arnold 1993). Managing a forest effectively as a commons depends on an associated knowledge commons with information ranging from data about use of forests, scientific information about impacts, and shared or disputed values about forests. Government agencies such as the US Forest Service are often charged with managing forests on public lands, guided by statutes and regulations such as the National Forest Management Act that provide a general management framework.

For managing forests on public lands, the governing statute, regulations, guidance documents, and other legal decisions designate lands as a unit of the national forest system and assign certain goals and values to guide management of the lands. These decisions provide the foundation for judgments that delineate the baseline Scenario 0. Some of these decisions are made by Congress or the Forest Service at the national level, while others are made more locally. At all levels, deciding what lands to designate as a national forest and what uses and values to prioritize for the forest requires information about the range of potential uses and benefits that can be derived from the forest and the values implicated by those uses and benefits. Thus, for example, historically, the Forest Service managed its lands primarily for the purpose of timber harvesting, but eventually received a mandate to manage forests for multiple uses, including recreation and environmental benefits in addition to resource extraction.

When the Forest Service's mission focused on timber harvesting, its management decisions focused on Scenario 1 and 2 issues of congestion and, in particular, determining how much timber harvesting was sustainable for a forest. If there was only one type of timber harvesting, this would raise issues of homogeneous congestion under Scenario 1. If multiple types of timber harvesting were in play – say, clearcutting and selective cutting – then Scenario 2 issues arise. In either scenario, the Forest Service needs descriptive information about the impacts of timber harvesting on forest productivity for future timber harvesting. Different stakeholder groups, including scientists, the timber industry, and environmental groups, are likely to have information to contribute to the understanding of how much timber harvesting a forest can sustain. Agencies sometimes employ formal mechanisms such as public comment and public meetings to elicit information relevant to their decisions. The information that stakeholders contribute is often not impartial, but instead reflects the normative priorities of the stakeholder that produces it. Thus, contestation over knowledge in the knowledge commons reflects disputes over physical resource use in the environmental commons. Having mechanisms that facilitate broad participation from all stakeholders and clear rules for how the agency treats the information it obtains through those mechanisms can increase stakeholders' perceptions of the legitimacy of the agency's decisions, potentially reducing conflict in the environmental commons.

Now that the Forest Service has a mission to manage forests for multiple uses, managing interactive effects among uses is an important part of its role. Some uses may conflict – for example, off-road vehicles may annoy hikers, and timber harvesting may at least temporarily displace wildlife. Other uses may benefit each other, such as when off-road vehicles use logging roads. Again, stakeholders are likely to contribute information that advances their agenda for the forest – for example, hikers complaining about the aesthetic impacts of logging.

When the Forest Service considers the positive and negative externalities of forest management, it is in Scenario 4. Logging may cause sedimentation of rivers and streams, impairing downstream water quality. Logging and recreation may contribute to the local economy, helping to sustain rural communities. To represent the broad public interest, the Forest Service needs descriptive information about these external impacts and also needs to reach an understanding of what value to attach to these different effects. Different stakeholder groups will generate relevant information consistent with their interests in uses of the forest.

In considering forests and other public lands management, we often think of the agency as a land manager, a label that indicates its responsibility for stewarding the environmental commons of the forest (or rangeland or wildlife refuge or state or national park). But these public lands managers also play an important role as managers of the knowledge relevant to stewarding the environmental commons. Debates about public land management draw on a wide variety of knowledge from various stakeholder groups. Because of the environmental commons–knowledge commons relationship, public lands managers must manage their knowledge commons well if they hope to manage their environmental commons effectively.

Public agencies often have rules and practices – some as formal laws or principles, some as informal norms – for what information and knowledge to consider in making decisions. These rules and practices should depend on the type of decision the agency is making, as indicated by our different governance scenarios. For example, if the Forest Service is deciding how much timber harvesting in an area would be sustainable (Scenario 1), this is primarily a scientific question and so scientific knowledge should be most relevant to the agency. Stakeholders will know this and attempt to cast the information they produce in scientific terms. The agency will have to evaluate the scientific merit of the potentially relevant information in the knowledge commons – for example, by assessing the methodology of the work that produced the information. By contrast, if the agency is deciding whether how to manage conflicts between off-road vehicle users and hikers (Scenario 3), it needs both descriptive information about how much off-road vehicles bother hikers and vice versa, but also normative information about how much value to place on off-road vehicle use versus hiking. For normative information, the agency has to undertake a different kind of evaluation – for example, determining the extent to which a comment represents the views of a broader group of stakeholders. The clearer and more transparent the agency can be about how it will treat different types of information, the more effectively stakeholders can structure their contributions to the knowledge commons.

Under administrative law principles, agencies often formally designate a body of knowledge and information as the administrative record on which they base their decisions. At least in theory, the agency's decisions must consider all knowledge and only knowledge in the administrative record. Stakeholders hoping to influence agency processes accordingly vie to get their positions supported by information in the administrative record. Agency processes such as comment periods and public meetings can reduce obstacles to stakeholder contributions to the administrative record, thereby enriching the quality of the knowledge commons. Whether the agency is able to leverage a robust knowledge commons into better governance of the environmental commons is a different issue.

This brief summary conveys only the tip of the iceberg regarding the interactions of environmental resource governance and knowledge commons governance in the context of public lands and administrative agency decision-making. Further research should examine the relationship between public lands and their associated knowledge commons, and in particular how agency practices for managing public lands and agency practices for managing associated knowledge commons can mutually support each other.

2.3.2 *Built Environment Examples*

We now provide an abbreviated look at how the insights from the previous section would apply to some familiar examples of built environments: roads and the living room.

2.3.2.1 Roads

Roads are an important infrastructure generally managed as commons (Frischmann 2012).[31] Governance of roads involves both the physical resource of the road infrastructure itself and an associated knowledge commons. The interaction of the two commons raises issues similar to the pasture example discussed in Section 2.

The baseline Scenario 0 presents the normative question of what roads to build and where to build them. Addressing this question requires considering information about the present and future transportation needs of the community, possible transportation options (which may include alternatives to roads, such as mass transit), and normative judgments about transportation as a fiscal priority compared with other pressing concerns.

Scenario 1 involves homogeneous traffic (e.g., similar-sized cars), which presents a basic congestion problem. Roads are not inevitably or always congested, but they can be, depending on capacity (supply) and demand patterns. Tolerating some congestion, especially at low levels, may be preferable or even necessary. Like the pasture, an individual vehicle's use of a road can impose externalities on other users – once there is some congestion, each additional vehicle on the roads increases travel times for other vehicles as well. When congestion reaches

[31] Road systems are complex and involve a polycentric governance with multiple decision-making entities. Different levels of government, different departments, and different geographic jurisdictions, as well as private entities, play different roles in managing and coordinating construction, maintenance, and use of a road system by different communities.

certain levels, for example, for certain routes during rush hour, sustaining the roads as useful commons may depend upon rationing or congestion pricing as mechanisms for dealing with anonymous crowding. The knowledge required for a community to choose among possible policy options for managing congestion and then to implement the chosen policy tracks the analysis described earlier for the pasture. Decision-makers will need to know information about resource capacity, number of users, the rate of consumption, pattern of consumption, rules-in-use, and monitoring.

Scenario 2 introduces heterogeneous traffic, such as different types of vehicles – say, cars and trucks. This complicates the descriptive details (e.g., different consumption rates, potentially different rules-in-use) but does not alter the basic analysis.

Scenario 3 involves interaction effects, for example, among vehicles (cars, trucks, and bicycles) and among use types (vehicles and pedestrians). Rules governing access to highways generally exclude bicycles and pedestrians to avoid interaction effects; communities deploy speed bumps and other traffic calming measures on residential streets for similar reasons. In addition to the knowledge requirements of other scenarios, new challenges arise: understanding how the interaction effects work, what the types of risks are for different users and types of roads (highways versus residential), and how to (de)prioritize across contexts. Managing this additional information may require new forms of expertise and the additional exercise of political (community) judgment. Further, strategic behavior in the generation and sharing of knowledge also becomes a more prevalent concern. As may be familiar to many readers, the politics associated with deployment of speed bumps highlights how the knowledge dilemmas for knowledge commons are not simply scientific or technocratic.

Finally, Scenario 4 surfaces the many positive and negative externalities associated with roads, beyond mere congestion effects among road users. Beyond their direct benefits and costs to road users, roads enable economically and socially productive activities (among different communities) that generate positive externalities (social surplus). These positive externalities provide a potentially important justification for managing road systems as commons rather than, for example, relying on toll roads. Roads also create negative externalities such as noise and pollution that impact neighboring communities. Information about these positive and negative externalities, and normative judgments about the consequences of their impacts, are potentially important to managing the road system for the benefit of the community.

As with the pasture example, the relevant decision-makers must determine which distinctions among road users matter and which do not matter and what this means for managing road congestion. These decisions may implicate different types of knowledge. For example, whether different types of vehicles contribute differently to congestion will determine whether traffic congestion is treated as homogeneous (Scenario 1) or heterogeneous (Scenario 2). This decision primarily depends on descriptive knowledge about vehicle use and its effects on congestion.[32] Other management decisions will depend on both descriptive and normative knowledge. For example, whether to apply preferential rules-in-use to electric vehicles may depend on the number of such vehicles on the roads, but also how much the public cares about pollution from gasoline-powered and diesel vehicles.

Despite the many differences between pastures and roads, each step in the analysis for roads triggers the same types of knowledge dilemmas and challenges summarized in Table 2.1. Our analysis of roads is admittedly cursory; we could write an entire chapter on this example alone. Still, the point is to reveal the shared features and spark interest in further exploration in the future.

2.3.2.2 Living Rooms

The living room of a home provides an overlooked everyday example of an environmental commons. Living rooms raise governance issues similar to pastures and roads.

The baseline Scenario 0 presents the question of how to use a particular room in a house – for example, as an office, dining room, or living room. The baseline decision reflects a commitment to shared space, shapes the set of complementary goods and inputs (e.g., furniture, design, decoration, and lighting), and also shapes expectations and social norms regarding the range of acceptable uses of the room.

Scenario 1 conflicts over the living room would involve issues of homogeneous congestion – for example, when a large group gathers to watch television. Managing congestion requires knowing how many people want to watch television, potentially including people from outside the home; the carrying capacity of the room, which in turn depends on people's aversion to (or preference for) crowding and seating preferences; and possible rules-in-use for managing the congestion.

Scenario 2 conflicts over the living room would involve issues of heterogeneous congestion – for example, children who take up less room on the couch than adults, or people who insist on sitting together. This requires additional information, but does not differ significantly from problems of homogeneous congestion.

Scenario 3 issues arise when different people want to use the living room for different purposes that conflict with each other – for example, when some people want to watch television and some want to read. Managing these conflicts requires additional descriptive information about the relationship between the conflicting activities – for example, how much television watching bothers readers – and also normative information about the relative weight of the activities.

[32] At the margins, decision-makers will have to exercise judgment about whether to overlook differences among vehicles and treat them the same (Scenario 1) or to take differences into account that treat different types of vehicles differently (Scenario 2). Politics also may influence the judgment; if truck drivers have enough political power, they may be able to influence decision-makers to overlook additional impacts that trucks have on traffic congestion, even if the differences may be descriptively significant.

Scenario 4 considers the broader impacts of how the living room is used. Perhaps noise from the television disturbs the sleep of other members of the household, or perhaps the living room can be used as a place for neighborhood children to socialize. If these externalities are important to the residents of the home, then making best use of the living room will require both descriptive and normative information about these external impacts of living room use.

Although the living room example may seem trivial (or even silly), it highlights the pervasiveness of commons governance in our everyday lives and the significance of knowledge and information to that governance. Accepted social norms and strong knowledge flows can make the living room a well-functioning environmental commons, and lack of communication can cause squabbles and divisions within the household.

2.4 BUILDING ROBUST COMMONS GOVERNANCE

So far, the discussion of the pasture, woodlands, roads, and living room examples have highlighted the commonalities among them. In particular, each type of environmental commons potentially raises different governance challenges, and each governance challenge for the environmental commons in turn has implications for associated knowledge commons. But there are important differences across commons resources as well, and these differences potentially have significant implications for the knowledge commons.

Compare, for example, a road system with a living room. Road systems are geographically dispersed, governed polycentrically by government agencies, and used by a very large number of people, often in the millions. Congestion and other interpersonal effects are highly complex and difficult to discern. Most users are relatively anonymous to each other and have only limited contact with the various public officials making governance decisions about the roads. Because they involve government agencies, decision-making processes for roads tend to be formal and bureaucratic.

The knowledge institutions that effectively manage the information needed to govern a road system reflect these features. Because of the complexity of the issues, expert professionals are hired to analyze traffic effects, environmental impacts, and economic costs and benefits of different options. Because road users are numerous, dispersed, and anonymous, rules-in-use are communicated through centralized and formal means such as highway signs. Because bureaucratic processes are involved, information is developed through formal mechanisms such as traffic studies.

Living rooms, by contrast, are a single space, governed informally, and used by the same small number of people for an extended time. Interactive effects are relatively easy for users to discern. The small number of users are socially cohesive, bonded as a couple, a family, or roommates. A small number of adults, often related, may exercise total control of living room use. Decisions tend to be made through social norms and custom rather than formal processes, and these customs are either well known to the users or easily communicated.

The knowledge institutions that manage living rooms reflect the features of a living room and contrast with those for road systems. Because of the informality of the decision-making and communication processes about use of the living room, the knowledge institutions are informal as well. Users come to their own understandings of living room use and communicate those understandings and their preferences directly to others in the home. Rules-in-use arise through social norms rather than formal process. Little communication about the rules is necessary.

If the living room example is modified slightly to the lobby of an apartment building or a common room in a college dormitory, then the features of both the environmental commons and the knowledge commons change as well. Residents in an apartment building are more anonymous to each other than people who live together in a home, requiring more formal processes of communication such as sending emails and posting signs. Residents may have only a limited understanding of how uses affect each other – for example, whether sitting with their dog in the lobby will bother anyone.

In theory, a well-functioning knowledge commons would contain all information and knowledge relevant to governing and using the associated environmental commons, and this information and knowledge would be easily accessible to all stakeholders in the environmental commons. Economists often assume perfect information as a precondition of a perfectly functioning market. In reality, however, information is costly to produce and to consume, and so a knowledge commons contains only some potentially relevant information, and the information in a knowledge commons is not perfectly available to all stakeholders in the environmental commons. A variety of barriers may impede access to a knowledge commons, including both access to produce knowledge that becomes part of the knowledge commons and access to consume knowledge that is part of the knowledge commons. Effective governance of a knowledge commons, which itself is important to governance of the associated environmental commons, thus requires attention to issues of access.

Some access issues arise because the cost of generating knowledge varies; some knowledge is easier to generate than other knowledge. In the hypothetical pasture, for example, it will be easier for sheepherders to understand the effects of congestion from their sheep than it will be to understand the effects of congestion from goats, and even more difficult for them to understand the effects that grazing has on downstream water quality. Without concerted efforts to find out about knowledge that is more difficult to acquire, decisions about the environmental commons – here, the pasture – will tend to depend on more readily available knowledge.

As observed in Section 2.3, as the complexity of an environmental commons increases, this increases the complexity of the associated knowledge commons. In Scenario 1, involving only homogeneous congestion, the associated knowledge commons can focus on sheep. As more interactions are introduced into the environmental commons – sheep, goats, donkeys, cows, and downstream water quality – the knowledge commons associated with the environmental commons becomes more complicated. Because generating, curating, and accessing information is costly, the costs of maintaining an effective knowledge commons increase as the complexity of the environmental commons increases. The relative costs of maintaining an effective knowledge commons should be factored into decisions about managing the environmental commons – in other words, one reason to confine use of the pasture to sheep, in our stylized hypothetical, is to avoid the cost of learning about sheep–goat–donkey interactions.

Knowledge commons are also unlikely to be neutral as to the interests in the environmental commons. Because existing uses of the environmental commons generate information naturally as a byproduct of the use, a knowledge commons will tend to include more information and knowledge about existing uses than about potential other uses. Because generating information, especially in accessible form, is costly, the information and knowledge in the knowledge commons also will tend to reflect the financial interests of stakeholders who have invested in creating and disseminating information favorable to their interests. Effective governance of the environmental commons may therefore benefit from institutional buffers that insulate the knowledge commons from conflicts in the environmental commons. Institutional buffers could take the form of, for example, publicly funded research to generate knowledge that would be underproduced by stakeholders in the environmental commons.

A well-functioning environmental commons–knowledge commons relationship supports effective governance of both commons. When knowledge commons and environmental commons are out of sync, this may pose a significant obstacle to effective governance. Ostrom (1990, 68–69) offers the example, described by McKean (1986, 565) of a situation in which Japanese villagers thought that their village leader had set a gathering season for forest products too late, thereby endangering their ability to obtain a type of pole they gathered from the forest and then used to support their gardens. The discrepancy between the villagers' understanding of the facts and the rules-in-use imposed by their leader led them to violate the rules despite the risk of severe sanction in the form of fines and forfeiture of what they had gathered. It is unclear from Ostrom's description whether the leader was correct or the villagers were correct, and in some sense it does not matter; conflicts in the knowledge commons led to a breakdown in the system used to govern the environmental resource.

Changing conditions also may have implications for governing both the environmental commons and the knowledge commons. Ostrom (1990, 88) noted that the stability of the system – for example, a consistent population of users – can contribute to effective governance. She pointed to the incentives that stability creates to act consistently with developed norms. A farmer who cares about his reputation in the community is more likely to comply with norms about water use for irrigation. But stability also supports effective governance of an environmental commons because stability allows the existing knowledge commons to support decision making and communication about the environmental commons. Changing conditions in the environmental commons, by contrast, may render knowledge obsolete, requiring updating of information (posing a challenge for managing the knowledge commons) or making decisions about the environmental commons with less information (posing a challenge for managing the environmental commons). Resilience in commons governance thus may require building an ability to respond to changing conditions in both the environmental commons and the associated knowledge commons.

2.5 CONCLUSION: FUTURE DIRECTIONS

Every environmental commons has an associated knowledge commons, and the interdependence of the environmental and knowledge commons means that neither one can be fully understood without the other. Effective governance of one also depends on the other, and conflict in one commons increases the risk of conflict in the other.

Future research should investigate these complex environmental commons–knowledge commons relationships. What are the implications of specific features of environmental commons for effective governance of the associated knowledge commons, and vice versa? For example, can some strategies prevent controversies in the environmental commons from infecting the associated knowledge commons, allowing for commonly accepted knowledge from which the community can draw in governing the environmental commons? Case studies exploring environmental commons–knowledge commons relationships can shed light on this question and point to governance strategies that productively manage the relationship between associated environmental commons and knowledge commons.

We also propose a retrospective empirical project that revisits and entails a meta-analysis of prior environmental commons studies. The aim would be to map the understudied and underappreciated knowledge commons implicit in many past studies of environmental commons.

There are also ample opportunities for additional case studies. In writing this chapter, we discussed and even drafted descriptions of many different examples, drawn from many different domains. Yet the GKC book of which this chapter is a part is its own entangled environmental commons–knowledge commons. There are many authors contributing shared knowledge, and there is only so much space in a book. And so, for brevity's sake, we held much in reserve. In closing, however, consider two examples that we hope inspire further research.

Digital networked environments on the internet are amalgams of knowledge resources (data, software, images, design, and so on) running on physical resources (hardware, connectivity infrastructure). A website, for example, can include text, images, video, design, and other content (knowledge resources) accessible on a screen (physical resources) as well as software code (knowledge resources) running on a computer (physical resources). To be a virtual environment that users visit, whether to obtain access to content or to interact with others, a website also depends on shared infrastructures for connectivity. Simply put, virtual spaces involve many shared resources, both tangible and intangible, often governed as commons. A social media platform, an email or Discord server, or even just a chat room presents many of the governance scenarios we have described. Communities that manage shared digital environments as commons often depend upon shared knowledge to deal with homogeneous congestion (e.g., too much information or too many users), interaction effects (e.g., bullying), and externalities (e.g., viral misinformation). Content moderation on digital tech platforms, such as social media, for example, must distinguish between interaction effects among platform users and productive use externalities associated with off-platform speech effects, even if sometimes both occur simultaneously. Of course, the extraordinary scale, scope, and speed of digital networked communications makes the governance challenges even more difficult, and this puts more pressure on the knowledge commons. As community members, users may play a limited role in platform governance; for example, flagging content that violates platform policies. Not surprisingly, tech platforms rely heavily on algorithmic systems to automate content moderation. These systems typically are highly opaque and often seem to displace potential knowledge commons. At the heart of many complex social dilemmas arising in digital networked environments are interdependent and evolving environmental commons–knowledge commons. We have only scratched the surface of this rich topic for future policy-relevant research.

Another area rich with environmental commons–knowledge commons interactions worthy of sustained study is public health. Consider, for example, the emerging global crisis of antimicrobial resistance (AMR), which impacts health, economic welfare, food security, and the global environment. In the twentieth century, penicillin and other antibacterials added years to life expectancy by preventing many infectious diseases (the major cause of death pre-antibiotics) and by enabling treatment of infections associated with surgery and other medical procedures. The global spread of AMR threatens to upend these incredible gains. AMR already hits hardest in low- and middle-income countries, where its effects are aggravated by inequity, but it also threatens high-income countries. Like climate change, AMR is a global-scale wicked problem that entails many interdependent environmental commons–knowledge commons. Antimicrobial effectiveness (AME), for example, is an essential public infrastructure for advancing public health and human flourishing. And AME implicates a body of knowledge about antimicrobial effectiveness, ranging from medical and public health studies to social norms of hygiene. Considering the challenge of AME in terms of infrastructure highlights the complex interactions between natural and built environments, knowledge commons, and public health, and it emphasizes how sustainability depends upon developing knowledge commons for sharing various knowledge resources globally to describe and diagnose shared resource dilemmas, devise potential solutions to manage collective action among diverse stakeholders, and engage different communities in a global conversation about normative priorities and values. A possible response to AMR would be to create a global institution of experts charged with compiling and disseminating consensus scientific information about AMR, similar to the Intergovernmental Panel on Climate Change (IPCC). Whether an IPCC-like institution would be effective for AMR/AME depends on a variety of factors regarding the technical, social, and political context of AMR. Like digital networked communications, the question of how knowledge institutions can contribute to addressing AMR warrants more examination and research.

3

Regenerative Authentication Credits

Truth as a Shared Resource within the ESG Knowledge Commons

Chris Draper and Simon Sun

3.1 INTRODUCTION

Barely ten minutes into the annual United Way Live United event at Prairie Meadows Racetrack and Casino in Altoona, Iowa, on May 10, 2023, KCCI Channel 8 News This Morning anchor Alyx Sacks told the crowd: "If you've attended this event in the past you might notice the lunches are being handled a little bit differently this year. Thanks a lot to the work by Prairie Meadows, any lunches that are not served today will be donated to our good friends at Urban dreams so thank you Prairie Meadows" (United Way of Central Iowa 2023).

The statement received warm applause as United Way leadership basked in goodwill from a community where the often unimagined reality that food insecurity could exist in the middle of an agricultural state pulled at the heartstrings of many local leaders. This publicly stated commitment, backed by a secured offtake agreement with Urban Dreams, a local nonprofit working to "overcome obstacles and uplift underserved and underrepresented people" in Des Moines, was a major change from the same awards event one year earlier.

The year 2022 saw many celebrated initiatives designed to fight hunger, from the Greater Des Moines Partnership's 15th Annual Hunger Fight (Zimmerman 2022) to the DSM Fellows Capstone Panel praising initiatives such as the Corporate Giving Garden on Farm Bureau's West Des Moines office campus (Greater Des Moines Partnership 2022). From the OpportUNITY Plan to Iowa Stops Hunger to the social media campaigns such as #NoHungerCentralIowa, hunger was an inequity that most civic leaders felt they could take on without fear of the common socioeconomic third rails in an overwhelmingly white state then grappling with its place in a pandemic-riddled society still reeling from George Floyd's murder in Iowa's northern neighbor. Ending hunger was an environmental, social, and governance (ESG) badge of honor that every local executive could wear proudly at a time when many Des Moines-based diversity, equity, and inclusion (DEI) directors felt required to intentionally censor words such as "diversity" from their public statements. Efforts to end hunger were an ESG currency that many felt comfortable trading in, and the United Way staked their claim that morning to the intangible value of feeding those less fortunate.

Yet, unlike in 2023, less than two hours after the 2022 Live United awards banquet kicked off, more than eighty meals that could have been donated to Urban Dreams that year were in the trash.

Aubrey Alvarez, the Executive Director of United Way-funded food rescue organization Eat Greater Des Moines (EGDM), who was preparing to take those meals to Urban Dreams in 2022, was brought to tears when Prairie Meadows staff intervened, preventing her from taking the perfect edible food to Urban Dreams, and instead threw all of the more than eighty meals into the trash right in front of her. Her tears led to anger at this perceived hypocrisy and fueled Aubrey to pen an emotionally stirring letter sent to EGDM supporters where she mused, "I'm regularly told is to 'be patient' … [but] how many more studies, data points, and personal stories will be enough for real change?" (Alvarez 2022).

By calling out Prairie Meadows banquet staff when writing, "asked if they really wanted this food to go into the garbage instead of to a person, their answer was a resounding yes" (Alvarez 2022), Aubrey had poked the eye of an organization to which United Way was indebted. By 2022, Prairie Meadows had given $2.1 billion over just six years to local nonprofits and organizations often supported by the United Way (Prairie Meadows 2022), including $1,000,000 to the United Way of Central Iowa directly in 2020 (Stewart 2020). On July 8, 2022, less than sixty days after Aubrey's call to action for EGDM supporters, United Way of Central Iowa Chief Community Impact Officer Renée Miller sent a letter saying they would no longer provide funding to support EGDM's efforts to end hunger in central Iowa (Ta 2022). No additional explanation was given in the letter, though when pressed, Axios was told the defunding was due to "EGDM staff that didn't align with United Way's "inclusive, respect-based work," according to a statement the organization sent to Axios that it declined to attribute to a specific person (Ta 2022).

United Way of Central Iowa pulling its funding left EGDM with an economic shortfall that exceeded more than half its senior leadership payroll. Less money meant less time to organize fewer resources to distribute, resulting in fewer people getting fed. For Aubrey, it meant many would go hungry because a few were embarrassed.

The core issue evident on May 9, 2022, at Prairie Meadows, which almost directly drove the nationally recognized battle pitting the Food Bank of Iowa against nearly every other nonprofit in Iowa fighting food insecurity,[1] is the fundamentally asymmetrical nature of ESG value realization and extraction. In short, small organizations such as EGDM struggle to receive fair compensation for the

[1] www.desmoinesregister.com/story/news/local/2023/08/03/the-food-fight-is-over-why-are-some-food-pantries-still-worried-about-new-food-bank-of-iowa-contract/70464881007/.

ESG value they create. Yet at the same time, donations to organizations that claim to create ESG value at scale rise exponentially even in the face of proven greenwashing or fraud. Food rescued by EGDM provides their donors with tax credits equal to the market value of the food being donated, a financial windfall for high-margin products such as bread, yet food rescue organizations struggle to convince donors that it is fair to share in the directly identifiable economic benefit those nonprofits provide. At the same time, donations to United Way of Central Iowa exponentially appreciated if donors believe food is being recovered even when it is being thrown away.

Unverified promises made in the opening remarks of a celebratory lunch to generate undue intangible value are at the heart of the greatest threat to ESG. Dependencies on opaque metrics compiled at scale are what lead to scandals such as Verra, where "more than 90% of [their] rainforest carbon offsets ... are worthless" (Greenfield 2023). Lack of ESG standardization for both carbon-based and noncarbon derived value is why verification costs often exceed $40,000 to create a tradeable voluntary carbon offset or credit typically worth less than $6 since 2022 (Carbon Credits.com 2023). These combinations of opacity and uncertainty lead to systems where evidence of effect is so difficult to prove that reputation is used as a proxy for verifying action. Yet when an organization is small, there is no benefit of the doubt, and even less access to the fair value being produced.

Despite its size, calculating EGDM's ESG value to its community can be done relatively straightforwardly. For example, Feeding America data shows that 7.3 percent of Iowans were food insecure in 2020 (Feeding America 2023). Closing the food security gap that year was projected to require $112,519,000 at an estimated cost of $3.05 per meal. With the average adult needing between 0.9 and 1.2 pounds of food per meal to feel satisfied, this could have been achieved by providing roughly 33 million pounds of food to 229,500 people. The food rescued by EGDM that went directly to reducing food insecurity during 2020 was enough to meet over 12 percent of that projected hunger gap (Eat Greater Des Moines 2023). Yet the cash donations supporting those executing the organization's mission barely exceeded $186,000 during that year. Using this Feeding America data as a benchmark, the EGDM team solved a $13.6 million problem for less than 1.4 percent of the expected cost.

The net ESG value created by EGDM in 2020 may have arguably exceeded $13.4 million, yet Aubrey struggled to monetize that intangible value. Like any small nonprofit, donor focus rested on covering and containing costs versus rewarding achievement. Food donors saw EGDM's services as a waste management alternative instead of EGDM being the source creating the near windfall tax credits – equaling the retail value of the food being rescued – providing outsized benefits to food donor bottom lines. Donor reluctance to fairly account for the value EGDM created led Aubrey to seek out ESG markets, yet food rescue never fit nicely into the plethora of nearly exclusively carbon-based ESG credits. While food rescue reduces the number of miles food had to be transported, reduces the energy required for production, and reduces energy conversion at any ingredient's source, a marketable greenhouse gas (GHG) reduction had too many variables to track. While rescuing the food prevented it from producing GHGs as it decomposed in a landfill, the true net impact compared with its consumption is difficult to truly evaluate. And calculating any GHG reduction estimation for the ESG benefit of feeding food insecure people is a challenge that many then consider void of any discernible starting point.

It was in this effort to find a path for monetizing the ESG value of EGDM food rescue activities that did not nearly conform to carbon-based equivalency calculations that Aubrey came across regenerative authentication credits (RACs) and the Human Impact Unit (Hu) to price them. Through two RAC auctions between fall of 2022 and spring of 2023, Aubrey was able to secure investment from individuals and organizations who would not have otherwise donated to EGDM, directly marketed the intangible value EGDM created instead of losing value by using a carbon-based intermediary, and proved an average market value of $3.53 per pound rescued. Through RAC sales, Aubrey had found a vehicle for moving from a donor appetite of $0.014 per dollar of ESG value created to a market paying a 16 percent premium over Feeding America estimates. For organizations such as EGDM, these kinds of RAC markets priced in Hu may end up being the equalizer that turns today's nonprofits from being the guests at galas or luncheons to the benefactors through fairly monetizing the intangible value they create in our communities.

3.2 ESG AS KNOWLEDGE COMMONS GOVERNANCE

3.2.1 *How EGDM Demonstrated the Broader Issues in ESG*

This chapter argues that the fundamental problem limiting community Trust in ESG efforts is its use of modeled data or secondary indicators to prove its Truth. In the case of the disagreement between EGDM and United Way, arguments could be made that EGDM was measuring ESG impact in pounds of food rescued, where United Way was measuring the number of participating organizations. In the ESG industry, more broadly, it will be argued here that the primary measure of success since 1997 has been tied to carbon when the majority of ESG goods does not have a meaningful carbon component. This lack of a carbon component requires valuations to adopt rather tenuous relationships as Truth that are later identified as being in conflict with the same community's interpretation of objective truth.

While it is commonly perceived that issues of double counting or "greenwashing" are typically products of fraud (Runyon 2022), the framing of limited ESG Trust being due to misaligned communication identified earlier is more likely. For example, very few projects directly model carbon emissions or sequestration, yet carbon credits are awarded and traded based on point estimates of metric tons of carbon. When estimation methods or the input data to these estimates change, which is common, the community interprets this as a modification of its previously accepted objective truth. This chapter argues that Truth must remain immutable in order to facilitate Trust.

Where ESG value is tracked without the use of carbon credit equivalency, historic deficiencies in the definitions of what constitutes ESG value have similarly damaged Trush by again misidentifying Truth that has the ability to align with the community's interpretation of objective truth. For example, the most common method that early ESG investors used to expand access was to invest in equities of publicly traded companies that were believed to embody the objectives of or were positively contributing to meaningful ESG outcomes. These types of secondary mechanism strategies do not guarantee the desired actions will be taken as seen with the Volkswagen emissions scandal (2015), Theranos fraud (2016), Wells Fargo fake accounts scandal (2016), and the Rio Tinto Juukan Gorge destruction (2020). Identically to carbon credits, these are examples where Truth was applied to items that were more variable than expected, leading to observations of the defined Truth that conflicted with the same community's perception of their objective truth, leading to losses in Trust.

These issues that emerge when Truth is applied as variables whose performance has a reasonable certainty that they will conflict with the community's interpretation of objective truth are addressed in this chapter. These issues are contrasted with the Hu valuation methodology and RAC asset, tools that more clearly define Truth using tangible, objective measures, and valuation estimations using relativistic comparisons of measurement units that directly reflect the ESG intentions of a valued action. It is argued herein that these two strategies reduce the prevalence of conflicts between any stated Truth and the community's ability to recognize it as objectively true.

3.2.2 *ESG Governance as Knowledge Commons*

ESG governance can be theorized through the linkage between an environmental commons (EC) and a knowledge commons (KC). As explained in Chapter 1, every EC has a corresponding KC for the purpose of managing the shared environmental resources. The relationship between an EC and its associated KC is bidirectional, creating an interdependency between EC governance and KC governance. "Knowledge" refers to "a broad set of intellectual and cultural resources." As Strandburg, Frischmann, and Madison explain, "The basic characteristic that distinguishes commons from non commons is institutionalized sharing of resources among members of a community" (Strandburg et al. 2017, 10). KC is an institutional approach to governing the management or production of a particular type of resource – knowledge (Strandburg et al. 2017, 10). Overall, KC is the institutionalized community governance of the sharing and creation of information, science, knowledge data, and other intellectual and cultural resources. This includes information, science, knowledge, creative works, data, and so on.

ESG can be perceived as a KC created to manage the EC. The environmental risks ESG aims to govern include declining biodiversity, pollution, resource scarcity; and potential climate change impacts, for instance (Gnanarajah and Shorter 2022, 1). ESG factors are considered to be an integral part of discussions about sustainability, "an approach that creates long-term shareholder value through managing opportunities and risks that derive from economic, environmental and social developments" (Gnanarajah and Shorter 2022, 1). ESG is typically fulfilled by reporting, such as publishing a sustainability report or disclosing data through their web pages, showcasing the company's ESG performance.

The March 6, 2024, adoption by the US Securities and Exchange Commission of "rules to enhance and standardize climate-related disclosures by public companies and in public offerings" (US Securities and Exchange Commission 2024a) represented another significant step towards the standardization of ESG and sustainability reporting. The preamble notes that the rules "were modeled on the [Task Force on Climate-related Financial Disclosure] TCFD disclosure framework … that provide a structure for the assessment, management, and disclosure of climate-related financial risks: governance, strategy, risk management, and metrics and targets" (US Securities and Exchange Commission 2024b, 37) and

> concepts developed by the [Greenhouse Gas] GHG Protocol for aspects of the final rules, as it has become a leading reporting standard for GHG emissions. Because many registrants have elected to follow the TCFD recommendations when voluntarily providing climate-related disclosures, and/or have relied on the GHG Protocol when reporting their GHG emissions, building off these reporting frameworks will mitigate those registrants' compliance burdens and help limit costs. (US Securities and Exchange Commission 2024b, 26–27)

When looking at the other frameworks referenced in the rule such as CDP Worldwide (formerly Carbon Disclosure Project), Sustainability Accounting Standards Board, and Global Reporting Initiative (GRI); or the United Nations Global Compact and its Sustainable Development Goals, the International Sustainability Standards Board International Financial Reporting Standards Sustainable Development Goals, or Climate Disclosure Standards Board framework, the underlying implication across these tools is the risks businesses will face in the future are due to climate change that is most likely a result of GHG emissions, which can be characterized using carbon dioxide (CO_2) emissions coefficients or factors (US Energy Information Administration 2024). These frameworks and tools provide access to a perspective that each reporting company will have a cost of someday dealing with the effects of climate change or must now pay a cost for helping to avoid it, with the latter seen in the regulations requirement that a company report on any "carbon offsets and renewable energy credits or certificates (RECs) if used as a material component of a registrant's plans to achieve its disclosed climate-related targets or goals" (US Securities and Exchange Commission 2024a).

The broad acceptance of climate change being the primary risk that ESG reporting is designed to characterize, and that this risk can be mitigated through GHG emissions reductions, has empowered a robust carbon trading industry. This industry of emissions reductions or carbon sequestration tracking and auditing, leading to a wide range of carbon offset or credit generation and trading programs or markets, has driven most to model any corporate value owing to ESG initiatives in terms of metric tons of CO_2 since that metric can be valued using efficient carbon markets.

The carbon data cycle typically goes as follows. First, firms communicate their carbon performance to stakeholders through a variety of channels (In and Schumacher 2021, 4). Firms can adhere to or fall under carbon emissions disclosure regimes, either mandatory or voluntary (In and Schumacher 2021, 4). Once a firm discloses its carbon performance, the data is then analyzed by third-party rating agencies, which act as intermediaries between company disclosures and investors seeking to access and use that data (In and Schumacher 2021, 4). These rating agencies create indicators and metrics based on the data provided by firms, distinguishing between high-carbon performers from low-carbon performers (In and Schumacher 2021, 4).

However, there are several issues with this model. First, while carbon data has been commonly used as an indicator, the majority of ESG goods do not have a meaningful carbon component, leading to a disconnect between ESG goals and actual environmental impact. Most ESG initiatives cannot be appropriately measured using CO_2 equivalence. For example, the primary value of food rescue is completely unrelated to carbon emissions reductions. The same can be said for water reclamation, habitat restoration, community literacy, or data governance, just to name a few. The disconnection between meaningful ESG efforts and the most popular method of valuing ESG as a function of carbon credits or offsets results in valuations that are either inaccurate or generally inappropriate for these "beyond carbon" initiatives.

Second, the lack of standardized metrics and reporting frameworks can result in inconsistent data, making it difficult to compare and assess the effectiveness of ESG initiatives across different organizations. Overall, there is an inconsistency of firm-originating carbon data (In and Schumacher 2021, 11). It is likely that companies take advantage of the current systemic inconsistencies (In and Schumacher 2021, 5). Firms have been found to employ a variety of methods for reporting both direct and indirect emissions under voluntary regimes (In and Schumacher 2021, 12). Rating agencies are themselves inconsistent, leading to low convergence between ratings (In and Schumacher 2021, 12). In fact, they are incentivized to highlight their climate mitigation activities or ambitions as more progressive than they actually are (In and Schumacher 2021, 12).

3.3 A POLYCENTRIC ESG KNOWLEDGE COMMONS GOVERNANCE: HU AND RAC

3.3.1 *Valuing ESG and Sustainability Efforts: Human Impact Unit*

The valuation challenge of ESG has sparked work on the Hu methodology, which was publicly introduced in a 2023 white paper (Gillibrand and Draper 2023). The Hu methodology starts from the assumption that ESG initiatives are intended to address conditions that exist owing to human actions or inactions. It then reasons that, if a normalizing denominator is found for directly comparing these previously disparate actions, valuations for actively traded initiatives such as carbon reduction or sequestration could be directly compared with beyond carbon efforts. This normalizing factor used to calculate a project's Hu is found by defining the size of problem (SOP) per citizen in the relevant community in terms of the impact's measurement units (Figure 3.1).

The SOP is typically a discoverable for many ESG challenges without much effort, as it is most similar to the serviceable addressable market or served available market common within entrepreneurial education (Blank and Dorf 2012, 226). Finding the SOP is most directly found by the practitioner posting the question: "How much of my fix for this problem would be required before the problem is solved?" For example, if an organization is looking to calculate its impact in Hu for every ton of plastic it removed from the ocean, the SOP would be the total amount of harmful ocean plastic, or 6.1 million tons as of 2019 (Gillibrand and Draper 2023). The more challenging aspect of the analysis is identifying the community that this SOP should be normalized against.

Given the core premise behind the Hu methodology, the community associated with the SOP should be defined as those who could have prevented the problem. In the example of ocean plastic waste, the challenge is fully identifying who truly was capable of preventing the problem. Since it is an international problem, it is the population of the world that is at fault? Or since children are likely not large contributors or capable of supporting laws that would have prevented such waste, should they really be included? Or should the community at fault really be those who are directly causing the waste, even though lawmakers could make the

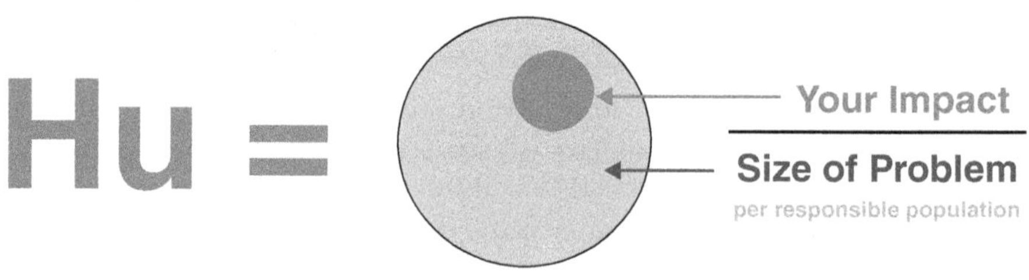

FIGURE 3.1 Human Impact Unit (Hu) normalization formula.

production of such waste far more risky with stricter laws? Or does it come back to the voting public since it is their ambivalence to the issue that enables inaction on the part of our governments? The fact that these are not straightforward questions, and are fraught with consequential trade-offs, provides context for the power of the Hu methodology when supporting the complex and uncertain challenges posed by ESG.

The immediate value of the Hu, though, is that normalizing the impact made by the SOP being addressed allows projects with no public market to price their impact using their Hu equivalence to active markets. For example, agricultural runoff is a significant ESG issue that requires meaningful intervention, yet meaningful impact is measured in nitrogen and phosphorus runoff reductions. Unlike other efforts where improvements can be modeled in GHG reductions, such as energy reduction measures in a commercial office building, the ESG benefit of reducing nitrogen and phosphorus runoff is the improved water quality. The fact that the true benefit does not have a carbon emissions link, even though clean water clearly improves the environment, means valuing this activity cannot use typical approaches that require carbon emissions factors. In the state of Iowa, the SOP for agricultural runoff pollution is massive. Runoff from the state of Iowa alone is estimated at just under 1.1 million tons of the nearly 2 million tons of nitrogen and phosphorus pollution that enters the Mississippi River each year as of 2019 (US Environmental Protection Agency 2023c), and has been modeled as the cause of more than 55 percent of the Gulf of Mexico dead zone (Eller 2018). This problem is one that can clearly be addressed through human intervention because its cause can be directly attributable to humans. The vast majority of agricultural runoff issues in the state of Iowa are caused by the approximately 143,000 producers as of 2022 who either directly pour the outputs of their field tile drainage systems directly into state waterways without any treatment, or the runoff is enabled by producers associated with operations that allow such practices to occur (Jordan 2022). By scoping the problem in this manner, the Hu methodology would attribute each individual classified as an Iowan producer as contributing 7.45 tons per year to expansion of the Gulf of Mexico dead zone. This normalizing factor would allow a project that sequesters 10 tons of phosphorus each year from Iowa rivers to define its impact as 1.3 Hu per year. Following a similar process using the average CO_2 emissions across the US and carbon credit pricing as of the first financial quarter of 2024 to find a value per Hu of $1,492.40 (Meidh Technologies 2023a) provides a basis for pricing the intangible value of a 10-ton reduction in phosphorus at $14,924. This approach still currently requires active markets such as carbon to provide a guide price, yet the Hu method allows that price to be directly related to the benefits provided in a manner that accounts for the cost and impacts on the communities impacted.

The ability for the Hu to provide a normalizing comparator across disparate ESG efforts is uniquely valuable. Yet an asset is only worth what someone will pay for

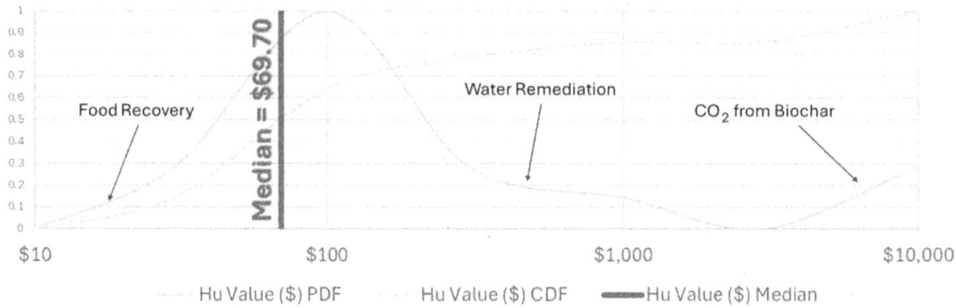

FIGURE 3.2 Hu valuation, in US dollars, probability density function and cumulative density function as of June 2024.

it. Reexamining the food rescue example from earlier, when the intangible value of EGDM efforts was actually auctioned, it fetched $3.53 per pound. Taking a national view of food rescue, one Hu can be calculated as being worth 23.4 pounds of food (Meidh Technologies 2023a). If accurate, this Hu estimate means the food recovery efforts performed by EGDM given the Hu valuation used in the agricultural runoff example given here should be worth $67.78 per pound versus the $3.53 per pound actually paid by bidders. Similar variations are seen when looking at various market estimates or use cases, as seen in the valuation distribution computed with June 2024 data (Figure 3.2).

This variation is definitely stark, but does not indicate the Hu model is ineffective. It indicates more that the means of transferring the intangible values associated with ESG efforts, and the evidence supporting the validity of the actions behind the projected values, is highly inefficient and must be better and more transparently understood.

3.3.2 *The Regenerative Authentication Credit (RAC)*

The paper "The Problem of Social Cost" by Ronald H. Coase (1960, 3) could reasonably be seen as the catalyst for the modern environmental credit and offset trading industry. Its proposal that applying property rights to pollution would encourage actors to efficiently control it through economic arbitrage (Coase 1960) appeared influential as the US Environmental Protection Agency (EPA) efforts to reduce sulfur dioxide and nitrogen oxide emissions saw the Agency introduce an "emissions trading system in 1977 that allows emissions from new sources to be offset by reductions from existing sources and later allowed for states to bank 'excess' emissions reductions" (Chandrasekhar 2023). This cap-and-trade strategy was first rolled out successfully with the Leaded Gasoline Phasedown program between 1982 and 1987. With concurrent advocacy around the Montreal Protocol system for tradable permits to reduce chlorofluorocarbon usage (Farber 2004), World Resources Institute land-based carbon-offset projects (World Resources

Institute 1992), and Project 88 efforts to explore cap-and-trade efforts more broadly (Stavins 1988), successful EPA programs for sulfur dioxide and nitrogen oxide were rolled out through the 1990s and early 2000s in the US (Schmalensee and Stavins 2015). While early offset discussions were broadly inclusive and wide ranging with regard to the environmental projects that could be solved, the Kyoto Protocol caused inertia to start building in 1997 towards GHG equivalency as the frame through which ESG has been primarily viewed since (Pearce 2021). For example, even the most recognized environmental offset programs of Renewable Energy Certificates introduced in 2001 for renewable electricity, Renewable Identification Numbers approved in 2005 for renewable liquid and organic fuels, and the Low Carbon Fuel Standard approved in 2009 to reduce the carbon intensity of liquid fuels in California are all use-specific proxies for carbon credits.

Even with the growth of voluntary markets since the 1999 launch of International Emissions Trading Association (International Emissions Trading Association 2023), most noncarbon markets have remained academic pricing exercises or conceptual secondary markets, with both typically slowed by the complexity of developing universally accepted models or standards. The realities of proving carbon claims has routinely left many calling for more standardization or Commodity Futures Trading Commission regulation (Fredman and Phillips 2022), yet the science of carbon and other environmental phenomena is not straightforward. It was in this environment that RACs were created in 2022 to address the core flaw seen in many carbon-defined offsets.

A RAC is a contract for transferring intangible ESG value from the originator to any future buyer (Figure 3.3). Each RAC is a combined document made up of the following components (Packin 2023):

- Redacted Evidentiary Documents. The originator has the right to choose what evidence of any claim it makes it included for public viewing. This evidence may be a redacted version of an unredacted copy, or some other form for presenting the sensitive information that is stored elsewhere.

FIGURE 3.3 Example of the four components that make up a RAC contract (from left to right): RTA, SOAO, RVD, and redacted evidence.

- RAC Value Definition (RVD). This document contains the definition of the intangible value represented by the RAC, the evidentiary document identifier (EDI) which is a Secure Hash Algorithm 256-bit (SHA256) hash of the unredacted evidence proving the actions that led to the generation of the defined intangible value, and lot size defining the number of units into which the RAC can be segmented. Between the ability to segment one RAC and for one action to have many different intangible values isolated in separate RACs, an identical EDI may be present in multiple RACs.
- Statement of Ownership at Origin (SOAO). This document identifies the owner of the intangible value at the time the actions associated with the RAC were taken, and the registrar who generated the RAC in the clearinghouse on behalf of the owner.
- RAC Transfer Agreement (RTA). This document defines the buyer and seller for a RAC, the terms of the sale, and identifies which RAC is retired as a result of the sale. In the case of lot segmentation, two new RACs would both reference the same retired RAC.

The RAC framework mimics a REC in two very important ways. First, the RAC separates the intangible value of an ESG action identically to a REC, requiring the prior owner to reference any work associated with the RAC to be considered "null work" in the same way that renewably generated electricity for which its RECs are separated is considered "null energy." Second, a RAC is built around proving the completion of a specific, tangible event in the same way a REC is directly associated with generated electricity. Additionally, the intangible value definition in the RAC mimics a feature retained from its predecessor, the Green Fuels Exchange Land Use Restriction Agreement that was first deployed in 2012 in support of a US Green Building Council Leadership in Energy and Environmental Design certification effort, of defining the intent of any actions taken without specifying or promising any specific effect or its magnitude.

This unique combination of features differs from most other offsets that reference a specific effect of a stated magnitude that can only be determined through modeling. For example, very few carbon credits are generated by direct observation of the emissions reductions they are citing. In the case of Verra, for example, the number, type, and characteristics of trees are audited, and the results of the audit are inputted into a model that projects the amount of carbon sequestered by the observed forest. This use of engineering judgment and modeling provides significant access to both error and fraud (Correa 2023).

Excluding intangible value or modeled estimations allows a RAC to avoid this access to errors or fraud. A RAC incorporates evidence about a directly observable, tangible action; allows the originator to define any fraction of the intangible values generated by that tangible action; and then depends on the market to independently define the RAC's value based on an analyst's estimate of certainty regarding the claimed action based on the reviewable evidence provided in the RAC. This approach directly acknowledges the existence of uncertainties that are typically buried in the models underlying traditional offsets and provides greater accessibility to markets. For example, a food rescue organization could generate a RAC stating 46,000 pounds-worth of strawberries were rescued, and the intangible value available for sale includes all benefits associated with feeding food-insecure citizens. Since operational standards and budgets vary widely in the food recovery space, the amount of evidence that may be available to prove these tangible actions could also vary widely. The RAC framework does not prevent any organization from generating a RAC with minimal evidence. However, if all that is provided as evidence in the case of a 46,000-pound rescue is an image of strawberries, it is expected that the acceptability of this evidence will be seen in the RAC's market valuation. In this case, it would be expected that anyone who purchases that RAC based solely on a picture of strawberries would reduce the price paid to account for any uncertainty regarding whether the amount of strawberries was actually received and the uncertainty regarding whether those strawberries made it to food-insecure individuals. Alternatively, if the food rescue organization were to instead include in the RAC a detailed document package identifying the bill of lading for the truck, the name and signature of the truck driver, the location of the offload location, and a signature of the recipient at offload, this type of a RAC would be likely to fetch a higher price.

The evidentiary variations cited in the food recovery example here would typically lead to calls for standardization. Yet the RAC framework assumes modern analytics can allow it to see even greater market efficiency by incorporating a "first principles" approach.

ESG RACs provides blockchain validated RAC contracts accessible via its clearinghouse. Technologically, ESG RACs:

- receives the thumbprint of evidentiary documents in the form of a SHA256 hash,
- commits that thumbprint token to the Trokt neopublic blockchain network (Meidh Technologies 2023b),
- builds a full RAC document that incorporates the evidentiary thumbprint and the redacted evidence defined by the originator,
- saves the combined RAC document so it is accessible in the clearinghouse, and
- writes the thumbprint of the combined RAC document back into the Trokt network.

This basic architecture and workflow of the RAC technology solution is presented in Figure 3.4.

This structure for generating a RAC allows the originator to control the level of transparency it feels it must meet in order to provide sufficient trust in its ESG

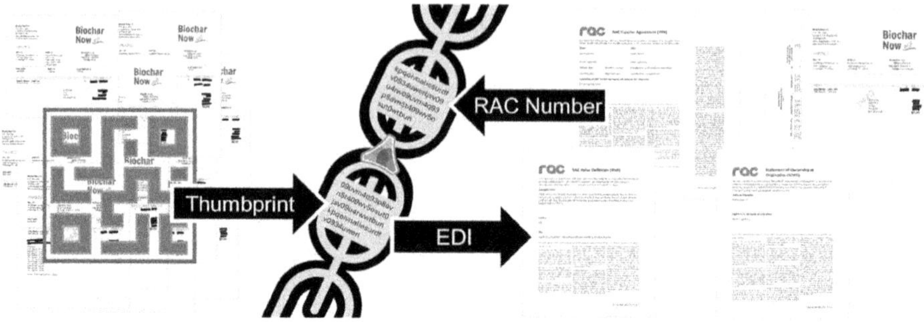

FIGURE 3.4 Process and technology involved in the creation of a RAC.

efforts to the market, while retaining full control over any information it deems to be commercially sensitive. When the intangible value represented by a RAC is sold, a new RAC is created by prepending an RTA that references the current RAC Number, and the new RAC Number of the new RAC is added to the Trokt network. This technique is commonly considered a "retirement" process. In order to provide the transparency needed that prevent double counting or "greenwashing," the old RAC number will remain in the system, yet the new RAC will identify that the RAC associated with that prior token no longer represents the intangible value of the associated action.

The relationship between the RAC and Truth and Trust as used in this chapter requires an understanding of the Trokt network and its Ostrom-inspired governance (Draper 2020). In the Trokt network, all data submitted into the network is equivalently valid, permanent, and contributes to how users perceive Truth within the network. However, each node is managed by its own community that develops its own standards for when validated data is sufficient for representing a Truth that should be incorporated and collaboratively protected by the Trokt blockchain network. The Ostrom inspiration behind the Trokt network constitution is seen in three major ways. First, each community representing each node is allowed to self-organize, defining the rules for membership, operations, and data validation. Second, these self-organized node governance committees are empowered with sufficient sovereignty to initiate their own actions that they deem best for managing the Truth associated with their contributions to the network. And lastly, the wider collective of communities is able to prevent the actions of one node if it is believed those actions would harm the value of the network or wider community. Figure 3.5 presents the primary components of network governance on the left that are responsible for generating what the network considers Truth.

The Trokt neopublic network differs from traditional public networks in that all Nodes must be preapproved like a private network, with any data payload arriving at any node being considered appropriate for replicating throughout the network. This differs from systems where a consensus protocol has the potential for

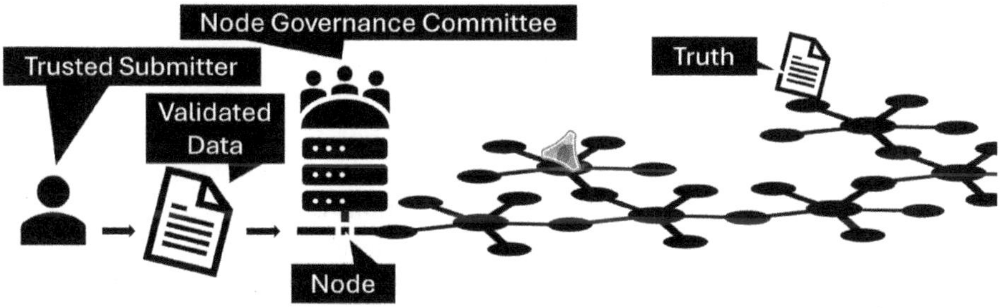

FIGURE 3.5 Structure of the Trokt network governance architecture.

rejecting an arriving payload for some reason. If a payload arrives at any node, it is considered validated data that is appropriate for replication.

The public component of the network is its node governance. Each node defines its own rules for what it considers data that is suitably validated such that its token should be allowed to be accepted and replicated within the Trokt network. Compliance is then required of the individuals who operate the system and send data packets of thumbprint tokens into the system. Once the thumbprint arrives and is replicated in the system, it is considered a representation of Truth.

3.3.3 *Truth as a Shared Resource*

RAC presents a compelling case where "Truth" is a shared resource within the ESG KC, governed *by* blockchain. The conception of Truth as a shared resource focuses on the fact that a token held in the system, by the nature of the network's immutability, is permanent. This permanence, meaning that one can prove the immutability of data since the time its thumbprint arrived at the system, does not mean that this system Truth will produce information that is acceptable to all members of the community. It is possible that the data represented by a token in the system can produce misleading or incorrect information either at the time or at some point in the future owing to the discovery of additional data or information. If this situation where items considered network Truth represent data that the community feels capable of generating false or misleading information, Trust in the system will rapidly erode. Because the governance structure counts on its member community to manage the quality of the data entering the system, with parties receiving a share of any financial gain that comes from wider use of the system, the Truth the system is generating can be considered a shared resource that will be eroded in value if overused or misused.

The notion of Truth has been discussed extensively in the marketplace of ideas theory, where the pursuit of Truth serves as an important purpose of speech. In 1644, John Milton, an English poet and essayist, wrote "Areopagitica" to induce Parliament to allow unlicensed printing. He articulated the seminal view that freedom of expression enhances the social good and that unrestricted debate would lead to the discovery of truth. In 1859, John Stuart Mill, an English philosopher and economist, linked liberty to the ability to progress and to avoid social stagnation in "On Liberty" (Smolla 1992). Mill argues that the suppression of opinion is wrong, whether or not the opinion is true: If it is true, society is denied the truth; if it is false, society is denied the fuller understanding of truth which comes from its conflict with error; and when the received opinion is part truth and part error, society can know the whole truth only by allowing the airing of competing views. In other words, society benefits from an exchange of ideas, and people could trade false notions for factual ones, but only if they could encounter them.

Justice Oliver Wendell Holmes further introduced the concept of the marketplace of ideas into American law, following John Milton and John Stuart Mill's discussion. In *Abrams v. United States* (1919), Abrams was accused of publishing pamphlets that criticized President Woodrow Wilson's deployment of troops and advocated a strike against munitions plants. The Supreme Court ruled that publishing such pamphlets during wartime was not protected by the First Amendment. Justice Holmes famously stated in his dissenting opinion that:

> When men have realized that time has upset many fighting faiths, they may come to believe even more than they believe the very foundations of their own conduct that the ultimate good desired is better reached by free trade in ideas- that the best test of truth is the power of the thought to get itself accepted in the competition of the market, and that truth is the only ground upon which their wishes safely can be carried out.[2]

This statement has been repeatedly quoted by different courts as the basis of the "Marketplace of Ideas Theory."

Under the marketplace of ideas theory, a functioning market requires two premises. First, the pursuit of objective "truth." All the major thinkers articulate the marketplace of ideas theory based on the concept of "truth." The marketplace of ideas is built on the *belief* that among all the information disseminated, some ideas are considered as true and others are considered as false. Properly understood, the marketplace of ideas is not linked to certitude that what actually emerges from the market is inviolable, objective "truth" (Smolla 1992). Instead, truth was never meant by "certainty" (Smolla 1992). Justice Oliver Wendell Holmes famously said that "certainty generally is an illusion, and response is not the destiny of man" (Holmes Jr. 1897, 8). Simply put, seeking "truth" is the intended goal while speaking.

Second, the market is functional: "Good ideas" will always survive challenges from lesser ideas. The value of the marketplace of ideas is its capacity to provide "the best *test* of truth."[3] The marketplace is not the end but the quest, not the market's capacity to arrive at the final and ultimate truth but rather the integrity of the

2 *Abrams v. United States*, 250 U.S. 616, 630 (1919).

3 *Abrams v. United States*, 250 U.S. 616, 630 (1919) (Holmes, J. dissenting); author's emphasis.

process (Smolla 1992). However, the ideas of the wealthy and powerful will have greater access to the market; the marketplace will inevitably be biased in favor of those with the resources (Holmes Jr 1897, 8; Barron 1967; Wellington 1979; Ingber 1984). As American philosopher Herbert Marcuse stated, "the concentration of economic and political power allows effective dissent to be blocked where it could freely emerge" (Wolff et al. 1969). In the mid 1940s, the Commission on Freedom of the Press also discovered that the press had become increasingly concentrated in the hands of fewer individuals. Therefore, the free market requires regulation, just as a free market for goods needs a law against monopoly (Chafee 1947). For instance, in "A Free and Responsible Press" (1947), the Hutchins Commission suggested the government finance new media outlets and that an independent government agency oversee press performance, and encouraged a subsidized and more-regulated media space, one in which a number of views could be disseminated (Commission on Freedom of the Press 1974).

Under the marketplace of ideas theory, objective truth is not only regarded as a shared belief but also as a shared resource. The puzzle within the marketplace of ideas is that empirically testing the proposition that "truth will triumph over error" would itself require some objective measure of what ideas are true and what ideas are false – a measurement that the marketplace theory itself forbids (Smolla 1992). However, this dilemma is the strength of this theory, which spurs us to accept the noblest challenge of the life of the mind: *never to stop searching* (Smolla 1992). As John Stuart Mill instructed, even when we are relatively confident in the truth of received opinion, "if it is not fully, frequently, and fearlessly discussed, it will be held as dead dogma, not a living truth" (Mill 1986). When conflicting dogmas offer themselves to the market as truth, the modern mind is most comfortable subjecting each to the intellectual acid bath of adversarial contest, for our intuition and experience reveal that truth may lie somewhere in between them (Smolla 1992). Practically speaking, we arrive at a suitably objective truth once belief in that truth can survive all rational objection.

An example of these issues in a more relatable context may be Truth Social, the social media platform launched on February 1, 2022, and used heavily by President Donald Trump. Conceptually similar to Trokt, users who are provided access to contribute to the network generate "Truths" that other people can read. The relationship between these "Truths" and the objective reality they represent or reference is defined by the operator who created the "Truth" in the Truth Social system. As "Truths" are added, the community's interpretation of how closely the information derived from the "Truths" contained in the network influences the level of Trust the community has in the network's ability to retain and protect the objective truth of its system Truth. Truth Social very clearly highlights the issues that arise when the community driving the network is able to see validity in its network Truth when the information accepted as objective truth by that community is in direct opposition to what other communities consider objective truth.

3.3.4 *Polycentricity in Addressing the Certain Level of Uncertainty*

The RACs approach – via Blockchain governance – offers an alternative governance approach from the traditional ESG approach. One important difference is that, as various scholars have identified, blockchain networks exhibit the attribute of polycentricity. Polycentricity is the concept of "multiple centers of decision-making, or multiple authorities, no one of which has ultimate authority for making all collective decisions," which has been recognized as the work of Vincent and Elinor Ostrom, in collaboration with researchers at the Ostrom Workshop at Indiana University (Stephan et al. 2019, 31). Blockchains are polycentric as "they are governed by rules that provide the basis for interaction in political, socio-economic systems, while establishing the social positions that different individuals may occupy according to their rights, obligations and empowerments to act in specific situations" (Bodon et al. 2019, 11). Alston and others further highlights that polycentricity is the defining feature of a permissionless blockchain network, where governments, too, are part of blockchain's polycentricity (Alston et al. 2021).

The polycentricity aspects effectively address the certain level of uncertainty within the ESG industry. ESG and the data underlying much of its quantification has typically struggled with the fact that significant uncertainty is unavoidable. For example, arguably the most successful initiatives at mobilizing climate action have levered the EPA ENERGY STAR program. In the retail space it is broadly known for appliance efficient ratings, and in the commercial building space it is the leading tool for energy, water, and GHG benchmarking among property investment funds. In states such as New York and California and some local jurisdictions any real estate transaction is required to provide energy data in the ENERGY STAR format, and many real estate brokers now voluntarily look to it as a means of third-party validation for communicating the energy usage and efficiency of a property. Its tools for commercial buildings are used by more than 300,000 properties across the US (US Environmental Protection Agency 2023b), nearly 95 percent of all households in the US benefit from an ENERGY STAR program delivered more than 840 utilities, and over 90 percent of Americans recognize ENERGY STAR (US Environmental Protection Agency 2023a). By nearly all accounts, ENERGY STAR is a widely recognized measure that has changed community behavior by offering an understanding of how to choose higher performing equipment and buildings. Yet even practitioners struggle to agree on how to evaluate the accuracy of the ENERGY STAR model. For example, the EPA notes on a frequently asked questions page in response to questions about ENERGY STAR model uncertainty that "there is no standard approach for combining those [model] uncertainties" into a single estimate across the model (US Environmental Protection Agency 2020), and academic research presents opportunities for improving various parameters by between 4.9 percent to 24.9 percent per parameter (Arjunan et al. 2020).

ENERGY STAR is a great example of a highly complex solution communicated effectively enough that its level of uncertainty is accepted within its relevant community, regardless of whether the community fully understands the underlying complexity or subtleties of the results it produces. Similarly, the RAC framework's lack of restrictions on intangible value definition and lack of standardization in evidentiary structure and visibility allows RAC originators to dynamically balance the competing forces that drive perceived value and acceptable price in markets where innovation is outpacing community knowledge. For example, originators of nonstandard commodities such as biochar are currently needing to balance how much evidence is visible in redacted form against what data if released would do commercial harm. In the case of the Biochar Now LLC RAC presented in Figure 3.3, the originator elected to provide sales invoices with pricing blacked out as evidence that a particular weight of a specific product was delivered for its stated use. As the Biochar Now LLC product has specific qualities that differentiate it from competitors, yet those qualities are not sufficiently defined by the broader industry to allow for specific definitions, the RAC was constructed in a manner that Biochar Now LLC felt an informed community member would have enough information to validate the type of biochar referenced in the invoices without providing any commercially sensitive specifics about the product. At the same time, for most individuals who considered purchasing all or a portion of that RAC, there was little concern that the product identified in the redacted invoices was not being deployed as intended when it was purchased. Owing to instances such as the Verra fraud highlighted earlier, the community has the ability to lose confidence that the full chain of actions from intent to implementation are completed. In this case of the Biochar Now LLC RAC, Biochar Now LLC believed the community would find the uncertainty that exists between the evidence that a product was purchased and the stated intent of how that product would be used once purchased would be accepted.

In environments more prevalent to pervasive theft of fraud, such as the fats, oils, and greases industry, this connection between an intended action and its completion can often be bolstered with photographic or video evidence that could also be referenced in or built into the RAC. For example, the GreaseTrack compliance software provided by RAC produces a quality label that is integrated into any renewable crude RAC as the redacted evidence (GreaseTrack 2024). This method of providing the community unique references that can be tied to any specific collection, with the images or other tracking data associated with that location collated in a manner that allows for their permanence to be validated using the Trokt neopublic blockchain network, and provides access to trust without full transparency (Figure 3.6).

Like the evidence provided in the Biochar Now LLC example, the valuation of a renewable crude RAC that provides a quality label as its public evidence is influenced by the perceived uncertainty that any token in the quality label may not be corroborated by the underlying evidence upon further investigation. Attempts to

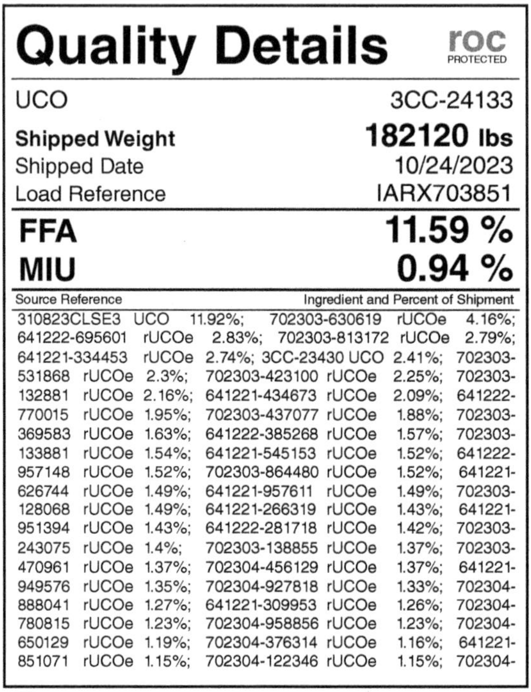

Quality Details roc PROTECTED

UCO	3CC-24133
Shipped Weight	**182120 lbs**
Shipped Date	10/24/2023
Load Reference	IARX703851
FFA	**11.59 %**
MIU	**0.94 %**

Source Reference — Ingredient and Percent of Shipment

310823CLSE3 UCO 11.92%; 702303-630619 rUCOe 4.16%; 641222-695601 rUCOe 2.83%; 702303-813172 rUCOe 2.79%; 641221-334453 rUCOe 2.74%; 3CC-23430 UCO 2.41%; 702303-531868 rUCOe 2.3%; 702303-423100 rUCOe 2.25%; 702303-132881 rUCOe 2.16%; 641221-434673 rUCOe 2.09%; 641222-770015 rUCOe 1.95%; 702303-437077 rUCOe 1.88%; 702303-369583 rUCOe 1.63%; 641222-385268 rUCOe 1.57%; 702303-133881 rUCOe 1.54%; 641221-545153 rUCOe 1.52%; 641222-957148 rUCOe 1.52%; 702303-864480 rUCOe 1.52%; 641221-626744 rUCOe 1.49%; 641221-957611 rUCOe 1.49%; 702303-128068 rUCOe 1.49%; 641221-266319 rUCOe 1.43%; 641221-951394 rUCOe 1.43%; 641222-281718 rUCOe 1.42%; 702303-243075 rUCOe 1.4%; 702303-138855 rUCOe 1.37%; 702303-470961 rUCOe 1.37%; 702304-456129 rUCOe 1.37%; 641221-949576 rUCOe 1.35%; 702304-927818 rUCOe 1.33%; 702304-888041 rUCOe 1.27%; 641221-309953 rUCOe 1.26%; 702304-780815 rUCOe 1.23%; 702304-958856 rUCOe 1.23%; 702304-650129 rUCOe 1.19%; 702304-376314 rUCOe 1.16%; 641221-851071 rUCOe 1.15%; 702304-122346 rUCOe 1.15%; 702304-

roc

FIGURE 3.6 Example of a GreaseTrack quality label that displays the probability of any specific collection event being contained in the total quantity shipped.

minimize this influence of uncertainty on value, which often manifests in a community as a lack of trust, can be seen in the design and implementation of the technology defining a RAC relative to its interpretation of Truth and relationships to Trust.

Transparency plays a crucial role in fostering trust within a polycentric system, as it enables various actors to share information openly, collaborate effectively, and hold each other accountable, thereby strengthening the overall governance structure. Trust serves as a central role in coping with dilemmas (Ostrom 2010, 661). As explained by Elinor Ostrom, "it is … the structure of the situation [that] generates sufficient information about the likely behavior of others to be trust- worthy reciprocators who will bear their share of the costs of overcoming a dilemma" (Ostrom 2010, 661). Such disclosure creates a foundation of mutual confidence, where participants are more likely to cooperate and contribute to the collective effort.

3.4 CONCLUSION

Exploring ESG value realization and the challenges of maintaining truth and trust within the ESG KC makes clear that the current frameworks, particularly those focused on carbon-based metrics, are insufficient for capturing the full scope and impact of ESG initiatives. These problems are best addressed by shifting towards more nimble, simplified presentations of the nuance required for meaningful ESG valuation such as the Hu offering valuation standardization for bespoke intangible value transfer contracts like RACs. These tools offer a way to authenticate and monetize the intangible value created by ESG activities, linking them to tangible, verifiable actions rather than abstract or speculative outcomes. By doing so, they provide a clearer, more reliable connection between ESG claims and their real-world impact, thereby enhancing transparency and trust within the community.

This chapter argues that industry must undertake a rethinking of ESG governance as a KC, where the management of environmental resources is intrinsically linked to the governance of the knowledge and truth that underpin ESG efforts. The concept of polycentric governance is particularly relevant here, as it recognizes the need for multiple stakeholders, each with varying levels of authority, to collaborate and share information openly. In this context, a balanced approach to auditable transparency is not just a desirable attribute but a crucial element for maintaining trust and ensuring that the shared resource of truth is preserved and respected.

The current approach to ESG valuation and governance must evolve to better reflect the diverse impacts of ESG initiatives. By moving away from an overemphasis on carbon metrics and towards frameworks that prioritize truth, transparency, and tangible outcomes, the ESG sector can more effectively align with community values and expectations. The adoption of information sharing tools such as RACs and analysis frameworks such as the Hu, combined with a commitment to transparent and accountable governance, offers a pathway to restoring and enhancing trust in ESG efforts. This, in turn, will ensure that the value created by these initiatives is recognized, respected, and appropriately compensated, paving the way for a more equitable and effective approach to addressing the critical ESG challenges of our time.

PART II

4

Linking Physical and Knowledge Commons in a Green Stormwater Infrastructure Program

Erik Nordman, Patrick J. Doran, Christian Glupker, Sam Haapaniemi, Elaine Isely, Paul Isely, Valerie Strassberg, and Shanyn Viars

4.1 INTRODUCTION

For more than a century, US municipalities have managed urban stormwater by moving it off site as quickly as possible through storm drains, ditches, and pipes. This paradigm primarily addressed stormwater volumes on site but exacerbated downstream flooding and water quality problems. The system of drains and pipes flushed sediments, oil, nutrients, and other pollutants – and in some cases, partially treated sewage – into nearby waterbodies in a pulse of stormwater (Debo and Reese 2002). Nonpoint source pollution, including stormwater runoff, is the largest remaining contributor to water quality problems affecting drinking water, recreation, fisheries, and wildlife (United States Environmental Protection Agency 2015a).

The National Research Council (2009, 5) noted that nearly all of the problems associated with urban stormwater "result from one underlying cause: loss of the water retaining and evapotranspirating functions of the soil and vegetation in the urban landscape." Roads and parking lots account for up to 70 percent of impervious cover in intensely urbanized cities and generate most of the city's stormwater.

A new ecological paradigm in stormwater management has emerged to recreate the "water retaining and evapotranspirating functions of the soil and vegetation" lost to urbanization. Often called "green stormwater infrastructure" (GSI), "low-impact development," or "nature-based solutions," the approach mimics natural hydrology by diverting stormwater runoff into well-designed rain gardens, bioswales, and other seminatural features. It also enhances biodiversity and community resiliency. Instead of a nuisance, stormwater becomes a valuable resource that is managed locally and integrated regionally (Debo and Reese 2002).

Many cities are experiencing more intense rainfall as the climate warms. In some cases, the rainfall increase is overwhelming the capacity of the drain and pipe infrastructure to move stormwater effectively off site (Waters et al. 2003; Kourtis and Tsihrintzis 2021). GSI can play an important complementary role to existing "gray infrastructure" systems by detaining and/or absorbing excess stormwater volumes to prevent flooding and reduce pollution. GSI refers to the systems and engineering practices that use or mimic natural processes to manage stormwater runoff. These include rain gardens, green roofs, permeable pavements, bioswales, and rainwater harvesting systems. GSI is designed to infiltrate, evapotranspire, capture, or reuse stormwater to slow down or prevent it from running into the sewer system.

On the other hand, green infrastructure (GI) is a broader term encompassing a wide range of natural and seminatural landscape elements. It includes parks, open spaces, trees, gardens, and other vegetation that provide ecosystem services such as air and water purification, temperature regulation, and wildlife habitat. While GI can contribute to stormwater management, it also has other environmental and social benefits, such as enhancing urban biodiversity, mitigating urban heat islands, providing recreational spaces, and improving mental health.

The monetized social benefits of GSI, in many cases, can exceed the costs (Nordman et al. 2018). However, the upfront costs are often borne by the property owners while the long-term benefits are shared with the broader community. The GSI practices can be on private or public property and the practices can be spatially extensive. These contribute to overall stormwater management challenges and increase public costs. Property owners have little private incentive to install GSI. For example, a rain garden can manage the stormwater from a parking lot, but it might reduce parking availability. Most of the benefits of on-site stormwater management occur to those downstream, not the property owner. The challenge for municipalities, therefore, is to devise institutions, from formal rules to behavioral norms, to encourage the adoption of GSI.

4.2 BACKGROUND

4.2.1 *Policy Context*

Stormwater degrades the nation's waters, but mitigating its effects has proved to be challenging. A National Research Council report identified three reasons why stormwater is so difficult to manage:

1. It is produced from literally everywhere in a developed landscape;
2. Its production and delivery are episodic, and these fluctuations are difficult to attenuate; and
3. It accumulates and transports much of the collective waste of the urban environment. (National Research Council 2009, 28)

Stormwater runoff causes water quality impairments in the nation's waters. Section 402(p) of the Clean Water Act identifies stormwater discharge as a point source of water pollution that can be regulated under the Act's National Pollution

Discharge Elimination System (NPDES). Operators of municipal separate storm sewer systems and for combined sewer systems for large and small urban areas and certain construction sites must obtain a NPDES permit. NPDES permits are also required for wastewater treatment facilities which may combine both wastewater and stormwater. The permit holders must create and implement stormwater pollution plans (National Research Council 2009).

Some states have opted to administer the NPDES permitting program themselves (United States Environmental Protection Agency 2020). In Michigan, the NPDES permitting program is administered by the state environmental agency, the Department of Environment, Great Lakes, and Energy. In southeast Michigan, including the city of Detroit, NPDES permit holders for stormwater include the Detroit Water Resource Recovery Facility (operated by the Great Lakes Water Authority) and the Detroit Water and Sewerage Department (DWSD) (Michigan Department of Environment, Great Lakes, and Energy 2019).

The US Environmental Protection Agency (EPA) designates the Detroit River as an Area of Concern (AOC) under the US–Canada Great Lakes Water Quality Agreement. The Agreement defines AOCs as "geographic areas designated by the Parties where significant impairment of beneficial uses has occurred as a result of human activities at the local level" (United States Environmental Protection Agency 2019). The EPA cites stormwater runoff as one of the contributors to the degradation of the Detroit River.

In 2017, Detroit mayor Mike Duggan created an Office of Sustainability to enhance collaboration among departments and agencies. One of its priorities was creating the Detroit Stormwater Hub to track GSI projects and improve education about stormwater management practices (Hughes 2020; City of Detroit n.d.).

Stormwater management in Detroit encompasses a combination of regulatory obligations and incentive programs to balance the need for infrastructural sustainability with encouragement for private property owners to participate in the effort actively. The nuances between the Post-Construction Stormwater Management Ordinance (PCSWMO), Drainage Charge, and Green Credit program form the crux of Detroit's stormwater management framework.

PCSWMO is a regulatory obligation designed to manage stormwater runoff post-construction. It requires new nonresidential development that "creates or replaces one-half acre (21,780 square feet) or more of impervious surface" to design and install stormwater management practices that infiltrate, evapotranspire, capture, or reuse a specific runoff volume. GSI practices are among these encouraged approaches. The goal is to minimize the impact of development on stormwater runoff rates and volumes and to reduce pollutants in the runoff. It is mandatory, and noncompliance can result in penalties.

DWSD requires additional onsite stormwater management on properties. Any new development or redevelopment must follow the PCSWMO.

Drainage charge is another regulatory obligation imposed on all Detroit property owners. The charge is based on the extent of impervious areas (that water cannot penetrate, such as rooftops, driveways, parking lots) on the property. The concept behind this charge is that impervious surfaces increase stormwater runoff, burdening the city's drainage system. Therefore, property owners with larger amounts of impervious surface area are charged more as they contribute more to the system's load.

The 2022 drainage charge was $678.28 per month per acre of impervious surface (City of Detroit Water and Sewerage Department 2023a). The city assumes that residential customers have downspouts that are disconnected from the stormwater system and discharge onto a lawn. Therefore, all residential customers receive a 25 percent "green credit" toward their stormwater charge.

Contrary to the aforementioned regulatory obligations, the Green Credit incentive program is designed to encourage property owners to reduce their drainage charges. It provides a financial incentive for property owners to go above and beyond the minimum requirements set out by the PCSWMO. The credits are earned by implementing GSI practices that reduce the amount of impervious surface and/or manage stormwater onsite beyond the volume required by the PCSWMO. By doing so, they decrease the amount of runoff that enters the sewer system and thus can reduce their drainage charge. DWSD offers a two-part credit of up to 80 percent of the drainage charge for property owners who reduce stormwater volume (40 per cent) and peak flow (40 percent). Volume reduction, or "retention," involves the permanent removal of stormwater volume from the system. Peak flow reduction, or "detention," involves the temporary storage of stormwater volume during wet weather events. This incentive program represents a proactive approach to stormwater management, encouraging property owners to contribute to the solution.

In summary, the PCSWMO and Drainage Charge are regulatory obligations requiring property owners to manage a specific volume of stormwater runoff and pay a fee based on their impervious area, respectively. The Green Credit program, on the other hand, is an incentive-based initiative that rewards new development for meeting the regulatory requirements by lowering their monthly drainage charge and motivates existing property owners and further development to exceed the minimum requirements of stormwater management and reduce their impervious area, which can lead to a reduction in their drainage charges. While the regulatory obligations ensure a baseline level of stormwater management is maintained, the incentive program fosters an environment of continuous improvement and greater involvement in sustainable practices.

Residents of Detroit, Michigan, are facing a growing problem of urban flooding. This issue is mainly due to the city's outdated water and sewer infrastructure, more frequent severe weather events, and other factors that are causing flooded basements and neighborhoods. A recent survey indicated that 43 percent of Detroit households experienced flooding between 2012 and 2020 (Sampson et al. 2021).

The root of Detroit's flooding issues is the outdated combined-sewer system, which accounts for 97 percent of the city's infrastructure. This system must be able to handle both sanitary flow during dry periods and runoff caused by storms during wet-weather events. Detroit was one of the last major cities in Michigan to adopt a PCSWMO, a measure that helps to reduce the impact of additional stormwater runoff from new private development. Additionally, the city was exempt from adhering to county stormwater regulations, which has compounded the issue.

Over time, this situation has increased the burden on the already overtaxed combined-sewer system. The cost of addressing these problems has fallen on the city's taxpayers rather than on the private developers who played a role in exacerbating the problem.

The aging infrastructure and intense rainfall also result in combined-sewer overflows (CSO) in which partially treated sewage flows into the Detroit and Rouge rivers. The Clean Water Act requires DWSD, along with the Great Lakes Water Authority, to implement a CSO control program. Detroit is using GSI as well as conventional controls to reduce its CSO discharges (City of Detroit Water and Sewerage Department 2022). A study of Detroit GSI by Thorsby et al. (2020) found that broader scale practices, such as bioretention basins, bioswales, and green roofs, had a larger effect on flood mitigation, especially when located at the upstream end of the storm sewer system. Smaller-scale systems, such as rain gardens, have a smaller mitigating effect. Webber et al. (2020) found a similar scaling effect.

The Green Credit program provides an economic incentive for property owners to reduce impervious surfaces by installing GSI practices. However, the economic approach may be insufficient. In Detroit, as in other cities, the drainage charge alone is often insufficient to change behaviors. Of the many thousands of properties in Detroit, only 268 GSI projects are listed in the city's database (City of Detroit Water and Sewerage Department 2023). Those property owners who do adopt GSI practices often do so for other, complementary reasons.

In this chapter, we use the Governing Knowledge Commons (GKC) framework, built on Ostrom's Institutional Analysis and Development (IAD) framework, to describe the complex institutions and motivations that influence the decision to adopt GSI practices.

4.2.2 *Institutional and Economic Perspectives*

Detroit's fee-based stormwater ordinance is founded on a rational choice model. Property owners must pay for stormwater they discharge into the municipal system based on the parcel's impervious surface area. The drainage charge also signals to the property owners that stormwater management is a scarce resource. The rational property owner is therefore expected to either reduce the amount of impervious surface (lowering the base charge) or manage the runoff (crediting against the base charge) as long as the present-value costs of on-site GSI practices are less than the present-value costs of the drainage charge.

Nordman et al. (2018) found that the net present values of the social benefits of many GSI practices exceed those of the costs in Grand Rapids, Michigan. From a social perspective, GSI can be an economically efficient choice for managing stormwater on-site. However, such practices still require the landowner to pay for the capital and maintenance costs while delivering benefits to those downstream in the sewershed. Drainage charges, as in Detroit, may shift the parcel owner's economic calculus in favor of adopting GSI practices.

The economic approach prioritizes technical knowledge and expertise with the goal of simplifying complex urban water issues. GSI implementation includes not only issues of power and expertise, but also of cultural values and leadership as well as structure and jurisdiction (Brown 2005). Carolyn Johns (2019) surveyed key informants in Toronto, Canada, about barriers to GSI implementation. She identified several key barriers including the urban form (land use, soil), political leadership, funding challenges, institutional challenges, lack of interdisciplinary knowledge and expertise, lack of community buy-in, and a culture that values gray infrastructure.

The decision to adopt and implement GSI practices to manage stormwater on-site is not merely an economic one, however. As several authors noted, the decision is embedded in a variety of institution contexts (Brown 2005; Mekala and MacDonald 2018; Johns 2019). Brown (2005, 465), for example, notes that "the technocratic structure of the administrative regime inherently privileges technical expertise and economic rationalism over an interdisciplinary alternative that values community participation in decision making and environmental sustainability." Harriden (2021) emphasized the role of Indigenous water knowledge in her critique of the highly engineered approach to stormwater management.

Mekala and MacDonald (2018) used the IAD framework (Crawford and Ostrom 1995; Ostrom 2009) to analyze the institutional context of GSI practices in Melbourne, Australia. Their institutional analysis identified several critical factors that affected GSI practices. The study region's decentralized and loosely coordinated planning and natural resource management agencies impeded the systematic implementation of GSI. The IAD framework helped to identify the lack of interactions and collaboration among key actors.

The stormwater drainage charge's economic approach assumes that parcel owners have access to the relevant information about the GI alternatives, have access to financing for the upfront costs of implementing GSI, have decision-making authority to implement on-site solutions, have access to technical knowledge or technical experts (engineers and landscape designers) who can design GSI systems that can be permitted and approved by DWSD, and understand how on-site stormwater management affects neighbors and communities downstream.

Our research questions are:

- How do economic incentives, like the drainage charge, affect the decision to adopt GSI practices?
- Do property owners know how to reduce their drainage charges using GSI?
- Is the knowledge about GSI practices widely available (a knowledge commons) or essentially privatized within design/engineering firms?

4.3 METHODS/CASE STUDY DESIGN

4.3.1 *Institutional Analysis*

This analysis builds on Haapaniemi et al. (2023) by situating the economic model within the GKC framework. The GKC framework extends Ostrom's IAD framework to describe the public goods nature of information (Ostrom and Hess 2006; Frischmann, Madison, and Strandburg 2014). In both frameworks, actors may consider economic costs and benefits within the action situation.

The GKC framework is a descriptive analytical tool that can help elucidate how knowledge is produced, shared, and managed. It can also identify and describe the collective action problems and key action arenas that emerge in various settings (Frischmann et al. 2014). The Knowledge Commons framework begins with a description of the study system including the resource characteristics, the attributes of the community, and what Ostrom called "rules-in-use." Rules-in-use are the working rules used by the community of resource users which may be different from those that are formally codified (Ostrom 2005). The action arena is the focal unit of analysis in the GKC framework as it is in Ostrom's IAD framework. The action arena comprises a specific action situation – for example, a decision to be made – and a particular set of actors. Ostrom (2005, 14) described the action arena as "the social space where participants with diverse perspectives interact, exchange goods and services, solve problems, dominate one another, for fight (among the many things that individuals can do in action arenas)." The resource characteristics, community attributes, and rules-in-use affect the action arena's structure and produce patterns of interactions. The GKC framework includes a feedback loop in which outcomes from the action arena can directly affect the resource characteristics. The patterns of interactions can affect both the study system and the action arena. Analysts may use evaluative criteria to assess the performance of the study system (Figure 4.1).

Ostrom (2005) further decomposed the action arena into component parts. Specific people (actors) may be assigned to positions or roles. The positions determine which actions may be taken. The actors may have limited information about the state of the system. Likewise, the actors in their positions may have limited control over the system. For example, the position may require an actor

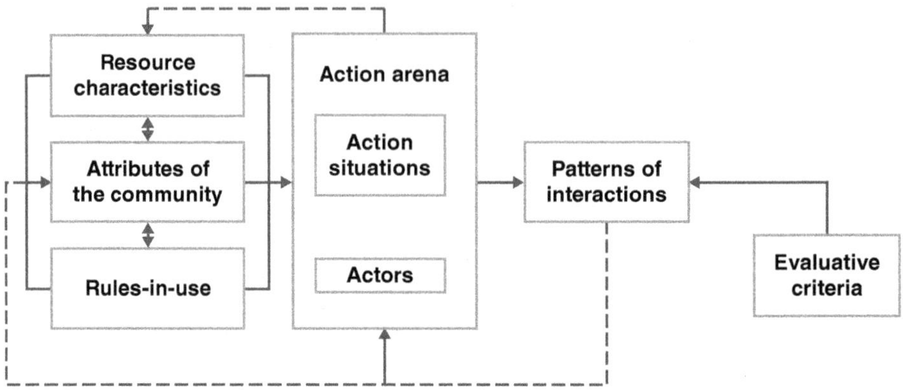

FIGURE 4.1 The generic Governing Knowledge Commons framework (Frischmann et al. 2014).

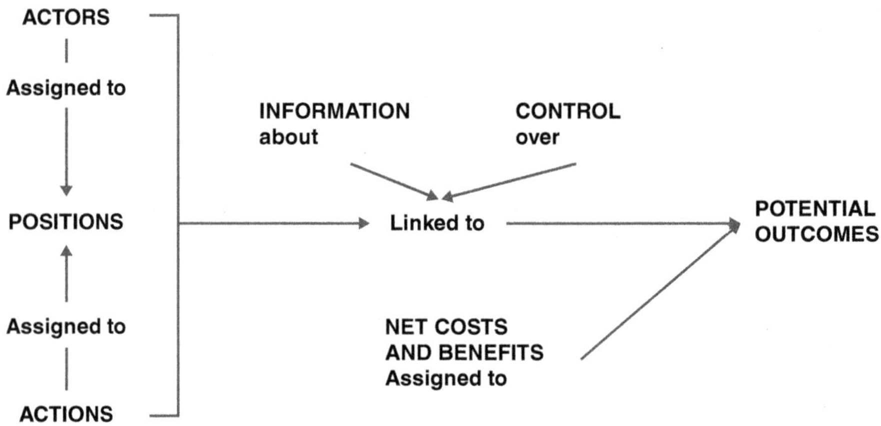

FIGURE 4.2 Action situation in the Governing Knowledge Commons framework (same as the Institutional Analysis and Development framework, Ostrom 2005).

to do something, may prohibit it, or may allow it. The information and control combine with the net costs and benefits to define a range of potential outcomes. It is these outcomes that generate the patterns of interactions seen in the primary level of the GKC framework (Figure 4.2). The patterns of interactions include the spatial distribution of GSI practices, amelioration of stormwater discharges, and economic development.

As Aagaard and Frischmann note in Chapter 2 of this volume, every physical commons has a corresponding knowledge commons. That is, the institutional arrangements that govern a shared natural resource, for example, rely on an institutional arrangement that governs how the knowledge about the resource will be acquired, communicated, archived, curated, or secured. Therefore, we decompose the stormwater management case study into two parts, one for the operational level management of stormwater and one for its corresponding knowledge commons.

4.3.2 *Types of Knowledge for GSI Implementation*

Ostrom and Hess (2007) described knowledge commons as comprising facilities, artifacts, and ideas. Facilities store the information as physical libraries and archives or as digital repositories. Artifacts are articles, books, documents, files, and websites that are housed within the facilities. The artifacts are the discrete resource units of the knowledge commons. Ideas are the nontangible content transmitted by the artifacts. Ideas are not physical and therefore are nonrivalrous. However, the artifacts that contain the ideas may be rivalrous.

However, not all shared knowledge is stored and transmitted through physical artifacts. Scholars increasingly recognize the importance of local and traditional ecological knowledge. Such knowledge may be developed, accumulated, and transmitted across years and generations without being written down.

In the case of Detroit's urban flooding challenges, there is a large body of formalized engineering knowledge. There is also local knowledge within the community about which locations are prone to flooding and how GI practices may or may not be effective (Carmichael et al. 2019). Successful stormwater management will require a flow of information between these types of knowledge systems.

4.3.3 *Benefit-Cost Analysis*

The empirical research presented here focuses on the net costs and benefits within the stormwater model's action situation. The research team was contracted by The Nature Conservancy – Michigan Chapter to analyze the "business case" for adopting GSI in Detroit. The team analyzed the capital and maintenance costs of constructing various GSI practices, the monetary value of the benefits, and the value of the avoided drainage charge. The benefit-cost analysis model was adapted from Nordman et al. (2018) and modified with appropriate Detroit values and adjusted for inflation. The additional benefit of CSO avoidance was included in the Detroit model. Data on the green and gray infrastructure projects from the participating property owners was provided by The Nature Conservancy.

Detailed methods for the economic analysis can be found in the report *Modeling the Business Case for Green Stormwater Infrastructure in Detroit, Michigan* (Isely et al. 2022). The report includes the benefits and costs of three GSI practices: rain gardens/restored wetlands; bioretention basins; and detention basins/underground storage. The monetized benefits included avoided CSO discharge, avoided pollution, flood risk reduction, avoided stormwater volume, and scenic amenity. Detention basins and underground storage reduce the peak flow of stormwater but do not reduce pollution nor do they reduce the total volume discharged. They do

TABLE 4.1 *Ecosystem service benefits provided by GSI types*

Ecosystem service benefit	Economic value ($/gal/year)	Rain garden / Restored wetland	Bioretention	Detention / Underground storage
Avoided CSO	$0.0354	Yes	Yes	Yes
Avoided pollution	$0.0069	Yes	Yes	No
Scenic amenity	$0.0019	Yes	No	No
Flood risk reduction	$0.0008	Yes	Yes	Yes
Avoided volume	$0.0003	Yes	Yes	No

From Isely et al. (2022)

not provide scenic amenities. Underground storage is not visible. Detention basins usually lack attractive plants that would be found in a bioretention facility, rain garden, or wetland (Table 4.1).

The team estimated the present value cost of managing stormwater including capital, annual operation and maintenance, annual drainage charges, and annual opportunity costs. The opportunity cost reflects the value of forgoing other productive activities (e.g., lost parking spaces). Costs were calculated over a fifty-year time horizon using a 3.5 percent real discount rate. We used a benefit-transfer approach to adapt cost estimates to the local conditions for Detroit. Cost estimates came from local GSI projects, published studies, and the Water Environment Resource Federation database.

The team used the US Environmental Protection Agency's Storm Water Management Model and data from both the National Oceanic and Atmospheric Administration and the Detroit Water and Sewerage Department's Stormwater Management Design Manual to estimate precipitation, stormwater volume, peak flow rates, detention, retention, and the Green Credit. The benefits and costs were applied to the volume of stormwater managed over the life of the practice.

The team evaluated fourteen properties where the owner installed stormwater management practices. The properties included two for-profit businesses, two houses of worship, and ten publicly owned properties.

The team analyzed the economic development impact of building GSI practices using the IMPLAN regional economic analysis software package. Installing GSI practices generates new economic activity through the hiring of designers and builders, buying supplies, and associated spending. In addition to these direct expenditures on GSI practices, economic development impact studies include indirect effects (purchases within the supply chain) and induced effects (increased economic activity generated by additional wages to laborers). IMPLAN reports economic development impact in three ways. First, it estimates the gross output. That is the total economic activity including the sum of the intermediate inputs and the value they add to the final good or service. Second, IMPLAN estimates labor income: the increase in wages, salaries, and proprietors' incomes that results from a change in demand. Third, it estimates value added which is equivalent to the industry's contribution to gross domestic product.

4.4 RESULTS

4.4.1 *Institutional Analysis of the Physical Commons*

Figure 4.3 provides an overview of the GKC framework as applied to the case of Detroit GSI.

Detroit receives an average of 33.7 inches of rain annually. The distribution of precipitation is fairly even with a low of 2.08 inches in February and a high of 3.72 inches in May. However, rainfall patterns are changing. Climate scientists expect "a significant increase in the magnitude and frequency of heavy rainfall events" and "relatively more pronounced changes for heavy hourly rainfall as compared to daily events" across Michigan (Kim et al. 2016). Recent weather events support these predictions. In 2014, intense storms caused $1.8 billion in flood damages in Detroit (National Weather Service n.d.). In June 2021, a single storm dumped more than 6 inches of rain on Detroit and surrounding areas, which resulted in widespread flooding (Rahal and Grzelewski 2021). The city's infrastructure is being overwhelmed by the increasing rainfall intensity. This leads to property damage and the discharge of untreated sewage as well as other pollutants.

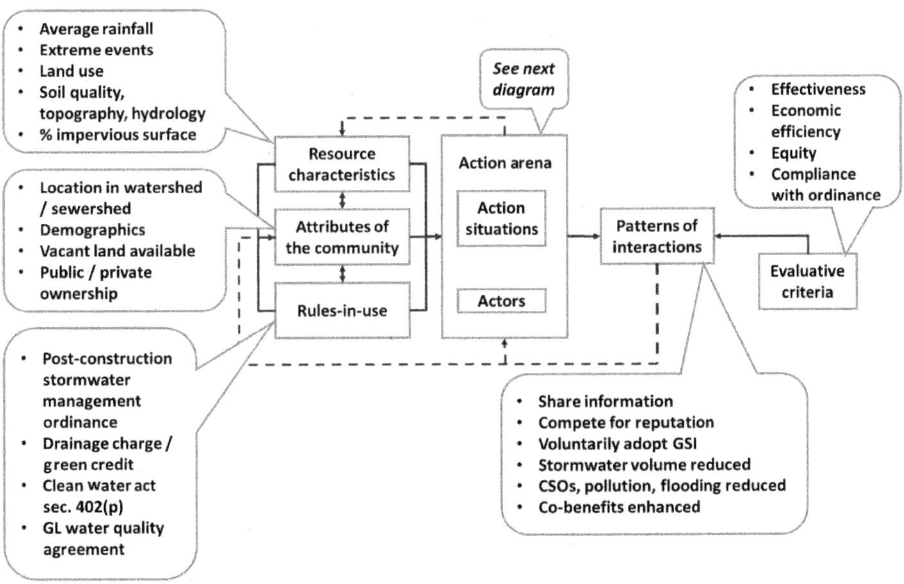

FIGURE 4.3 Institutional analysis of the physical commons for stormwater.

Stormwater management is an environmental justice issue. More than 42 percent of Detroit residents reported experiencing home flooding resulting from rainfall between 2012 and 2020. Renters were more likely to experience flooding than homeowners (Sampson et al. 2021). Detroit residents report that repeated or severe flooding induces stress, anxiety, anger, and frustration (Sampson et al. 2019). The City of Detroit owns many vacant parcels that can be used for neighborhood-scale GSI practices.

The drainage charge requires property owners to pay a fee for the property's unmitigated impervious surface. Property owners may reduce their drainage charge by installing GSI practices and reducing stormwater runoff. The formal drainage charge stems from higher order, collective choice rules including the Clean Water Act Section 402 and the Great Lakes Water Quality Agreement.

The action situation involves the decision to reduce stormwater runoff by implementing GSI practices (Figure 4.4). The actors are the property owners, which include residential owners, small businesses, large corporations, nongovernmental organizations, faith communities, and municipal government entities. Additional actors include engineering design firms and developers. The actors may serve in positions such as sole decision-maker, manager, board member, or administrator. The actions include choosing a method of stormwater management (including not managing and paying the drainage charge), providing information about GSI practices, setting behavioral norms, and creating and enforcing rules.

The actors rely on information about GSI practices to aid their decisions. Information about GSI practices is publicly available through the City of Detroit,

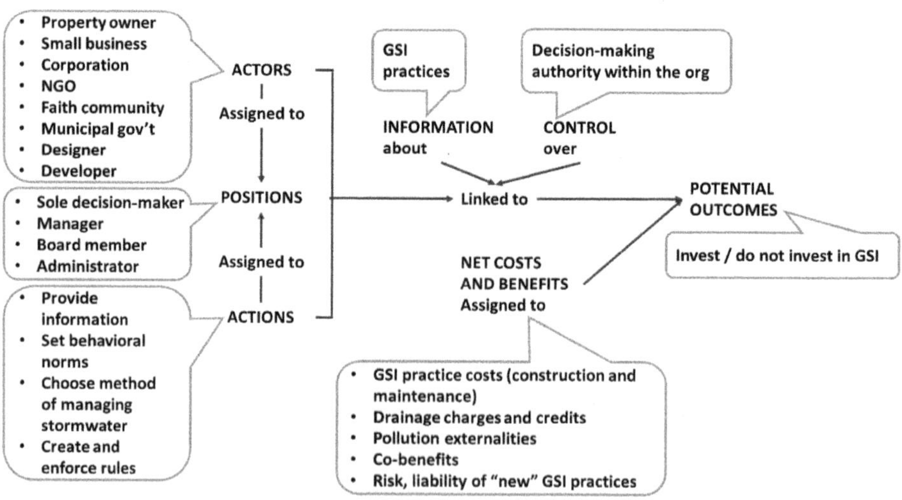

FIGURE 4.4 Annotated action situation for green stormwater infrastructure in Detroit, Michigan.

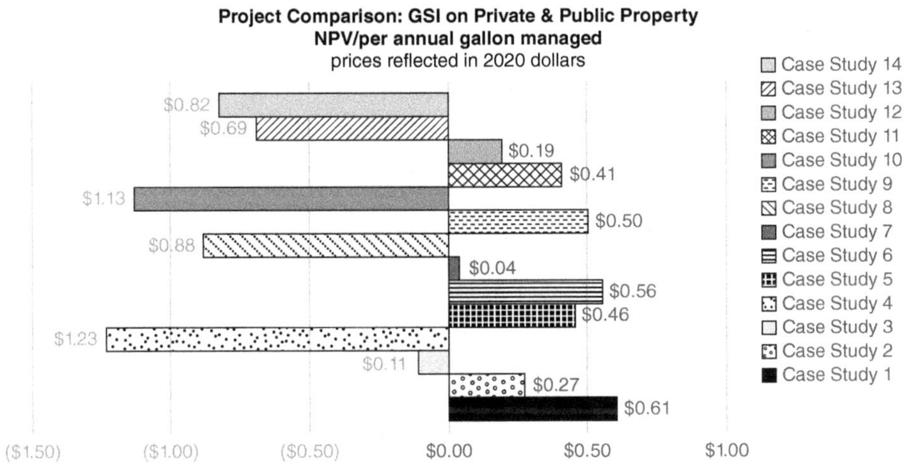

FIGURE 4.5 Net present values for fourteen green stormwater infrastructure practices in Detroit, Michigan.

nongovernmental organizations (NGOs) such as The Nature Conservancy, local universities, and other organizations. The engineering design firms and developers may also have information, especially highly technical information, about GSI practices. As noted in the "positions" section, some actors have control over whether to install GSI practices. Others play an advisory or consultative role.

Of the fourteen cases studied, eight had a positive net present value. That is, the discounted lifetime benefits exceeded the discounted lifetime costs. Positive net present values ranged from $0.04 to $0.61/annual gallon managed. The cases with negative net present values ranged from $-0.11 to $-1.23/annual gallon managed. These calculations included both private benefits (reduced drainage charges) and public benefits (reduced pollution and flooding) (Figure 4.5).

The two GSI practices installed by private businesses (Cases 1 and 2) had positive net present values. Case 1 involved a 20,230 ft^2 detention basin adjacent to a manufacturing facility. The present value of the benefits exceeded $4.8 million. However, the present value of the private financial benefit (avoiding drainage charges) ranges from $276,371 to $555,476, depending on whether outflow is enforced. The estimated credits were based on modeled stormwater management performance. In some cases, these models showed an outflow rate greater than what was allowable for credit. But since this is model-dependent we estimated credits as a range, with the higher bound not including that enforcement and the lower bound including it. In Case 2, the property owner installed subsurface detention (underground storage tank). The total benefits had a present value of $535,515. The total present value costs were $368,848. The individual financial benefit (avoiding drainage charges) ranged from $3,715 to $39,671. The property owner indicated that the decision to install the underground tank was made at corporate headquarters, not by the local management team. In both Cases 1 and 2, the present value of the individual financial benefit is significantly lower than the present value of the costs. Most of the benefit from the GSI practice accrues to the public, not the property owner. Even though the projects have positive net present values for the community, the property owner does not recoup the costs of the GSI over its lifetime.

Cases 3 and 4 involved houses of worship. In Case 3, The Nature Conservancy initiated the project by developing a pilot project with Sacred Heart Church. This historic faith community is nestled in Detroit's Eastern Market District. With its large parking lots, the church faced flooding challenges and steep drainage charges exceeding $16,000 annually. The Nature Conservancy worked with Sacred Heart Church to design and implement a bioretention/rain garden that not only manages stormwater, but also improves traffic flow and walkability, increases biodiversity, and fosters creative placemaking (Figure 4.6). The Nature Conservancy plans to use the Sacred Heart Church GSI practice as an example that can inspire other property owners. The Nature Conservancy and Sacred Heart shared detailed construction plans and costs with the team. The bioretention basin/rain garden had a total present value benefit of $1,147,089 and a total present value cost of $1,261,077. Therefore, the net present value was negative at $-113,988, in part demonstrating the difficulty of retrofitting sites.

Similarly, another faith community in Case 4 constructed a bioswale/rain garden to manage its stormwater and reduce its $24,000 annual drainage charge. The GSI project had a total present value benefit of $299,336 and a total present value cost of $637,241. The project had a negative net present value of $-337,906. In both cases, the property owners were faced with high construction costs. The projects variously required moving utility infrastructure, removing and replacing pavement, and/or other costly retrofits. In Case 3, the additional benefits of improved traffic flow and walkability were not monetized. In Case 4, the bioswale is relatively shallow and provides limited stormwater capture and infiltration capacity. Therefore, the monetized value of the benefits was relatively low as well.

Cases 5–14 involved public properties managed by the City of Detroit. These practices include large-scale wetland restoration and bioretention retrofits at

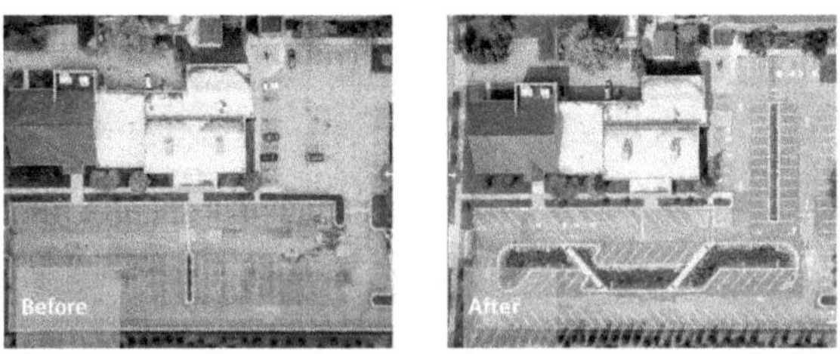

FIGURE 4.6 Before (left) and after (right), the bioinfiltration/rain garden construction at Sacred Heart Church, Detroit, Michigan.

public parks as well as neighborhood-scale rain gardens on vacant lots, bioswales along streets, and permeable pavement. Six of the practices analyzed had positive net present values and four had negative net present values. Those with positive net present values generally provided many amenities, such as recreation and aesthetic quality in addition to managing stormwater. Those with negative net present values either had high construction costs owing to retrofits or provided few cobenefits. For example, a project using permeable pavement effectively managed stormwater. However, permeable pavement does not provide any scenic amenity. Another bioretention practice on a vacant lot was sized to capture more runoff, but the practice was not yet connected to the street. Another bioswale practice was shallow and captured a small amount of stormwater relative to its construction costs.

The action situation leads to a pattern of interactions. In this case, property owners use the information they must decide whether to install GSI practices. To date, only 268 properties have chosen to install a GSI practice. Many of these are publicly owned by the city (Table 4.2). The most common practice (disconnected impervious) simply means that the property's impervious surface does not drain into the stormwater system and is therefore exempt from the drainage charge. The second most common practice (downspout disconnect) involves letting stormwater discharge onto a pervious surface instead of flowing directly into the storm drain. Neither the disconnected impervious nor the downspout disconnection

TABLE 4.2 *Number of Detroit properties using various GI practice types*

GI practice type	Number of properties
Disconnected Impervious	105
Downspout Disconnection	42
Bioretention	31
Multiple	21
Subsurface Detention	14
Water Harvesting	13
Rain Garden	13
Permeable Pavement	8
Bioswale	6
Green Roof	5
All Stormwater Stays On-site	3
Rain Barrel	2
Subsurface Infiltration	2
Surface Detention	1
Stormwater/Constructed Wetland	1
Other	1
Total	268

FIGURE 4.7 Geographic distribution of GSI practices in Detroit, Michigan.

involve actively constructed GSI practices. After accounting for those, only 121 properties actively manage stormwater on-site using GSI. The GSI practices are spread throughout the city (Figure 4.7).

Constructing GSI practices generates economic activity across the region. The results of the IMPLAN economic development impact indicate that each $100,000 in GSI practice construction leads to $183,779 in gross output, $164,903 in earnings, and $190,726 in value added.

4.4.2 *Institutional Analysis of Knowledge Commons*

Figure 4.8 summarizes the GKC framework for GSI in Detroit. The basic concept of GSI has been around for decades and thus may be considered common knowledge. For example, the US EPA (United States Environmental Protection Agency 2015b) promotes GSI practices through its Soak Up the Rain program, which includes webinars, posters, and other resources in the public domain. DWSD provides publicly available information for property owners on how to reduce drainage charges through GSI (Detroit Water and Sewerage Department 2020). Numerous NGOs, such as the West Michigan Environmental Action Council and The Nature Conservancy, provide general and Michigan-specific information about on-site stormwater management using GSI. The Detroit Stormwater Hub Advisory Group is an especially important coalition of organizations working on GSI in some capacity (https://detroitstormwater.org/about-us).

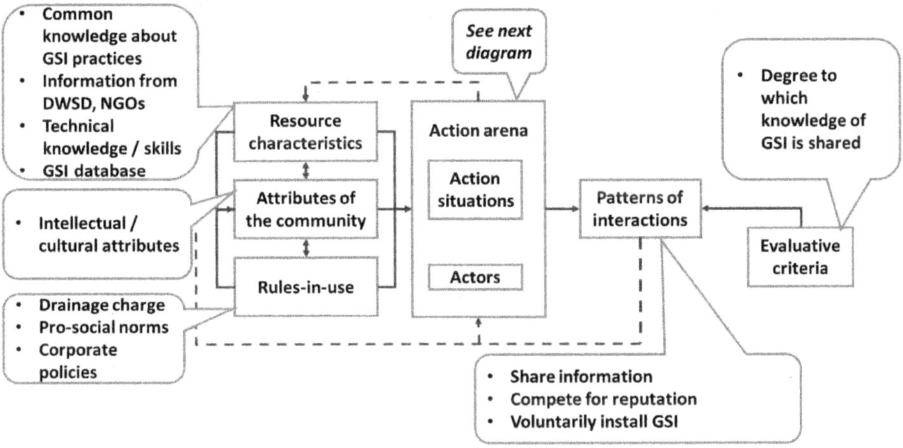

FIGURE 4.8 Knowledge commons for GSI.

However, Detroit property owners can only obtain a drainage charge reduction (up to 80 percent) if their GSI practice is designed and installed by a professional engineer. The professional must certify that the practice meets the standards set in the Post-Construction Stormwater Management Ordinance (City of Detroit 2020b) and Stormwater Management Design Manual (Detroit Water and Sewerage Department 2022). This technical knowledge is a critical resource for managing stormwater, yet may be difficult to access for many property owners, especially residents.

DWSD also maintains two publicly accessible online databases. One is the DWSD Impervious Surfaces Public Viewer (https://detroitmi.gov/webapp/impervious-surfaces-public-viewer). The website features an interactive map of all impervious surfaces within DWSD's service area. Anyone can locate properties, view the impervious surfaces, and inspect the details. DWSD has a procedure for property owners to correct the calculation of impervious surface. DWSD also maintains an online map of all registered GSI projects (https://detroitstormwater.org/). The map includes information about the GSI location, type, area managed, and other key attributes.

The intellectual and cultural attributes of the community members vary greatly. Property owners may have a high level of sophisticated, technical expertise about GSI or may know very little. Government/municipal properties and commercial/industrial properties account for about half of all GSI installations (Table 4.3). This suggests that these property owners have a high degree of knowledge about GSI practices and the capacity to seek out qualified installers. The city has 322,906 housing units of which 232,492 (72 percent) are single family homes. Yet only fifteen residential properties have installed GSI practices (Census Reporter 2021). Residential properties already receive a 25 percent credit, and it would be difficult to manage enough runoff on a typical residential lot to achieve more than that.

TABLE 4.3 *GSI installations by property owner type*

Owner type	Number of properties	Percentage of total
Government	61	22.7
Commercial	43	16.0
Industrial	24	9.0
Faith-based	16	6.0
Residential	15	5.6
Nonprofit	14	5.2
Municipal (libraries, etc.)	8	3.0
Educational institute	2	0.7
Owner type unknown	84	31.3
Total	268	100.0*

*The percentages do not add up to 100.0 because of rounding.

The drainage charge and Green Credit are two of the more formal rules-in-use within the knowledge commons. The drainage charge and Green Credits are price signals alerting all property owners to the scarcity of stormwater management services. Less formally, some property owners take prosocial actions to encourage others to adopt GSI. This is especially true of the sixteen faith-based communities. Sacred Heart Church, for example, has an informative kiosk explaining how its rain garden works. The rules-in-use may also include corporate policies. In Case 2, the retailer installed an underground detention tank because of corporate policy. Some sections of the city have master or framework plans that address stormwater. For instance, the Eastern Market Neighborhood Framework and Stormwater Management Network Plan includes plans for significant GSI as new development comes into the area. This would be reiterated through the city permitting process (City of Detroit 2020a).

The action situation within the knowledge commons describes the choice whether to share information about GSI practices (Figure 4.9). Sharing information, such as engineering techniques and construction costs, may encourage others to adopt GSI practices. On the other hand, sharing might jeopardize valuable intellectual property. The actors include DWSD, various NGOs, property owners, and the design and engineering firms that install GSI. Property owners can be thought of as "consumer producers" who, when they install GSI, coproduce stormwater management services with DWSD, the public service provider. NGOs such as The Nature Conservancy can act as information brokers who can share knowledge that might otherwise be proprietary or hard to find. DWSD and design/engineering firms create knowledge about the costs, benefits, and operations of GSI when they design and install projects. Finally, all property owners share knowledge when they engage in the market transaction of the drainage charge.

Actors then consider the information about GSI practices and their organizations' protocols over information sharing. They assign costs and benefits to the

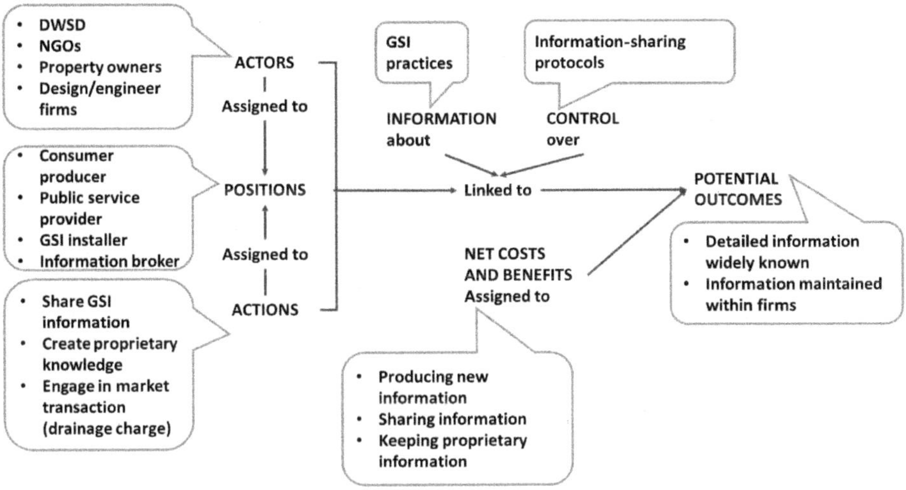

FIGURE 4.9 Summary of the stormwater knowledge commons action situation.

actions of producing new information, sharing information, and keeping information proprietary. This can include not only the costs and benefits of whether to share, but of how much and when. Potential outcomes include a range of information availability from widely known details to secured, proprietary information.

4.4.3 KNOWLEDGE COMMONS PATTERNS OF INTERACTION AND EVALUATIVE CRITERIA

Repeated decisions within the action situation result in a pattern of interactions. The organizations decide how much GSI information to share. But in doing so, they also engage in prosocial activity that can inspire others to act. Those organizations that are willing to share information may be held in higher esteem by their community members. Most importantly, the pattern of interactions will lead to some property owners installing practices. The evaluative criterion at this level is the degree to which GSI information is shared.

4.5 CONCLUSIONS

Detroit's stormwater drainage charge is a price signal. It informs the property owner that stormwater management is a scarce resource and provides an economic incentive to reduce stormwater runoff. However, the fourteen GSI cases we reviewed showed that the discounted benefits of avoiding the drainage charge did not exceed the GSI practices' discounted construction and maintenance costs. Either the drainage charge is too low to incentive the property owners to reduce runoff, or the costs are too high. The social benefits of GSI, on the other hand, often do exceed the construction and maintenance costs. As a result, only 268 properties have been documented to include GSI practices out of the many thousands of properties across Detroit.

The GKC framework enables us to explore more than economic motivations for implementing GSI practices. For example, our cases included two faith communities. Both stated they have a focus on environmental stewardship that stems from their religious missions. Part of that stewardship also entails sharing knowledge about GSI practices and encouraging others to install what they can. The Sacred Heart rain garden in particular is located in a district that emphasizes the use of GSI, is highly visible to the community, and includes informative kiosks. The Nature Conservancy worked closely with Sacred Heart and the team of designers and builders to construct the project.

The drainage charge's economic model provides that price signal regarding stormwater management. But acting on that signal requires property owners to be aware of the alternatives. The Nature Conservancy team consulted with many property owners who installed GSI practices. Most of them declined to share their GSI projects' details. Some GSI projects are relatively simple, such as a rain barrel or small rain garden. These can be done by the homeowner but may not manage much runoff or achieve much credit. However, constructing a rain garden for a parking lot, for example, requires significant technical expertise and equipment. The anecdotal information gathered from these conversations suggests that many property owners, large and small, do not know how to reduce their drainage charges with GSI practices. Many design and engineering firms tend to have expertise in specific GSI practices and stick to what is most familiar to them. In the case of one of the commercial buildings, the decision to install an underground storage tank was made at corporate headquarters, not by the local manager. Therefore, the drainage charge's price signal may not work as well as intended.

Our research questions were:

- How do economic incentives, like the drainage charge, affect the decision to adopt GSI practices?
- Do property owners know how to reduce their drainage charges using GSI?
- Is the knowledge about GSI practices widely available (a knowledge commons) or essentially privatized within design/engineering firms?

Our research has shown that the lifetime discounted benefits of avoiding the drainage charge are less than the lifetime discounted costs of constructing and maintaining GSI. However, the additional value of the cobenefits, including avoided pollution, avoided flood risk, and scenic amenity, provide substantial benefits to society. Therefore, the net present value GSI is, in many cases, positive when the social benefits are included. The drainage charge alone is insufficient to encourage private property owners to install GSI practices.

Many property owners do not know how to reduce their drainage charges using GSI, and knowledge about GSI practices is not widespread. This information is held by a select set of technical experts – engineers and landscape designers. The Nature Conservancy collaborated with Sacred Heart Church to install a demonstration practice that effectively managed stormwater from the church's parking lot. The project's high cost was related to the complexity of moving utility lines and other nonstandard expenses. Highly visible projects such as those at Sacred Heart and the City of Detroit properties may educate residents and property owners about GSI practices.

5

Co-Curating Institutional Data on Climate Change-Induced Loss and Damage via Expert Panels

Implications for the Environmental Knowledge Commons

*Mathew Kurian, Yu Kojima, Wa'ed Alshoubaki, Sekela Twisa, and V. Ratna Reddy**

5.1 INTRODUCTION

The resilience of socioecological systems is the ability of biophysical systems that are exposed to hazards to resist, absorb, accommodate, adapt to, and transform and recover from effects of climate events in a timely and efficient manner, through institutional interventions that preserve and restore its essential basic structures and function (Jaramillo and Destouni 2015). In 2019, the increasing frequency, intensity, and duration of droughts and floods impacted an estimated 1.4 billion and 1.6 billion people respectively and nearly 95 percent of infrastructure losses reported between 2010 and 2019 were due to water related disasters (United Nations 2023). Climate change induced changes can include reparable loss and irreparable damage to habitats, income and livelihoods, recreational opportunities, cultural heritage, and personal self-worth (Byrnes and Surminski 2019).

The transport and energy sectors are by far the biggest contributors of greenhouse gas emissions responsible for rising global temperatures, but the agriculture sector in the global south is disproportionately affected by the impact of droughts and floods because of the size of populations reliant on the sector for food security (Campbell et al. 2017). It is therefore remarkable that in 2018, 93 percent of climate financing went towards measures that focused on mitigating emissions of greenhouse gases. There are opportunities to pursue cobenefits through cross-sectoral

* The authors benefited from their participation in the Belmont Forum project on cyber-enabled disaster resilience supported by the US National Science Foundation, United Kingdom Research and Innovation, and São Paulo Research Foundation. The authors also benefited from participating in an international evaluation of the Big Data Platform of the Consultative Group on International Agriculture Research (CGIAR). As Consortium Lead of the Belmont Project, the lead author thanks Adelaide Nardocci at the University of Sao Paulo, N.K. Goel at Indian Institute of Technology, Roorkee, Christopher Scott at Penn State University, the late Kent Portney of Bush School of Government and Public Service, Texas A&M, Anjenetta Raymond of the Workshop in Political Theory and Policy Analysis, Indiana University, Bloomington, and Ahmed Degu at Makelle University for research collaboration.

coordination because, for example, many water management interventions in fields of water reuse and climate smart agriculture can advance both mitigation and adaptation goals (United Nations 2023).

Paradoxically, while 90 percent of countries prioritize action on water for adaptation in their nationally determined contributions for climate financing, 50 percent of countries reported that they do not have the formal national mechanisms to facilitate cross-sectoral coordination that is critical to ensure resilient socioecological systems (United Nations 2023). Crucially, national mechanisms are sustained by norms (shared values), institutions (rules), and organizations (ministries and departments) responsible for design of policy frameworks that formalize the implementation of operational guidelines relating to environmental conservation (Harris et al. 1995; Ostrom 2009).

5.2 MONITORING CLIMATE RESPONSE: IMPLICATIONS FOR DATA, INFORMATION, AND KNOWLEDGE

The discussion on "country readiness" or preparedness is premised on the notion that the use of improved assessment approaches, tools, and methods can generate the evidence that is required to design and deploy technologies and management systems that would restore climate resilience.[1] This is because conventional assessment techniques are unable to accommodate for institutional contexts where technology and financing produce nonlinear outcomes on account of heterogeneous responses of beneficiaries to project interventions (Dorward et al. 2005). The problem is compounded by development planning that is unable to capture feedback about the recursive effects of interventions, thereby blunting the ability to coordinate institutional response to climate events through reform of management information systems (MIS) (Kurian and Kojima 2021).

Environmental changes are nonlinear, nonmonotone, and seldom recursive. This is because interactions of the agency with a wider political ecology are dynamic enough to produce diverse responses and erratic courses which cannot be addressed by postulates of rational action or fixed models alone.[2] Consequently, conventional environmental models have been unable to account for poor coordination between the proposed technical/management options and the fact that environmental outcomes are often shaped by uncertainty and changes that arise in the policy

[1] The Green Climate Fund (GCF) established in 2010 under the auspices of the United Nations Framework Convention on Climate Change to assist developing countries mitigate and adapt to the effects of climate change has acknowledged the difficulty of disbursing funds can be mitigated through improved monitoring systems that focus on ameliorating the concerns of member states over the terms of private sector financing and the quantum and sequencing of grants and loans (IEU 2022).

[2] We refer to political ecology as a framework that perceives the interactions between environmental resources and society as being the result of negotiations involving agents with varying power and interests that often finds expression at different scales of contestation.

environment.[3] As a result, case studies alone may not be sufficient to unpack the functioning of commons resources such as forests, irrigation systems, livestock pastures, or groundwater basins (Turral and Kurian 2010). In this chapter we discuss two methodological innovations, trade-off intensity (TI) and typology assessments, that can unleash insights on structural variables that intersect with forces of history, reputation, hierarchy, and culture to produce changes in collective behavior (such as stall feeding of cattle or rules for irrigation water rotation) and have an ameliorating impact on environmental and social outcomes in the context of climate change. For this purpose, we rely on an analysis of five cases of common pool resources management combined with an expert panel review of climate loss and damage in Jordan to discuss their implications for the knowledge commons framework.

5.2.1 *Reflections on the Institutional Analysis and Development (IAD) Framework*

It is in this context that we believe that scholarship on the knowledge commons can support institutional analysis that informs policy and decision-making. By "knowledge commons" we refer broadly to commons arrangements (e.g., data repositories) for overcoming various social dilemmas associated with sharing and producing information, innovation, and creative works (Ostrom and Hess 2006). These commons arrangements could furnish protocols that enable the co-curation and joint use of a wide range of knowledge resources such as scientific data, open-source software (e.g., R), and machine learning approaches (Frischmann et al. 2014). The adoption of a knowledge commons framework could revolutionize the use of case studies and agent-based modeling to better inform policy processes by aligning data, models, and data transformation tools (e.g., composite indices) with open-data principles: Findable, Accessible, Interoperable, and Reusable (FAIR) (Poteete et al. 2010; CGIAR 2021).

5.2.2 *IAD Framework: Implications for the Knowledge Commons in the Context of Climate Change-Induced Loss and Damage*

The knowledge commons framework borrows from the IAD framework with the objective of providing a systematic approach to case study design that would enable comparisons and aggregation of lessons across a wide range of institutional contexts. The ultimate objective of the exercise is to provide a basis for developing theories to

[3] There is a common assumption of linearity between construction of irrigation infrastructure and improvements in agricultural productivity that can result from managing soil runoff efficiently. Similarly, it is assumed that cooperative management of environmental resources is more effective than private entrepreneur-led collective action – monotonic understanding of the causality between agency behavior and environmental outcomes. However, empirical experience suggests otherwise: Soil conservation interventions can have repressive effects on livelihood strategies and hence targeted populations suffer from less diverse diets. This is because weak feedback loops between project implementation and policy design made it difficult to modulate the regressive impact of higher tax rates on incentives for community level collective action (nonrecursive effects).

explain the emergence, form, and stability of the observed cases and to eventually design models that can inform institutional design (Strandburg et al. 2014). Some have claimed that the IAD framework is pretheoretical, in that it stops at delineating a broad set of elements (and relationships among these elements) that could be used to analyze all types of settings relevant to the framework. Nevertheless, the framework was novel for its attempt to open a theoretical space for researchers from a wide range of disciplines to explore social dilemmas surrounding the commons.

Furthermore, by engaging the policy realm especially through the design principles that distinguished successful natural resources management, the framework emphasized the importance of evaluative criteria. Ostrom (1991, 239) argued that "rather than conceptualizing rule-governed choice as more important than rational choice, a general approach would attempt to explain how both rules and anticipated consequences affect behavior and outcomes." This would presuppose a synthesis that involves two layers: first, rules determine the choice of available choices, while rational choice determines which of these options is selected. Second, rationality extends to the choice of rules. "To be rule-governed, the rational individual must know the rules of the games in which choices are made and how to participate in the crafting of rules to constitute better games" (Ostrom 1991, 242). Ostrom was quick to point out in this context that "history, institutions and cultural traditions will play a more significant role in the evolution of rational choice theories in the future than they have in the past" (Ostrom 1991, 242).

Ostrom (1998) introduced important elements of history in her analysis through the incorporation of concepts of reputation, trust, and reciprocity to better understand the rational choice theory of norms (Tarko 2016). According to this account, "levels of trust, reciprocity and reputations are positively reinforcing which also means that decrease in any one of these can lead to a downward spiral" (Ostrom 1998, 13). This is an important advance, especially from the point of view of monitoring programs on climate change adaptation since instead of explaining levels of cooperation directly this approach links structural variables to an inner triangle of trust, reciprocity, and reputation, and how these in turn affect the levels of cooperation and net benefits. The International Forestry Resources and Institutions (IFRI) research project led by Elinor Ostrom played an important role in advancing the policy dimension of the IAD framework. The three goals of the IFRI project were to (1) enhance interdisciplinary knowledge of institutional trajectories with specific reference to forest stewardship, (2) provide a methodology to ground-truth aerial data and spatially link forest use to deforestation and reforestation, and (3) improve assessment capabilities of participating countries (Kurian and Kojima 2021).

5.2.3 *The Political Economy of Commons Management*

IFRI explored ways to link research talent in each country and provide opportunities to collect information, build models, and influence policy change, which is as necessary as tree planting to combat deforestation. IFRI also pursued a strategy of starting with small-scale studies that identify the simplest concepts in which a process occurs so that particular processes can be studied on-site, starting with the most observable (read exhibiting extreme trade-offs) and moving to more global strategies (read based on cross-country comparisons) (IFRI 1997). The second concept which IFRI pursued was the development of "cost-effective prototypes of coupled models" (IFRI 1997, 7). As the IFRI experience suggests, assessments of institutional trajectories can be both time-consuming and rely heavily on continuous funding. In this sense, the IFRI project was ahead of its time in emphasizing the importance of sharing knowledge resources, and combining and coordinating preexisting resources to generate new knowledge, ethics, and modalities of data sharing and open data principles. The enormous advances that were made by IFRI to emphasize the evaluative power of IAD should, however, not prevent us from pursuing an important question: What innovation in the forms and reuse of data themselves could accommodate for a more dynamic storytelling using expert opinion to illuminate metaphor, history, and analogy in explanations of the commons? This would necessitate an engagement with factors of political economy to better understand structural variables and the effects of social difference and change in affecting commons outcomes.

5.3 USING EXPERT PANELS TO MONITOR TRADE-OFF INTENSITY IN CLIMATE ASSESSMENTS

Institutions are key to ensuring a balance between planetary health and the needs of a populace for basic services – water, energy, and food. Governing climate change induced losses is essentially about (1) understanding overall policy trade-offs, (2) delineating hotspots of extreme trade-off intensities, (3) prioritization of hotspots depending on the magnitude of losses and damages, and (4) institutional response to extreme TI. This is why we argue that an iterative process of theory led evaluations of climate programming can improve the governance of losses and damages. In this section, we will begin by describing how a composite index can be employed to operationalize hotspot mapping to support analysis of trade-off intensities.

5.3.1 *Constructing a Loss and Damage Index for Soil and Water Conservation Programs*

Most scientific models do not appreciate the fact that case study evidence cannot be persuasive in policy design because it is unavailable in a format usable by decision-makers (OECD 2008). By working with typologies, we seek to improve upon conventional methods by developing multidimensional models of socioecological systems instead of crafting theories of change purely based on analyzing nodes and density of social networks in public agencies (Deutsch et al. 2021). Second, instead of relying on massive data collection without engaging with feedback emerging from the policy process, we propose working with composite indices that rely upon expert panels to inform the design of policy/fiscal instruments (Kurian and Kojima 2021). Finally, by undertaking an analysis of TI we embrace political ecological realities to explain the differences in the institutional response given the impact of losses and damages on the livelihoods of communities affected by climate change.

5.3.2 *Why Institutional Mechanisms are Crucial for Monitoring Climate Resilience Policies*

Both the first (Laos) and fourth (India) typologies illustrate contexts where the impacts of agricultural interventions resulted in unexpected adverse impacts owing to ineffective institutional response, which was reflected in an inability to adapt to changing market trends and trade policies. In typology 1, losses arising from soil erosion which had the potential to aggravate flooding in upstream catchments (the commons) elicited a response in the form of Improved Fallow technology that was promoted by the Consultative Group on International Agriculture Research (CGIAR). This management option was developed by the CGIAR in response to persistent poverty and soil erosion, which was partly triggered by intensive cultivation coupled with rainfall variability. Under a policy environment where Laos was transitioning from state ownership of land to private land titles, however, we found that trade policy orientation aggravated agricultural intensification in the context of rainfall variability. A lack of cross-sectoral coordination among multiple ministries/departments was compounded by the absence of multifaceted information on crop yields and conditions in labor markets and absence of credit and insurance support to enable farmers to adapt to changes in trade policy orientation (Stevenson and Vlek 2018).

Typology 4 (North India) demonstrates the losses and damages in food security (nutrition) in which people suffer from less diverse diets, which is aggravated by soil run-off (a commons resource) caused by intensified land use. The case illustrates how agricultural development challenges are layered, necessitating a longitudinal analytical framework to capture such relationships. The typology also suggests that an absence of intermediate financial schemes that could enable farmers to adapt to changed market conditions combined with a failure to coordinate multipronged policy directives involving trade, agricultural production, and rural development through the mechanism of an MIS that collects and synthesizes data has the potential to aggravate losses and damages in the context of increased frequency, duration, and intensity of climate change-induced flooding events.

There is a common assumption that reusing safely treated wastewater for agricultural production increases productivity and hence enhance livelihoods and protects ecosystem services (soil quality in particular) for peri-urban communities in the developing world. Typologies 2 and 5 address this assumption from global (case 2: global sustainable development goals, SDGs) and regional specific (case 5: South India) perspectives by focusing on water reuse models. Typology 2 demonstrates the public health risks arising from the use of untreated wastewater (irrigation as a commons resource) are aggravated by flooding that can impact small scale aquaculture and farming. On the other hand, typology 5 highlights the damage evident in impacts for public and environmental health (soil contamination). In both cases, these losses and damages occurred owing to flooding events caused by malfunctioning of sewer infrastructure that is aggravated by storm drain overflows in cities. In addition to the nonalignment of national financial instruments for the delivery of water and sanitation services with global targets, there is limited synchronization of roles and skills among concerned ministries/departments and an absence of information on the effects of water pollution on livestock and human populations.

Typology 3 (Tanzania) represents another variant of the losses in public health and livelihoods arising from deteriorating water quality. While typology 2 focuses on urban water and sanitation challenges caused by frequent flooding events, typology 3 deals with a similar developmental challenge in the context of rural water supply which has become unreliable owing to cumulative siltation of infrastructure (a commons resource) caused by agricultural intensification and exacerbated by frequency of dry spells. Both typologies 3 and 5 showcase variations on a similar theme whereby water scarcity exacerbated by flooding (typology 5) and dry spells/drought (typology 3) causes deteriorating health of human populations and the environment, thus adversely impacting the livelihoods of vulnerable communities.

5.3.3 *Typologies of Climate Change-Induced Loss and Damage Stress*

A failure to effectively coordinate institutional response by addressing a critical mass of financing and technology, capacity, and information will likely generate losses in the planetary, institutional, and political ecology domains.

1. **Soil Conservation (Flooding events in upstream catchments)**
   Agricultural Development Intervention Areas:
   - Food security (production)
   - Poverty reduction
   - Environmental health

   Losses in Institutional Response (IR) Domain:
   - Soil loss owing to agricultural intensification causing increased flooding

   Losses in Biophysical Condition (PT) Domain:
   - Vulnerability of region to soil erosion intensified

   Losses in Political-Ecology (PE) Domain:
   - Trade policy orientation induces agricultural intensification, resulting in shrinking livelihoods

2. **SDG 6.3 Urban Water Quality (Flooding events in urban environments)**
   Agricultural Development Intervention Areas:
   - Urban water and sanitation
   - Public health
   - Environmental health
   - Livelihoods

   Losses in Institutional Response (IR) Domain:
   - Untreated wastewater induced by flooding heightens public health risks

   Losses in Biophysical Condition (PT) Domain:
   - Frequent flooding events cause damage to wastewater treatment infrastructure

   Losses in Political-Ecology (PE) Domain:
   - Flooding events intensify public health (water quality) risks and damage livelihoods dependent on small-scale aquaculture and farming
3. **Water Quality in Rural Water Supply (Frequency, duration, and intensity of dry spells)**
   Agricultural Development Intervention Areas:
   - Livelihoods
   - Environmental health
   - Public health
   - Rural water supply

   Losses in Institutional Response (IR) Domain:
   - Nonfunctional infrastructure results in deteriorating drinking water quality

   Losses in Biophysical Condition (PT) Domain:
   - Siltation caused by agricultural intensification and exacerbated by frequent dry spells damages water supply infrastructure

   Losses in Political-Ecology (PE) Domain:
   - Public health expenditure rises due to poor water quality and unreliable water supply, leading to decline in income from poultry raising and kitchen gardens
4. **Soil Runoff (Frequency, duration, and intensity of flooding events in upstream catchments)**
   Agricultural Development Intervention Areas:
   - Livelihoods
   - Environmental health
   - Irrigation
   - Poverty reduction
   - Food security (nutrition)

   Losses in Institutional Response (IR) Domain:
   - Nonfunctional infrastructure results in unreliable irrigation services, adversely affecting diet diversity and nonfarm livelihoods

Losses in Biophysical Condition (PT) Domain:
- Siltation caused by agricultural intensification and worsened by frequent flooding damages irrigation infrastructure

Losses in Political-Ecology (PE) Domain:
- Secular decline in local revenues from agriculture (farming/livestock rearing) and urban tourism (which relies on water sourced from rural catchments)

5. **Peri-Urban Water Reuse and Soil Contamination (Flooding events in urban environments)**

Agricultural Development Intervention Areas:
- Public health
- Environmental health
- Livelihoods
- Peri-urban agriculture
- Urban water and sanitation

Losses in Institutional Response (IR) Domain:
- Public and environmental health damage due to malfunctioning sewer systems caused by storm drain overflows

Losses in Biophysical Condition (PT) Domain:
- Soil contamination from the use of untreated peri-urban wastewater in agriculture

Losses in Political-Ecology (PE) Domain:
- Public health (water quality) risks from use of untreated wastewater in agriculture and impacts on nonfarm employment

Let us now turn to discuss the outlines of a Climate Induced Loss and Damage Agriculture Stress Index (CILDAS) index that can be employed to monitor climate losses and damages. We will employ typology 3 (Tanzania) as an example. As you recall, the typology highlights mitigation of extreme trade-offs between agricultural intensification and the quality of water supply. A CILDAS index can reflect this trade-off through a conceptual model of three sub-indices: (1) Political Ecology (PE); (2) Institutional Response (IR); and (3) Planetary Threshold (PT). Index construction starts with the PE component. The level (high, medium, and low) of TI for the effects of agricultural intensification (i.e., cropping intensity, fertilizer use), and water quality (i.e., turbidity, coliform bacteria) can be expressed through the selection of PE indicators that can range from public health to tourism revenues and livelihood loss.

The second step involves IR-assigning weights for three elements (siloes, thresholds, and critical mass) to map the institutional response to varying levels of TI. Finally, the contextualization of planetary thresholds in the form of PT can be drawn from biophysical data (rainfall, temperature, rates of land cover change, etc.). The combination of these three elements can express system-level stress on account of losses and damages of targeted regions/jurisdiction and their potential to aggravate slow onset events (e.g., droughts), noneconomic losses (e.g., the disappearance of certain crops from diets, loss of self-worth, and biodiversity loss), and loss of revenue streams for government agencies responsible for managing the poverty environment nexus (Dasgupta et al. 2005).

5.3.4 *Illuminating the Political Ecology Context through Analysis of Trade-Off Intensity*

A loss and damage assessment framework should view institutional response to climate change-induced losses and damages as the outcome of negotiations involving groups with disparate power across administrative jurisdictions which ultimately shapes policy design, implementation, and monitoring. Adoption rates of soil and water conservation technologies in turn are influenced by the interaction with the larger political ecology context, an issue which is rarely articulated in climate financing programs. This is why we employ the concept of TI to understand the levels of stress that biophysical systems place on the magnitude and scope of institutional responses to climate threats. By combining analysis of biophysical stress and institutional response, we can specify the institutional capacity that needs to be developed given the landscape of economic trade-offs between environmental, social, and institutional priorities at any given time. Trade-off intensity analysis to monitor the effectiveness of climate financing programs.

Planetary Threshold (PT)

- Temperature trending towards extremes
- Rainfall/precipitation trending towards extremes
- Quality of water resources trending positive
- Quality of energy services trending positive
- Rates of land cover change trending towards extremes
- Rates of soil erosion/flooding/fires trending towards extremes
- Natural resource use per-capita trending towards extremes

Trade-Off Intensity (TI)

- Incidence of nutritional insecurity per-capita trending towards extremes
- Secular changes in agriculture contribution to gross domestic product and employment trending towards higher variability
- Hydropower/water discharge rates trending towards higher variability
- Secular changes in labor demand and supply for agricultural operations trending towards higher variability
- Cropping intensity rates trending towards extremes
- Rates of land use change trending towards extremes
- Volumes of agricultural input use for (fertilizers, pesticides, mechanization) agricultural operations trending towards extremes

Institutional Response (IR)

- Resource allocations towards infrastructure operation and maintenance trending towards higher variability.
- Projected staffing and training on World Economic Forum (WEF) climate adaptation trending negative.
- Criteria for disbursement prioritizing operation and maintenance of climate smart agricultural infrastructure/technology trending negative
- Projected changes in trade policy with implications for WEF climate adaptation trending negative.
- Extent of official recognition of TI for data in MIS trending negative.
- Projected fiscal trends with implications for asset distribution for resource poor in agriculture sector trending negative.
- Secular changes in agricultural terms of trade trending negative.

The challenge of engaging context-specific data to support analysis of TI can be effectively addressed by aggregating the views of expert panels using a sliding Likert scale. Such an exercise will serve to valorize data and models that inform decisions based on projections made by project, census, or statistics bureaus of a given jurisdiction.

5.4 USING EXPERT PANELS IN JORDAN TO EXAMINE PERCEPTIONS OF CLIMATE RISK BASED ON A MULTIDIMENSIONAL MODEL

The country of Jordan is situated in Southwest Asia and experiences a semiarid climate. A significant portion of its land (approximately 75 percent) is covered by desert, and the majority of its regions receive minimal rainfall each year, with levels averaging under 50 mm (MOPIC 2017). Jordan's natural and energy resources are limited, and the country endures frequent existential water shortages (The World Bank 2022). The irreparable damage caused by the harsh weather, severe winds, temperature fluctuation, and heavy rains increases the vulnerability of infrastructure and utility systems in Jordan, most of which are outdated and fragile. Indeed, the irreparable damages and losses have affected the Jordanian socioeconomic sector, and this vulnerability has led to decreased crop production and reductions in some households' income (Ministry of Environment 2021). Climate-related factors have caused some agricultural regions in Jordan to experience a reduction in income by 10–20 percent (Ministry of Environment 2021).

Many other factors are involved in defining policy choices and various systems, cultures, institutions, and environmental factors limit the capacity of policymakers to consider the evidence (Stoker and Evans 2016). As previously discussed, the conventional assessment techniques cannot adequately deal with the contextual changes and provide the required evidence to monitor changes and deal with the adverse effects of climate change. Therefore, we developed a local panel of experts consisting of six academics, scholars, and practitioners who specialize in environmental studies from three public universities in Jordan, strategically located in the north, central, and southern regions of the country. We also included policymakers who possess expertise in climate change adaptation in Jordan. Although we aimed to include female experts in the panel, no one expressed interest in joining. To maintain no more than six members, some have expertise in multiple areas, such as working with climate change governmental projects and academia (see Appendix A for details).

5.4.1 *Data and Methods*

We assessed the climate change-induced loss and damage in Jordan's soil–water–food systems and agriculture sector through a targeted web survey. We embedded the survey link in the experts' recruitment email, which directed the respondents to the platform to complete the questionnaire. We developed the regional analysis based on the geographic and topographic characteristics, dividing Jordan into three main climatic regions: the Ghor region (lowlands), the Highlands, and the Badia and Desert region (FAO 2020); see Figure 5.1. The assessment process involves three main steps. First, we identified Jordanian regions at high and low risk of climate change-induced loss and damage in soil-water-food systems. Second, we conducted a TI analysis by administering a twenty-three-question weighted binary questionnaire. The questions were derived for each of the variables listed under institutional response, TI, and planetary thresholds (Table 5.1) derived from the CILDAS model. Responses for most unlikely were scored 0 points while those indicating highly likely were scored 10 points. Third, we compared the results of the first two steps to determine any differences (see Appendix B).

5.4.2 *Implications for the Environmental Knowledge Commons Framework*

According to the experts' evaluation of the most vulnerable climatic region, the Highland regions, which extend to the north and south to the east of the Ghor region, have the highest risk of climate change-induced loss and damage in soil-water-food systems. The Jordanian highlands are divided into three main portions: north, central, and south. The north portion is bordered by the Yarmouk River to the north and the Zarqa River to the south, both of which are tributaries of the Jordan River (Shoup 2007). Irbid and Ajloun are the two biggest cities in this region. The central portion, known as the Balqa Heights, extends from the Zarqa River in the north to Wadi al-Mujib in the south. Amman, the capital city of Jordan, and the towns of Al-Salt and Madaba are located in this area. The south portion is known as Jabal al-Sharat, and includes the largest city in this area, Al-Karak, which is located near the southern end of the Dead Sea (Shoup 2007). Most of Jordan's population and major cities are located in the highlands, which has the highest potential for rangeland in Jordan (FAO 2020).

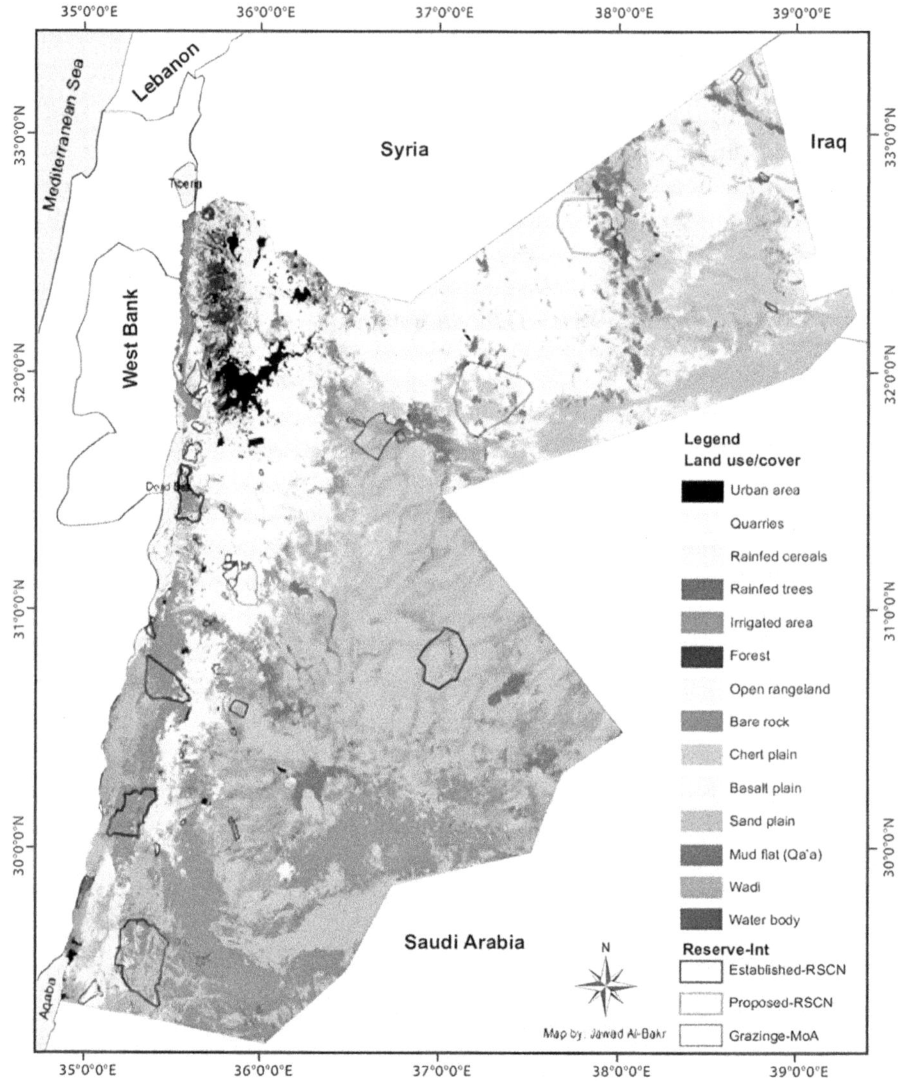

FIGURE 5.1 Regions covered by expert assessments in Jordan.
Source: Aligned National Action Plan to Combat Desertification in Jordan, 2015–2020

Moreover, the experts have revealed that among the three climatic regions, the Badia and desert regions have the lowest risk of climate change-induced loss and damage in soil-water-food systems. This region stretches across an area of around 70,000 square kilometers and experiences an annual rainfall ranging from 50 to 100 mm. The southeastern part of the region is classified as a true desert, with an annual rainfall of less than 35 mm (FAO 2020). This vast landscape covers approximately

TABLE 5.1 *Regional-wise summative assessment*

Region	Planetary threshold (A)	Institutional response (B)	Trade-off intensity (C)	Total score (A)+(B)+(C)*
Lowland region	186	266	267	719
Highland region	312	257	231	800
Desert and Badia region	498	523	498	1,519
Section total score	996	1,046	978	
Country score				3,038

Note. *A higher total score may be an indication that the loss and damages are significant.

80 percent of the country and is home to unique archaeology, ancient history, and various fragile ecosystems (World Bank Group 2016). The Badia region is also home to Bedouin livestock breeders, many of whom are nomadic. However, numerous factors such as settlement, drought, and overgrazing are causing damage to their lands, jeopardizing their income earned from herding and agriculture (The World Bank 2016). Jordan's Badia region is home to crucial groundwater reserves and resources, including the Al-Azraq basin and Disi aquifer (The Hashemite Fund for Development of Jordan Badia 2023). The largest and most improvised governorates in the Badia and desert are Ma'an and Mafraq.

In light of experts' assessment of biophysical conditions, TI, and institutional response, we conducted a regional-wise summative assessment to identify the climate change-induced loss and damage. Table 5.1 indicates that the Desert and Badia region experienced the most significant loss and damage owing to climate change, followed by the Highland region.

It is worth noting that the experts' general assessment of Jordanian regions regarding which are considered at high and low risk of climate change-induced loss and damage in soil-water-food systems is discrepant from the regional-wise summative assessment of the TI analysis. We identified several reasons for this discrepancy, including the well-articulated assessment factors of the TI analysis, which enabled experts to specifically identify the lack of governmental intervention to deal with climate change.

The taxonomic approach of the trade-off analysis made experts leverage the comparative basis of the adverse effect of climate change among Jordanian regions. Ultimately, we argued that the intersection of the TI analysis and the Jordanian regional division provides insightful indicators that experts can use to assess the adverse effects of climate change in light of the Jordanian government's uneven allocation of resources among Jordanian regions. Notably, the majority of developmental resources are directed towards the central region and specific sectors, whereas other marginalized areas such as the south and east regions, which are known as Desert and Badia in our analysis, receive less attention.

5.4.3 *Predicting the Effect of Rule Changes*

It must be pointed out that given the "non-linearity and complexity of many action situations, it is challenging to predict the precise effect of a change in a particular rule" (Ostrom 2009, 239). This can be viewed as a limitation of the rational choice theoretical framework. Furthermore, the tendency to assign all authority to a central agency is based on a false assumption that only a few rules need to be considered and that only experts know these options and can design optimal policies. But the renewal of back casting approaches and the emergence of supervised machine learning has expanded the avenues for experts and non-experts alike to be engaged in building a consensus based on prior knowledge of commons dilemmas. This would fit in well with Ostrom's optimism about the drama of the commons and how it can be enriched by enabling people to act "pro-socially" in the interest of fairness and increasing welfare in general (Ostrom 2000). More broadly, this would also address calls to make climate justice a reality by addressing issues of distributive (resource allocation), recognitional (local knowledge), and procedural (fairness in decisions) representation in the exercise of rules that govern the curation and use of environmental models (Rose 1997; Dasgupta et al. 2005).

To pursue thinking along these lines, we argue that analysis of TI can promote intersectoral policy coordination by actively tracking changes in weights for variables of institutional response: threshold capacity, critical mass of financing, and technology and information siloes. The constitution of periodical expert panels has the potential to support a robust monitoring ladder that informs the pilot testing of policy instruments such as guidelines, notifications, standards, circulars, and directives. Such an approach can overcome some of the shortcomings that relate to the discrepancy between market and nonmarket prices for cost and benefit analysis, key category analysis, and the concerns that have been expressed about the subjectivity of scoring and weights in climate assessments (ND-GAIN 2020; United Nations Framework Convention on Climate Change 2021). We acknowledge that the subjective nature of finding a consensus among experts may involve power hierarchies that are embedded in differences in disciplines, gender, and affinity to policy positions. Therefore, it is pertinent to inquire about the extent to which supervised machine learning can mitigate the excesses of political calculations of expert panel members with regard to the "majority view" on certain questions that involve the allocation of weights by professionalizing the exercise whereby the views of experts are aggregated to arrive at a consensus. This new frontier of rational choice theory has implications for managing the transformation of data into knowledge and information for decision-making with implications for the knowledge commons framework. An implicit assumption of such an endeavor will be that "humans are fallible learners who seek to do as well as they

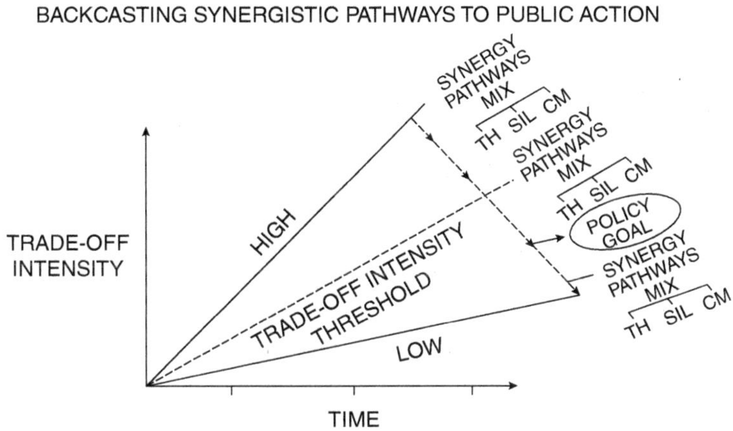

FIGURE 5.2 Monitoring institutional response to climate change-induced trade-offs.
*TH: Thresholds, CM: Critical mass of technology and financing, SIL: Siloes
Source: Adapted from Kurian and Kojima 2021

can give the constraints that they face and who are able to learn heuristics, norms, rules, and how to craft rules to improve achieved outcomes" (Ostrom 2009, 7).

In practical terms, back casting can help overcome the limitations regarding predicting the effect of rule changes. For one, for every model of institutional change (e.g., CILDAS), it would be possible to view possible interventions along the spectrum of high to low TI by identifying a threshold criteria. Depending on the policy goal – whether it is to lower or increase TI, institutional reforms may target the three elements of our CILDAS model – capacity thresholds, information siloes, and critical mass of technology and financing.[4] From a monitoring perspective, knowledge commons research should be able to draw upon expert panels to predict the effect that changes in each of these can have on overall outcomes in complex, nonlinear systems. Second, as a sequel and once sufficient cases have been organized, knowledge commons research could inform the design of institutional rules that can be piloted using distinct phases and transition points for each of the three intervention areas – siloes, thresholds, and critical mass (see Figure 5.2). This approach would overcome some of the limitations of the IFRI database-driven strategy that made limited contributions to the design of institutional rules in a real-world setting, thus minimizing its impact on policymaking.

[4] For an interesting Android app that aims to construct expert panels using the CILDAS model for agriculture to generate a visualization of climate change-induced losses and damages, see https://theclimatepanel.org.

5.5 CONCLUSIONS

The climate loss and damage discussions have laid bare the tensions in financing adaptation efforts worldwide. Third world agriculture bears the brunt of the effects of emissions responsible for droughts, fires, floods, and heatwaves. While it is acknowledged that intersectoral coordination that addresses normative and institutional change is crucial, experience shows us that policy and science are slow to respond to signs of crisis. Elinor Ostrom was responsible for offering a third way that emphasized the importance of organizing collective action for the management of commons resources. This chapter reviews five cases of the natural resources commons to argue that the knowledge commons can offer pathways for organizing data, models, and information to create the basis for evidence-based decision-making. This presupposes that important questions of distributive, procedural, and recognitional justice are addressed.

We have previously inquired in *Governing the Nexus* (Kurian and Ardakanian 2015) why good science does not translate into good policy. The answer is that political economy considerations play an important role in deciding which scientific problem gets priority. Ostrom's conceptual framework attempted to overcome some of the limitations of the game theory, transactions cost, and rationality postulates of public choice theory. By underlining the importance of reputation, repeated interactions, and trust, Ostrom attempted to incorporate "pro-social" elements into her framework. We revert to her reformulation of the rationality postulate described as follows: "to be rule governed, the rational individual must know the rules of the games in which choices are made and how to participate in the crafting of rules to constitute better games" to base our call for the use of expert panels and supervised machine learning in designing better games with an eye on extracting lessons for policymakers. This is why we think the environmental knowledge commons framework can contribute by furnishing protocols where university-led research and science in general can contribute more directly towards the design of monitoring frameworks for climate adaptation (Ostrom and Hess 2006).

Though not statistically significant, our use of a small group of experts in Jordan reveals that an exclusive focus on the biophysical domain would not suffice when addressing the challenges of climate losses and damages. Instead, a methodological framework that attempts to capture the political economic pressures of decision-making using the concept of TI can prove to be more effective in guiding climate investments. Depending on the policy goal – whether it is to lower or increase TI, institutional reforms may target the three elements of our CILDAS model – capacity thresholds, information siloes, and a critical mass of technology and financing.

From a monitoring perspective, knowledge commons research should be able to draw upon expert panels to predict the effect that changes in each of these can have on overall outcomes in complex nonlinear systems. Second, as a sequel and once sufficient cases have been organized, knowledge commons research could inform the design of institutional rules that can be piloted using distinct phases and transition points for each of the three intervention areas – siloes, thresholds, and critical mass. This approach would overcome some of the limitations of the IFRI database-driven strategy that made limited contributions to the design of institutional rules in a real world setting, thus minimizing its impact on policymaking.

Terminology List

- Agent-based modeling: A type of computer simulation that models the actions and interactions of individual agents to understand the behavior of a system as a whole.
- "Back casting": Environmental back-casting takes one of the imagined futures as a given and asks what conditions produced it. In contrast of forecasts, back-casting would not focus on being predictive but instead emphasize the importance of posing the most relevant question, challenging conventional assumptions, shaking up mental models of how the world works and encouraging cognitive flexibility to consider outliers in statistical analysis. Back-casting-oriented research is focused on lowering the costs of monitoring environmental and social outcomes through a focus on mitigating trade-offs, feedback and social learning drawing upon co-curation of data based on locally defined indicators of quality, affordability, coverage and/or service reliability. For details, see Kurian and Kojima (2021, chapter 4 – Experiential Learning Via Environmental Backcasting).
- Composite indices: Measurements that combine several different factors into a single score.
- Cost-effective prototypes of coupled models: Affordable early versions of systems that combine different types of models, like economic and environmental models.
- Cumulative siltation of infrastructure: The gradual build-up of sediment in structures like dams or ports over time.
- Environmental changes: Environmental changes are defined by the conditions of institutional and environmental synergies. They are non-linear, non-monotone and seldom recursive. In a view of the conventional policy assumptions, institutional and environmental outcomes would demonstrate features characterized by the standardized response of consumers/users (monotone), the interaction between environmental resources and institutions are sequential and in fixed course (linear), ensured by well-coordinated and regularly updated institutional feedback mechanisms (recursive). In reality, however, institutional and environmental outcomes often exhibit diverse response of consumers/users as shown for instance, poor adoption rates of technical and management options recommended by global public goods research (non-monotone), dynamic course on the interaction between environmental

resources and institutions which often the conventional assumption in the policy challenged by unforeseen uncertainties contained in the biophysical processes (non-linear) and ill-coordinated/weak updating feedback mechanism of institutional effects on environmental outcomes reflected in budgetary, strategies, staffing and information sharing (non-recursive), preventing effective multi-sectoral coordination in view of changes in the larger political and economic landscape. It is argued therefore, that institutional resilience is advanced when governance systems have developed the capacity to address these effects of non-linearity, non-monotony and recursiveness in design, implementation, monitoring and evaluation of public policy interventions (Kurian and Kojima 2021, 9–13, 103).

- Extreme trade-off intensities: Areas or situations where the choices between different options are particularly difficult or consequential.
- Ground-truth aerial data: Verifying information collected from aerial or satellite imagery by checking it against direct observations on the ground.
- Institutional trajectories: The paths that organizations or systems of rules take as they change over time.
- Peri-urban: Areas immediately surrounding a city or town, often a mix of rural and urban characteristics.
- Pre-theoretical: Ideas or frameworks that come before a fully developed theory, often used to guide initial research.
- Sliding Likert scale: A way of measuring opinions or attitudes that allows for a range of responses, usually from strongly disagree to strongly agree.
- Structural variables: Factors that are fundamental to how a system is organized and that influence its behavior.
- Trade-off intensity: The degree of difficulty or importance of choices between different options, especially when improving one area might worsen another.
- Typology assessments: Methods of categorizing things based on their similarities and differences.

PART III

6

Building a Sustainable Space Knowledge Commons

Laetitia Cesari and Simon Sun

6.1 INTRODUCTION

Knowledge of the space ecosystem – encompassing both objects and activities – has raised numerous concerns among state and nonstate actors, as the scope and significance of operations conducted in Earth orbit, and beyond, continue to expand. The question of knowledge is bound up in this discussion about identifying the nature of spacecraft and understanding the purpose of their operations and maneuvers. Knowledge is hardly monolithic, especially when considering the range of operators, military, governmental, or private, that can carry out space activities. Some spacecrafts are operated to support military operations. Different operations require different types of understanding. Just because a space operator is conducting a benign operation does not mean it is not testing other capabilities. A brief analysis of trendlines shows the need for knowledge and understanding by states, private operators, and observers to coordinate space activities better. Both information-sharing about and monitoring of the space domain continue to gain relevance owing to the multiplication of actors and spacecraft. Experts regularly share their concerns regarding unidentified space activities, disruptive maneuvers, and lack of transparency and cooperation.

From observation of astronomical phenomena and launches of a handful of objects to outer space, space activities now range from the provision of space applications enabled by single space systems or constellations of interconnected space objects to the conduct of scientific investigation on the Moon or other planets. For a variety of stakeholders, including public authorities, military forces, commercial operators, and civil society, contributing to and maintaining awareness of developments within outer space is essential (Borowitz 2022). This awareness facilitates informed decision-making, enables proactive responses to emerging trends, and supports alignment with practices in the field for better coordination and traffic management between operators. Consequently, stakeholders are actively developing various approaches to gather interpretable and actionable space-related data, either by utilizing proprietary tools or engaging in collaborative efforts. These initiatives reflect a strategic commitment to generating insights that inform decision-making and drive effective responses to emerging developments within outer space. Space-related data can concern both artificial objects (human-made spacecraft) and natural objects (resources on a celestial body, or a satellite body itself, such as a meteoroid, a planet or satellite, or an asteroid).

While there is currently no harmonized or standardized format for data collected and shared globally, whether by public or private entities, expanding access to space-related data to include more participants and possibly sharing more comprehensive data and services globally can foster continuous dialogue and trust-building. The work conducted by analysts and interpreters to process various resource forms and assess data quality is essential to ensure the information's reliability and usefulness. Sharing data underscores the potential for diverse contributions, not necessarily from those with direct data collection technology but from various fields that can enhance decision-making and algorithm development (Kostopoulos 2019, 9). Interoperability allows for the creation of a cohesive and usable picture of space activities. Using such space-related information does not bar other stakeholders from their capacity to use it. Rather, it contributes to general knowledge, and also helps verify the reliability of the data. The advantage of such platforms is that they provide reliable information, the dissemination of which does not prejudice the national interests of individual countries while protecting the interests of space operators.

However, information may not be shared, leading to the issue called the tragedy of the anticommons. Unlike the tragedy of the commons, where shared resources are overused to the point of depletion, the tragedy of the anticommons arises when multiple parties hold rights to exclude others from a resource, paradoxically leading to its underuse. This sheds light on how fragmented control and excessive exclusion rights can hinder efficient resource use, slow innovation, and limit access to valuable assets, ultimately resulting in missed opportunities. In the context of space knowledge, the tragedy of the anticommons may arise owing to concerns about security and national defense, intellectual property considerations, or international competitiveness – particularly when entities or nations aim to secure strategic or economic advantages.

If too many community members keep information secret or make it inaccessible, this not only causes cooperation between stakeholders to fail but also prevents the positive developments that making knowledge available enables. For instance, limited access to information restrains possibilities to anticipate risks and threats and better plan future space operations. In addition, it increases the costs of access to training and community participation, slowing down opportunities for progress and the willingness to participate and contribute to the community. Moreover, intellectual property limitations could hamper access to the general public, including civil society, the scientific community, and other governmental organizations. This is especially considering the growth of private actors in the space arena. Our goal is therefore to understand the interest of communities with the technology to collect data in sharing it, in order to advance cooperation between stakeholders, strengthen the sustainability of activities, and possibly benefit from the expertise of other members of the community (Ghosh 2007, 218).

In the rapidly evolving space sector, where the proliferation of private actors and technological advancements are redefining the dynamics of space governance, the development of a sustainable space knowledge commons is essential, by addressing the challenges of fragmented data sharing, such as the tragedy of the anticommons, and fostering strategic, economic, and scientific collaboration.

This research defines space knowledge commons, in this context, as the collection and sharing of space data for the safe and secure conduct of space activities, to foster long-term sustainability. We advocate for diverse space data-sharing proposals to establish various space knowledge commons that can be analyzed under the governing knowledge commons (GKC) framework. The goal is to ensure the mitigation of risks of disruptions and incidents, and the reduction of threats and misperceptions between space actors. It conceptualizes the notion of sustainable space knowledge commons for stakeholders to manage use and exploration of outer space. The GKC framework provides a useful research tool to ensure the safe, secure, and equitable use of outer space for current and future generations.

This chapter begins by examining the tragedy of the anticommons in space knowledge, offering an in-depth analysis of the factors that disincentivize information-sharing among actors. It then explores the concept of space knowledge by differentiating between space data and space knowledge, examines the context of space data, and presents a case study on space traffic management (STM). Lastly, it introduces the notion of sustainable space knowledge commons from three perspectives – strategic, economic, and scientific – and outlines the community involved. The goal is emphasizing the critical role of space-related data in promoting sustainable exploration and utilization of outer space, including safe and secure operations.

6.2 THE TRAGEDY OF ANTICOMMONS IN SPACE KNOWLEDGE

The governance of space data is particularly important given the increasing presence of private actors in the space arena, including companies such as SpaceX and Blue Origin, which lead in satellite launches and reusable rocket technology; Astroscale, which focuses on orbital debris removal and sustainability; Virgin Galactic and Blue Origin, which have ventured into space tourism; and Planet Labs and Maxar Technologies, which specialize in Earth observation and satellite analytics. Additionally, companies such as Axiom Space and Sierra Space are advancing space habitats and human exploration, while Eutelsat's OneWeb and SpaceX's Starlink are revolutionizing global connectivity with satellite constellations. These private actors significantly shape the governance, sustainability, and equitable use of space resources, gathering more knowledge about space.

Currently, there are no formal rules applicable to the international community concerning how space-related knowledge should be collected, used, shared, or protected. Because copying and sharing digital information is relatively cheap and easy (Kellerer et al. 2019, 715), it would be much more difficult to totally block access to space data than to manage the supply of it to communities. Although the presence of space assets orbiting the Earth cannot be concealed from telescope owners, trajectory prediction is a complex endeavor and precise operations conducted by space operators are rarely publicly shared. Various interest groups have formed and dissolved over time, comprising operators, governmental entities, and experts, contingent not only on available technologies but also on the vested interests at play.

The increasing number of stakeholders involved in space activities and the multiplication of objects launched to outer space makes space data collection dynamic and complex. The multiplication of objects in space, the miniaturization of technology, and novel operational techniques all contribute to this complexity, making it difficult to interpret and verify certain activities (Ben-Itzhak 2022). Criteria for data quality, including timeliness, completeness, uniqueness, consistency, validity, and accuracy, are essential so they can be exploited with other sets of data to form relevant pools of information for a large number of players, so they do not rely on incomplete or outdated data.

However, the limitation of proprietary data collected by operators and the tendency to fiercely protect access and use of this information, motivated by intellectual property and economic and strategic stakes, lead to fragmentation of data availability. Manufacturers and operators may consider that protecting spacecraft designs and operational data can protect their competitive advantage on the market and prevent unauthorized replication or reverse engineering, and also ensure that their activities remain secure from unauthorized use. Each operator, seeking to increase the value of its own investments and avoid sharing its valuable analyses, limits access to this data, preventing maximum exploitation of its collective potential. So, although many players have access to fragmented data, the lack of cooperation and sharing mechanisms hampers synergy and innovation.

The theory of the tragedy of the anticommons proves to be useful here. As Garrett Hardin proposed in his 1968 essay, tragedy of the commons happens in a situation where individuals, acting in their own self-interest, deplete or overexploit a shared resource, leading to the resource's eventual degradation or collapse (Hardin 1968; Ostrom 1990; Ostrom 1999). In contrast, as Michael Heller explains, underuse in an anticommons is the "mirror image of overuse in a commons" (Heller 2013, 12). The tragedy of the anticommons arises when multiple owners are each endowed with the right to exclude others from a scarce resource, and no one has an effective privilege of use (Heller 2013, 18). When there are too many owners holding rights of exclusion, the resource is prone to underuse. Heller's theory was initially proposed to describe post-1990 developments in Moscow, where many buildings remained empty because potential users had to secure the agreement or permission of multiple agents, each with the power to exercise a right of exclusion (Heller 1998, 633–641). Heller and Rebecca Eisenberg further applied the tragedy of the anticommons theory to biomedical research (Heller and Eisenberg 1998). Patent holders, through exclusive licensing, exploit rental value, hindering follow-on developers from realizing potential gains. This stifles development and, ironically, undermines the very purpose of patents: to incentivize research investment.

In the context of space knowledge, we draw on the theory of the tragedy of the anticommons to describe the lack of data sharing, particularly in light of the growing involvement of private companies. We identify three key driving forces behind this phenomenon: national security and national interests, intellectual property concerns, and the pursuit of strategic or economic advantages.

First, regarding security and national interests, certain information concerning satellites placed in orbit to support military operations or test new space capabilities cannot be made public. These satellites, often equipped with advanced technologies, play a crucial role in intelligence gathering, secure communication, and support for strategic missions (Bataille et al. 2022, 9–13). Revealing details about their nature, position, or capabilities could compromise the security and effectiveness of ongoing military operations and expose space infrastructures to the risk of sabotage or espionage by threat agents (Garino and Gibson n.d., 274). Operators also ensure they retain exclusive rights to critical information, so they maintain a strategic advantage for future activities and exploration efforts. Moreover, as military and dual-use technologies are sensitive data, states can implement measures to prevent adversaries and competitors from acquiring critical technologies, promoting defense and security. Confidentiality around these programs is, therefore, essential to preserve technological superiority and national sovereignty. As such, some operators prefer to keep information about their space assets out of the public's eyes.

Second, various intellectual property measures can be put into place. These include patents for inventions implemented through software, particularly those involving novel algorithms aimed at solving real-world problems or offering technical advantages, such as predicting space assets trajectories or innovative computing technologies for data processing. Additionally, copyrights protect original works of authorship, such as software code (Malloy et al. 2003). Many of the problems, dilemmas, and limitations are to be found in the data-collecting and data-processing procedures. Moreover, access to pools of information is generally exclusive, given that space data often carries confidentiality or is protected under intellectual property law. There may be attempts to limit or restrict access and impose some rules and standards to data collection and utilization processes to increase the quality of pools of information generated for specific purposes, such as collision avoidance mechanisms (Buchs et al. 2023, 374–383).

Third, while data sharing is essential for the advancement of science and international cooperation, it needs to be balanced by appropriate safeguards. Indeed, once analyzed, data can be exploited for competitive purposes, particularly by entities or nations that might seek to gain a strategic or economic advantage when planning their activities. This preserves the interests of data collectors while ensuring that the information disseminated serves the common good without compromising the strategic or economic benefits associated with space exploration. Moreover, it provides a guarantee that the information shared is verified and contextualized, thus avoiding the propagation of incomplete or misinterpreted data that could harm further research or space security. This is particularly relevant in the context of the exploitation of space resources. Although access to extraction technology is minimal nowadays, as is humankind's ability to travel in outer space and fully exploit natural space resources, it would be appropriate to work on raising awareness of the risks of overexploitation of resources (Cheney 2024, 353–358). To a certain extent, limiting the dissemination of data about space resources, including their nature, location, quantity, and role for an operator's space activity, can help to avoid arousing the interest of competitors (Cilliers et al. 2023). Here, data dissemination, access to information, and pointers to areas of interest are considered through the lens of the collection and extraction of space resources to mitigate, in the long term, the degradation of certain celestial bodies.

Here is an example involving satellite operators that demonstrates the tragedy of the anticommons. For strategic economic reasons, satellite operators – whether they are planning to launch a single satellite or an entire constellation – need to develop innovative technologies and obtain the best possible orbits. These orbits, which have become precious resources, are fiercely contested as they determine the quality and efficiency of the services provided by these satellites. To protect their market position and secure their competitive edge, operators are careful to keep their projects and technologies secret. Premature disclosure could allow competitors to capture the most strategic orbits or copy innovative business plans, jeopardizing their profitability and technological lead. Intellectual property plays a central role in the processing and valorization of data: In a context where considerable resources are invested in its collection and analysis, the data obtained, often through advanced technologies and sophisticated processing methods, have great value not only as economic assets but also as strategic tools for states. Because of their potential to influence economic prospecting and strengthen strategic positions, operators place a premium on protecting this data and the analyses derived from it, in order to maintain a competitive edge. Protecting intellectual property makes it possible to preserve the results of these efforts and investments, while limiting access by competitors or the general public to information likely to offer a competitive advantage or compromise national interests.

Operators, meaning to protect their investments and maintain a competitive edge, may be reluctant to share valuable data or participate in collaborative initiatives that could compromise their proprietary analyses. Although resources exist, their use is hampered by too many barriers to access them efficiently, reducing their overall usefulness. This phenomenon can lead to wasted opportunities for scientific advancement, economic decision-making, and collective security. To remedy this situation, collaborative regulations facilitating a balance between intellectual property protection and strategic data sharing are needed (Sankar et al. 2024; Seeds 2024). This would make it possible to utilize these resources optimally while preserving the competitive advantages and strategic interests of the various stakeholders.

There is a clear need for more space data sharing. The lack of a precise policy for data collection, sharing, and ensuring reliability poses a significant challenge to the management and regulation of space and technological information. The United Nations proposes general guidelines to states for operators' practices (United Nations Committee on the Peaceful Uses of Outer Space 2019). States and observers are also working on potential legal structures for activities in the exploration, exploitation, and utilization of space resources (United Nations Committee on the Peaceful Uses of Outer Space 2021). However, each actor, whether state or private, can adopt its own protocols for data collection and processing, leading to a heterogeneity that complicates international cooperation and transparency. The lack of specific standards on what is to be shared and how to certify data reliability and integrity raises crucial questions of trust and security (Baseley-Walker and Weeden 2010). Without harmonized certification and verification mechanisms, it is difficult for states and operators to guarantee the quality and relevance of exchanged data. This can lead to discrepancies in data interpretation and decision-making, potentially affecting national security and geopolitical stability.

6.3 SPACE DATA, SPACE KNOWLEDGE, AND THE ESSENCE OF DATA SHARING

6.3.1 *Space Data and Space Knowledge*

Access to space data benefits various stakeholders, including space operators, whether governmental or nongovernmental, to international organizations, agencies, academic institutions, and civil society (Reed et al. 2022). Until recently, data about objects located in space and activities conducted beyond the Earth's atmosphere has only been accessible to a small number of space operators, both governmental and nongovernmental. While users are not necessarily the ones collecting and analyzing space data, they benefit from it for various reasons, particularly the planning and management of their present and future missions in outer space and the long-term sustainability of space activities. Managing and governing space data raises several questions: What qualifies as space data (i.e., what information is relevant)? What are its origins (i.e., how is it collected)? Who are the users (i.e., who can access and process it)? How is it utilized (i.e., how is it employed)? And what are its applications (i.e., for what objectives)?

Under the knowledge commons literature, a meaningful distinction exists between data and knowledge. It takes a broad and inclusive view of "knowledge" for purposes of researching common governance, referring to human-generated material at any position that situates "data" at the lowest level, "information" and "knowledge" at intermediate levels, and "wisdom" at the highest level (Madison 2024, 320). This recognizes that knowledge is a product of what legal systems consider "counts" as a knowledge resource, and the character of cultural resources is frequently embedded in feedback loops at multiple levels (Madison 2024, 321).

Here, we distinguish between "space data" and "space knowledge." The term "space data" does not refer to the sensing of the Earth's surface, but rather to data relating to the space environment, including, but not limited to, natural resources characteristics and location and human-made objects' characteristics, orbital specifications, trajectories, and orbits. Space data ranges from raw information about outer space to the management, dissemination, preservation, and utilization of such data. Whether they generate such data or not, stakeholders need to access this resource and find a shared understanding of opportunities, benefits, and limitations regarding the joint use of this pool of information. Eventually, because of the multiplication of activities and the increasing need to coordinate between emerging and traditional actors, it may come to a point where the international community will have to address common management and governance. These resources are collected as a source of information about space-based natural elements, assets, and phenomena, as well as human activities and human-made objects, both functional and nonfunctional, including their components. Space data also relates to the mechanisms in place, starting with conversion of analog measurements to digital content, after data collection by relevant entities, to create information and share related knowledge, and also manage, disseminate, analyze, and preserve such data.

It is critical to note that the mere presence of data does not imply its active collection. Rather, sensing data is an activity that can only be carried out by a limited number of entities equipped with the necessary technical capabilities. Its processing and storage also rely on dedicated platforms, and compliance with existing transparency measures depends on states' willingness to share information about national space activities and assets with the international community (MITRE Corporation and Aspen Institute 2022, 5–6). For example, the Republic of Korea introduced plans to develop a space surveillance network combined with the KEPLER (Korea Enhanced Platform for Lowering spacE Risk) project, an advanced system that combines data from optical, radar, and laser sources to enhance situational awareness. During the 2025 United Nations Committee on the Peaceful Uses of Outer Space scientific and technical subcommittee session, the Republic of Korea unveiled the system's architecture, introducing Spacebook, a dedicated database for observing, collecting, analyzing, and managing space data. This platform is complemented by the Space Risk Warning Portal, designed to disseminate critical information to users (Choi 2025).

There are also initiatives to identify, label, and catalog natural resources and geological features regarding celestial bodies, including the Moon (Lunar and Planetary Institute, n.d.; Chinese Academy of Science 2024). Several projects initiated by private satellite operators and observers aim to better understand space (i.e., Space Data Association and Jonathan's Space Report) and states started to develop platforms to foster space situational awareness policies and develop STM mechanisms (Lal et al. 2018, 14–16).

The data can be analyzed and converted into valuable information, aiming to mitigate risks, reduce misperception and miscommunication between stakeholders, and anticipate critical scenarios. For example, they can be used to track the trajectory of objects in space and calculate the probability of collisions, thus contributing to the safety of space activities. In addition, these analyses can be used to identify the presence of specific resources on celestial bodies, facilitating the planning of future activities or the development of resource exploitation strategies (Clerc et al. 2025, 298–299). This transformation of raw data into usable information is fundamental to valorizing it and supporting strategic decisions that are both accurate and timely (Bonvino and Giorgino 2024).

After collecting data, identifying their type, and checking their reliability, the next step is to ensure relevance and focus on areas of mutual interest to stakeholders (Patriarca et al. 2019, 201–211). This process should integrate both protocols for data quality, interoperability, and formatting to ensure consistency and ease of use and tools for data import, analysis, and visualization, which allow contributors to upload data and users to interact with it meaningfully. Furthermore, knowledge gaps exist, as some operators prefer not to make public certain strategic and military uses of outer space. Thus, the objective here is not to list and classify all human made objects and natural resources present in orbit or on celestial bodies, nor the space phenomena or activities conducted in orbits, but rather to identify how knowledge of these different elements is acquired, shared, and used, and to what purpose.

These resources, ranging from voluntary shared data to actively collected facts and measurements, have diverse characteristics. Despite the existence of transparency measures and incentives to exchange information, it is the detection of data through sensing technology and calculations that is of real interest. Ensuring access to accurate, complete, reliable, relevant, and timely data is made easier if all entities with sensing capabilities make space data available, so the resulting information is properly exploited. In addition, renewed interest in space operations and applications through the deployment of large satellite constellations in low Earth orbit (Blount and Cesari 2023, 147) and projects to extract natural space resources from celestial bodies (Guyomarc'h 2023, 6) are prompting states and various operators to carefully analyze the space environment before planning and designing their space projects and missions.

Generally, space data access and management tend to be more and more open to a larger part of the population. Being part of a community, as is the case with governmental entities or satellite operators in particular, facilitates access to this type of information. There are not necessarily any particular barriers to capturing data, apart from access to observation technologies (Ortega et al. 2023, 18–19). However, their analysis and the knowledge that can be derived from it may be subject to protection measures to prevent access by strategic competitors.

The development of space knowledge commons, as a whole, involves the collection and sharing of space data to support the safe and secure conduct of space activities, ensuring long-term sustainability. It relates to relevant information beneficial for projecting human activities and fostering the long-term sustainability of space activities (Porras 2019). For instance, knowing space objects' trajectory and orbital parameters is important for adequate coordination between operators operating satellites in orbit. Its goal is to mitigate risks of disruptions and incidents while reducing threats and misperceptions among space actors. Creating knowledge commons based on space data involves developing a shared, accessible resource that enables multiple stakeholders to contribute, access, and build upon collective knowledge. Because sensing space data requires having scientific instruments and observation tools such as optical telescopes or radars, all information about outer space is not necessarily accessible to the public (Weeden et al. 2010). However, as observation instruments become more affordable and accessible, and computers become more powerful and numerous, some information can be shared as open source, notably by online user communities and members of civil society, research centers, universities, and so on (Renault et al. 2022, 24; Ortega et al. 2023, 31–33).

6.3.2 *Data Sharing as an Essential Attribute of Knowledge Commons*

Knowledge commons is governance by a community or collective of shared knowledge, information, and data resources, searching out instances of shared knowledge, information, and data that prompt the need for governance (Madison 2024, 308). As explained by Madison, "Knowledge commons research begins with the assumption that sharing knowledge, information, and data effectively is both a substantial public policy challenge and an enormous policy opportunity, not only emerging from questions surrounding contemporary data, software, artificial intelligence, and the like, but also building on equivalent questions of long pre-Internet, even Homeric standing" (Madison 2024, 304).

Data sharing is an essential attribute of the governance of knowledge commons. Certain data collection instruments and pools of information exist to catalog the conduct of human-led activities in outer space or the presence and characteristics of space natural resources that could be of value to the market. Cataloging natural space resources is crucial for scientific purposes and improvement of research. It can also help operators know where these resources are to ensure successful missions and resource collection and plan how resources might be collected, managed, and utilized in outer space, particularly on celestial bodies (Clerc et al. 2025, 301–303). Space-data collection can serve to identify, describe, and possibly quantify resources in order to create a detailed map locating valuable materials on the Moon or other celestial bodies, for both scientific and economic purposes. Opening access to information on the state of celestial bodies, their composition, and the elements that make them up or are located on them may raise concerns about the uncontrolled and unrestricted extraction of natural resources for commercial purposes alone. Gathering and analyzing space-related data, and more specifically cislunar data, is important for states aiming to foster scientific research and future growth and economic activities.

From a space governance perspective, data sharing occurs in two contexts: first, among partners, and second, by making data accessible to the public.

6.3.2.1 Data Sharing Among Partners

First, sharing related information with international partners not only improves global engagement and expands international cooperation but also enhances space situational awareness to maintain a foundation for responsible behaviors in space. Overall, it gives incentives to implement robust communication and navigational infrastructure to support safe and sustainable activities in space (White House 2022). On this basis, partners and competitors working on space mining activity can develop collectively understood norms with regards to acceptable, prohibited, or tolerated actions for stakeholders in specific situations, supported by enforcement measures and specific consequences in cases of noncompliance (Christensen et al. 2019).

Sharing space data efficiently and profitably requires the establishment of rigorous standards and coordination mechanisms. For these mechanisms to be reliable, rational, and usable, it is essential to establish a global normative policy defined by clear and commonly accepted standards. These standards may include guidelines on how to collect, process, and verify space data to guarantee both its quality and reliability. In the absence of such standards, publicly shared information may contain errors or be incomplete, which can undermine decision-making and trust between stakeholders.

It is, therefore, necessary to adopt certification mechanisms that guarantee the quality and integrity of space data before it is shared. This includes the introduction of international standards for data processing and dissemination, such as technical validation protocols and detailed documentation practices. In addition, enhanced coordination between the various players – be they governments, international organizations, or private entities – is crucial to ensure that space data is interpreted uniformly and that differences are minimized. This coordination can take the form of bilateral or multilateral collaborations, information-sharing forums, and the implementation of centralized platforms where verified space data can be deposited and consulted according to precise rules.

Ultimately, effective space data sharing, based on common standards and solid coordination, will not only promote better information use but also avoid the pitfalls associated with misinformation and errors of judgment caused by inconsistent or unverified data. However, for both public authorities and the private sector, data collection can be complex and costly. This difficulty stems largely from the technical and financial obstacles required to develop and maintain data collection infrastructures. Having one's own collection capabilities implies access to advanced technologies and substantial financial resources to build, operate, and update the necessary infrastructure. These include sophisticated sensors, robust communications networks, and high-performance data processing systems. The cost of research and development to remain competitive adds a further layer of complexity to the establishment of such an infrastructure.

Sharing and receiving space data from other operators requires integration into a network or group where trust and cooperation are established. Membership in these networks guarantees that data can be exchanged using common secure protocols. Membership in such groups implies commitments, such as compliance with sharing standards and protection of sensitive data, which can limit operators' freedom to manage information independently. Coordination and interoperability between different systems and collection methods are essential to ensure the consistency and efficiency of the space data exchanged.

Governance and sharing mechanisms are generally set up by both governmental and nongovernmental entities because exchange of information between operators and common governance reduces miscommunication, misperceptions, and mistrust. In that case, access to data can be granted to a part of the user community or be available to the general public so they can extract and use data (Hess and Ostrom 2007, 52). Companies, members of civil societies, state operators, and other stakeholders can use space data openly shared as nonrivalrous resources, even though not all information is shared, as some is kept secret for an operator's competitiveness for economic, strategic, or military reasons.

6.3.2.2 Public Information

Publicly available information is a crucial mechanism for data sharing, contributing to the development of a space knowledge commons. Specific legal instruments, such as the Convention on Registration of Objects Launched into Outer Space (United Nations 1975), require states to provide information to the United Nations Office for Outer Space Affairs (UNOOSA) (United Nations Office for Outer Space Affairs 2024). States generally grant licenses to space operators who request them, authorizing them to launch objects to carry out their operations. Furthermore, the International Telecommunication Union (ITU) regulates spectrum and orbit for space radiocommunication services (ITU n.d.). To this effect, it records in the Master International Frequency Register frequency assignment and orbital information for space stations onboard geostationary and nongeostationary satellites used or intended to be used in order to ensure efficient, rational, and cost-effective utilization of orbital and spectrum resources, considered as limited resources (ITU n.d.). These transparency requirements proposed at the multilateral level help estimate the number of objects in the various orbits. However, this is a declarative mechanism, and many objects launched to outer space are not registered or information provided is incomplete or erroneous (Hertzfeld 2021, 241). While it is possible for states to share data related to their national space objects in the multilateral context to UNOOSA and ITU (Masson-Zwaan et al. 2024, 242–248), there is no real standard format or particular obligations regarding data quality, accuracy, or completeness. Furthermore, there is no obligation to share data about natural objects and phenomena in space or about how human activities alter celestial bodies (Chen).

Open access information or publicly available data, including that managed by the United Nations register, can serve as a valuable alternative or complement. With the growing presence of private actors, such disclosure is increasingly essential. These data enable operators to obtain information without incurring significant initial collection costs. However, its reliability and level of detail can vary. It often requires additional verification or cross-checking and trust between all stakeholders. Public space-related data plays a crucial role in informed decision-making but must be handled with care to avoid errors owing to outdated, unreliable, or inaccurate information. When space data is made public without the source being identifiable, it may include erroneous or poorly processed information. This may be due to differing collection methodologies, varying levels of accuracy, or failure to apply rigorous processing protocols. The absence of a common validation and certification policy also leads to differences in space data interpretation, making it difficult to align stakeholders on consistent conclusions or to develop harmonized policies.

Open access makes it possible to monitor and verify operators' compliance with national obligations, ensuring responsible behavior in outer space, in conformity with the licensing states' international commitments. In the event of an incident, such as a collision, more open access to data helps clarify the circumstances and facilitates access to redress for victims, enabling a fairer and more transparent resolution. Finally, for future exploration activities and scientific progress, open data is essential. It supports the building of a shared knowledge base about outer space, which is essential for understanding and exploring it more safely, securely, and sustainably. This international cooperation and knowledge sharing ensures that space resources are used responsibly, benefiting both current missions and future generations.

6.3.2.3 Case Study: Space Traffic Management

STM serves as a compelling example of why data sharing is critical in space activities. In terms of regional STM, data plays a key role in the surveillance, tracking, and coordination of objects in orbit (Oltrogge and Kerr 2024). For example, the European Union is exploiting a network of terrestrial sensors, including radars and telescopes, to monitor and track space objects. This Space Surveillance and Tracking System (EU SST) aims to prevent the risk of collisions and track the trajectory of space debris to ensure the safety of satellites and space missions (McKnight 2019, 101–107).

Through this EU SST program, the European Union has also called for the development of space debris mitigation services for space safety and sustainability. (Committee on the Peaceful Uses of Outer Space Scientific and Technical Subcommittee 2023; Council of the EU 2023) By providing data and using its technological capabilities, the European Union seeks to enrich the pool of information available to the space community. These efforts aim to make monitoring services more transparent and accessible, aligning the European Union's approach through open public service (Moranta et al. 2020). This would enable private operators and space agencies from various countries to access the data they need to navigate safely in space, plan their missions, and avoid collisions (Moranta et al. 2020).

The integration of European efforts with other systems, such as that of the US, is an essential aspect of the overall STM coordination. The US, through the US Space Surveillance Network (Chatters and Crothers 2009, 249–258), manages a sophisticated network of sensors that continuously monitor space and provide critical data for STM. By working in partnership with players such as the European Union, the two systems can share complementary data, improving accuracy and global coverage (Stickings 2019, 8–9). Such collaboration also overcomes the geographical limitations of individual sensors, ensuring a more comprehensive and coordinated view of the space situation (Ortega et al. 2023). This articulation can be achieved through common platforms and bilateral or multilateral agreements, where data from both systems are exchanged according to defined protocols. Harmonization of data collection and analysis methodologies helps to enhance the reliability of shared information. Initiatives such as sharing best practices and developing common standards ensure that integrated data from European and American systems can be used consistently by all players in the space sector.

The ultimate aim of this international cooperation is to create a space situational awareness environment that is global and integrated, reducing the risks associated with space activities and supporting the sustainability of in-orbit operations (Oltrogge and Christensen 2020, 432–438). This could lead to better coordination for proactive debris mitigation, orbital conjunction management, and future space mission planning while promoting safer and more efficient use of space for future generations.

On the private sector level, the Space Data Association (SDA) plays a significant role in bringing together various satellite operators to encourage the sharing of data essential to the safety and integrity of the space environment. The SDA is a collaborative initiative that enables operators to share valuable information on satellite position, trajectory, and status to minimize the risk of collisions and disruptions in space. It emphasizes the sharing of reliable operational data and promotes best practices across the industry (Muelhaupt et al. 2019, 80–87).

The SDA approach is distinguished by the fact that it is a closed service reserved for a limited number of operators who agree to participate on a reciprocal basis. This means that members must not only receive information but also contribute their own data concerning their satellite fleet, trajectories, and life expectancy, among other information, to enrich the collective knowledge base. This fosters an environment of mutual trust, where the exchange of information benefits all participants and helps to enhance the safety of space operations (Oltrogge et al. 2024, 342–361).

Participation in the SDA gives operators access to accurate, up-to-date data on space traffic, reducing the risk of collisions and enabling better maneuver planning for collision avoidance. In addition, this approach promotes the harmonization of STM methods in the private sector. It helps to complement the efforts of government systems such as those of the European Union and the US. By promoting best practices and facilitating secure and efficient data sharing, the SDA supports not only flight safety but also the long-term sustainability of the space environment.

This reciprocal sharing structure demonstrates the importance of private collaboration in STM, particularly when coordinated with public initiatives to create a more comprehensive and resilient surveillance ecosystem. The bottom line is that initiatives to share space data, whether from the public or private sectors or from collaboration between the two, highlight both considerable challenges and promising opportunities. On the part of public-led initiatives, the focus is on establishing robust infrastructures and open services to provide reliable data for safety and STM. However, the absence of common standards on an international scale complicates the coherence of exchanges and the quality of shared data while leaving the door open to divergent interpretations and the risk of errors (Stauch et al. 2016).

On the private side, the reciprocal and reliable sharing of data between operators can significantly improve space safety and coordination between satellite operators. However, these private initiatives remain limited in terms of access and participation and rely on trust and reciprocity, which may exclude important players that do not meet these criteria. The main challenges of these various initiatives include the need to develop harmonized standards, ensure data reliability and accuracy, and coordinate effectively between multiple stakeholders with varied interests. The issue of intellectual property and data protection also remains a major concern, influencing how and to what extent data can be shared.

At the same time, the opportunities offered by structured and coordinated sharing of space data are considerable. They include better management of space traffic, reduced collision risks, more efficient mission planning, and the possibility of developing global strategies for space debris reduction. Cooperation between public initiatives and private efforts could create an integrated and resilient space ecosystem. Such collaboration would be essential to ensure not only the immediate safety of space activities but also the long-term sustainability of outer space and, by extension, their security, a common asset essential to the continuation of space use and exploration. Because the space environment, particularly in low Earth orbit, can undergo rapid changes, space operators constantly need up-to-date information to be aware of a situation and conduct their activities safely, with a comprehensive repository of space data.

6.4 BUILDING A SUSTAINABLE SPACE KNOWLEDGE COMMONS

6.4.1 *Overview*

The purpose of the GKC framework is to prompt systematic study of resource-sharing practices, as the research program is pragmatic rather than ontological (Madison 2024, 317). The Ostrom literature makes an important distinction between a "framework," a "theory," and a "model." A framework identifies, categorizes, and organizes factors considered most relevant to understanding a phenomenon. A theory, in contrast, proposes general causal relationships among subsets of these variables or categories, designating certain factors as particularly significant while treating others as less critical for explanatory purposes. Finally, a model specifies the specific functional relationships among particular variables or indicators, hypothesizing their operation under well-defined conditions (McGinnis 2011, 170). The goal of the GKC framework is to invite researchers to explore knowledge commons governance by addressing clusters of interrelated questions, designed to be examined and answered systematically (Madison 2024, 308).

Different from the Institutional Analysis and Development (IAD) framework, "resources" in the GKC context are not tangible or "biophysical." Instead, the framework focuses on knowledge, or information that is non-depletable (Madison 2024, 309). It also does not make the assumption that "actors" are individuals operating on a rational decision-making basis (Madison 2024, 309). Generally, teams of experts are dedicated to the planning, management, and overall control of space activities, under the supervision of public authorities. The terminology in that schematic partially corresponds to the terminology developed by the IAD framework, particularly its emphasis on "rules-in-use" (referring to formal and informal rulesets that define the relevant community and its practices) and "action arenas" (contexts in which relevant actors repeatedly interact concerning shared resources) (Madison 2024, 309). However, a key difference lies in the interaction of various variables. Unlike the IAD framework, the outcomes of a given pattern directly influence the input variables, potentially leading to the destruction or sustainability of the resource (Strandburg et al. 2017, 15). These outcomes can also drive modifications to the rules-in-use if the community is dissatisfied with the results.

Overall, we advocate for space data-sharing policies to build various knowledge commons, where these different case studies can be effectively analyzed under the GKC framework. The creation, sharing, and maintenance of common resources and the structures controlling them or facilitating their appropriate use enable all stakeholders to ensure the smooth running of our activities. It also enables the development of rules or norms of behavior in the space environment. As such, the international community is already working on encouraging states to adopt responsible behavior in their use.

This is especially important because of the proliferation of private entities in space governance. Entities such as Starlink, Leolabs, Planet, Look Up Space, CFSCC, USSPACECOM, JSC Vimpel, and SeeSat-L have directly shared space data concerning space assets and activities on different platforms, either open such as Space Track or AstriaGraph or more confidential. Even though this practice might raise intellectual property concerns, this type of open access without costs or permissions does not prevent these platforms from retaining copyright over the work they provide (Wang et al. 2022, 13).

In addition to existing private initiatives, the European STM platform currently under development and mentioned earlier is supported by space-based data (Moranta et al. 2020). The US, meanwhile, has a legal structure for space situational awareness. This is also an opportunity for the military, which sees outer space as a strategic operational domain, important to their operations.

Information about the situation in orbit is useful for satellite operators to calculate collision probability or plan future operations. Generally, the analysis of space data enables better management of traffic, anticipation of collision risks, and identification of the areas in which operators can place space objects, especially in low Earth orbit and medium Earth orbit. Geostationary orbits have been under constant scrutiny ever since operators first realized their economic benefits: Placing an object in geostationary orbit means not having to move it, or reorient it frequently, because of its Earth-like orbit (Sato et al. 2021, 331–338). In nongeostationary orbits, it is more complex to identify the objects that are placed, and their trajectory, speed, altitude, and other characteristics linked to their placement (Borowitz et al. 2021). Moreover, not all satellites can be remotely piloted, some are no longer functional, and the presence of debris can cause damage to satellites (World Economic Forum 2021). Only some satellites or space objects can be maneuvered to avoid collisions or simply redirect their antennas to conduct their activities. Therefore, identifying the characteristics of different resources with as much space-related data as possible is essential for obtaining useful and reliable information. Increasingly, this information is being collected and analyzed by a number of categories of experts and researchers (i.e., Space Data Association and Jonathan's Space Report). Sharing space data therefore facilitates coordination between different space operators and, more generally, improves the efficient management of space traffic.

To date, mechanisms for collecting, sharing, and managing space-related data are used to assess the risk of in-orbit collisions in an efficient, temporal, and precise way, to reduce false alarms and missed events, and to reduce the time and resources devoted to this type of assessment by the various operators. This also minimizes the risk of confusion and conflicting decisions between operators while quickly finding solutions to avoid the risk of interference and collision (Silverstein 2023, 18–21). In terms of ensuring the investment of time and resources in this type of operation, opening up this information and access to a wider community of observers would perhaps enable greater efficiency and the development of best practices for stakeholders. Without such a mechanism, there is no standardized format for these data, analysis, sharing, and prevention of more reliable and accurate results.

6.4.2 *Building a Sustainable Space Knowledge Commons*

6.4.2.1 The Boundaries of Space Knowledge: Strategic, Economic, and Scientific Considerations

One fundamental question when conducting GKC research is to define what constitutes knowledge commons. Intangible knowledge resources are not naturally defined by boundaries that limit their use. Instead, it is constructed, rather than discovered, and it operates through at least two resources – either embedded in the tangible form, or shaped and regulated through law and other social practices (Strandburg et al. 2017, 13–14). In the context of patents, for instance, the "claims" define the boundaries (Strandburg et al. 2017, 14). These boundaries are partly within and partly outside the control of members of a knowledge commons, giving rise to a series of social dilemmas (Strandburg et al. 2017, 14).

Space knowledge is inherently valuable but not neutral – it serves both scientific and strategic purposes. On the one hand, analyzing data and conducting research advances space exploration and science. On the other hand, leveraging data for strategic and economic considerations helps markets project revenues, assess investments, and evaluate associated risks (OECD 2024, 6–7). This is a question of social ethics that can be the subject of discussion and study to determine acceptable levels of safety for public expectations, while taking into consideration the desire of certain states to develop their space economy either with extraction technologies in their own way or with all the capacities and logistical systems that surround it.

Here, we utilize "sustainability" as a key term to draw the boundaries for space knowledge commons (Space Data Association 2024). In other words, sustainability becomes a primary goal for space data-sharing policies and serves as a determining factor in deciding what should or should not be shared. Sustainability is a major topic regarding the responsible use and exploration of outer space. It is intrinsically linked to space safety and security, as a debris-saturated and poorly managed orbital environment greatly increases the risk of collisions and accidents, jeopardizing not only ongoing space missions but also the infrastructures on which many terrestrial services depend. Relevant and reliable data on space situations and activities is essential to ensure a sufficient level of safety and security. This is where the concept of sustainability in our understanding of knowledge commons becomes relevant – space data, when shared and accessible for the purpose of space sustainability, can be considered as knowledge commons. The notion of sustainable space knowledge commons encourages the international community to share critical information that strengthens the coordination and collective management of outer space. Reasoned sharing of data on the position and trajectory of space objects, as well as on debris management, contributes to better risk anticipation and faster, more effective response to potential incidents (Space Data Association 2024).

The notion of "sustainability" should be a central aspect of various policies for space data sharing. Within the GKC framework, it serves as an important objective behind different rules-in-use. This concept implies that these data become collective resources, which, when properly managed and exploited, benefit the entire space community and beyond. The importance of knowledge commons for space data is threefold, covering strategic, economic, and scientific aspects.

From a strategic point of view, knowledge about the launch operation of a rocket and the encounter of space satellites should be shared, which gives an operator, whether governmental or nongovernmental, a complete and precise awareness of the situation around its assets. This knowledge is essential for ensuring the safety and integrity of space missions by making it possible to monitor nearby movements and operations and prevent incidents such as collision risks or unauthorized maneuvers, among which are threatening close approach (West 2023). This ability to anticipate and react proactively strengthens the operator's sovereignty and operational security. The goal is to prevent miscommunication, misunderstanding, misperception, and the rise of tensions between States. (United Nations Institute for Disarmament Research (UNIDIR) 2022).

From an economic point of view, access to space knowledge on space maneuvers, of the trajectory, and the position in orbit, is essential for investment planning and optimization. Private and public operators need reliable data to design missions, decide on the best orbits to use, and assess environmental conditions before launching satellites. Moreover, in the context of increasing competition for the exploitation of outer space, information on the distribution of debris or the viability of a future satellite's location can make the difference between a fruitful investment and a considerable loss. Concerning space resource exploitation, the availability of data about celestial bodies, such as the Moon or asteroids, can be used to assess the profitability and feasibility of extraction missions.

With regard to scientific exploration, shared space knowledge on specific celestial bodies in terms of the location and the chemical composition would create a collective knowledge base and facilitate international collaboration to understand outer space, celestial bodies, and improve the study of the universe. This includes the knowledge of specific celestial bodies in terms of the location and the chemical composition. States tend to address this from a scientific point of view – however, future discussions, informed by eventual technology developments, may lean towards an economic point of view. Identifying resources present on asteroids or other celestial bodies, detecting new objects, and analyzing their composition are essential elements for scientific research. These knowledge commons enable the scientific community to work more efficiently, exchange ideas, and push back the frontiers of space research. This stimulates innovation and fosters discoveries that can have beneficial applications on Earth, such as improving space technologies, understanding the universe or even technological spin-offs in medicine and engineering.

6.4.2.2 Community

Managing and accessing space data as knowledge commons represents a crucial opportunity for strategic, economic, and scientific development. However, realizing this potential depends on stakeholders' ability to develop standards, share infrastructures, and strengthen international cooperation to ensure that these commons are sustainable and accessible while protecting the specific interests of each stakeholder.

Utilizing the GKC framework requires a comprehensive understanding of the community involved. Key questions include identifying community members, defining their roles, and assessing the degree of openness toward different stakeholders and the general public. Establishing standards to assess data quality and predict potential outcomes is crucial for organizing information and connecting it to the growing number of space activities (Hess and Ostrom 2007).

Overall, the community managing space data as a knowledge commons comprises space data providers, policymakers, users, space operators, civil society members, the scientific community, governmental organizations, private entities, international bodies, and technology developers, each contributing uniquely to ensuring sustainability, security, and accessibility. This diverse and interconnected network highlights the complexity of aligning interests, establishing governance frameworks, and fostering collaboration to address the shared challenges and opportunities of managing a sustainable space knowledge commons effectively.

The increasing accessibility of observation tools and computational power contributes to the rise of communities focused on outer space (Ortega et al. 2023). The growing awareness of the importance of space sustainability and safety has underscored the need for collaborative efforts. Space data – ranging from voluntarily shared information to actively collected measurements – possesses diverse characteristics. While transparency and information-sharing mechanisms exist, advanced sensing technologies and analytical tools play a crucial role in ensuring access to accurate, reliable, and timely data. Entities with sensing capabilities should make their data available to enable meaningful exploitation and support strategic planning. Recent developments, such as deploying large satellite constellations in low Earth orbit (Blount and Cesari 2023) and initiatives to extract resources from celestial bodies (Guyomarc'h 2023), have further highlighted the need for comprehensive data analysis to guide project design and mission planning.

State and private stakeholders are becoming more involved in space operations to ensure safety, security, and sustainability. Sharing data allows these parties to coordinate activities effectively, reduce collision risks, and contribute to a stable outer space environment while reaping strategic, scientific, and economic benefits (Foust 2019). For both state and nonstate actors, access to shared data promotes mutual understanding and facilitates cooperation on shared objectives.

Information providers, policymakers, and users all have important roles. Providers include those who collect, process, and disseminate data, as well as those offering supporting software, hardware, and infrastructure. Policymakers often operate within self-regulated communities, promoting transparency and encouraging information exchange among stakeholders (Hess and Ostrom 2007). Users range from individuals accessing digital content to organizations employing this data for operational purposes.

These interconnected groups typically function at different levels of the knowledge commons, where locally managed information pools are globally utilized. Ensuring that the data remains relevant requires proper categorization and classification, avoiding interference with trade secrets or sensitive military strategies.

In consideration of the law, international legal frameworks impose significant responsibilities on states for their space activities. Under the Outer Space Treaty (1967), states are internationally liable for damage caused by their space objects (Article VII) and must avoid interfering with the activities of other states (Article IX). National space laws further impose licensing conditions, including administrative, legal, financial, and technical obligations on operators. These regulations ensure smooth operations and minimize in-orbit risks.

Space operators, meanwhile, bear responsibility for minimizing their impact, coordinating with others, and contributing to the overall safety and sustainability of space. Given the rapid pace of developments, particularly in low Earth orbit, the creation of a comprehensive repository of space data is essential. Such repositories could enhance collision prevention and post-event analysis while supporting governmental and nongovernmental entities alike (Alfano et al. 2022).

While many platforms for sharing space environment data are developed by operators and entities directly using the information, other groups – such as civil society, scientific communities, and governmental organizations – play significant roles. These groups contribute to multilateral discussions by clarifying complex issues, conducting research, and reducing tensions in space (Cesari 2022). Their involvement helps ensure that space data is collected, analyzed, and shared to address emerging challenges and foster stability.

In conclusion, the effective management of space data as a knowledge commons relies on the collaboration of a diverse and complex community. This intricate network of stakeholders, each with unique roles and perspectives, underscores the importance of fostering cooperation, establishing clear standards, and maintaining transparent governance to ensure the sustainability, security, and accessibility of space data for the benefit of all.

6.5 CONCLUSION

Since the advent of space activities, various actors have strived to monitor activities in outer space to better anticipate future space missions and protect their assets from threats and operational risks. Nowadays, advancements in technology, including more optical telescopes, radar systems, and computing power. Space data collection tools involve diverse technologies, such as radars and tracking dishes, either based on Earth or placed in outer space.

As space-related data are exploited in pools of information by different stakeholders, they are shared differently depending on whether they relate to public operations or confidential and sensitive space missions. Community of users determine mechanisms for designing, sharing, and managing space data based on their characteristics and how this resource can serve different stakeholders, whether private or public, national, regional, transnational, or international.

Even though these technologies provide data that can be used to survey areas of interest, each of them has inherent limitations and biases and no single sensor provides an absolute and ubiquitous truth of the space situation. Furthermore, stakeholders and the general public cannot continuously and persistently observe every object all the time or share information about their objects in real time. However, despite these challenges, space-related data are very useful for various purposes, including the development of safety mechanisms and the planning of space mining activities. Therefore, aggregating data helps gaining a clear understanding of space activities. When the provision and management of space-related data have beneficial implications for all, it can lead to the qualification of knowledge commons.

In recognition of the rise of private actors in space, we are concerned about the potential occurrence of the tragedy of the anticommons, where information is withheld by private companies. We identify three key driving forces behind this phenomenon: national security and interests, intellectual property concerns, and the pursuit of strategic or economic advantages. We then explore the concept of knowledge commons, identifying what it means to share data and why it is important in the context of space data. To define the boundaries of space knowledge commons, we utilize the concept of sustainability and advocate for the development of a sustainable knowledge commons, emphasizing data-sharing policies. The GKC framework is flexible and well suited as an analytical tool for policies related to the collection, processing, and use of space data. The term "sustainability" should encompass economic, strategic, and scientific considerations, driving the rules-in-use within the framework. Furthermore, we outline the community involved, which can be effectively analyzed using the GKC framework to inform and enhance future policy analysis.

If the provision and management of spatial data have beneficial implications for all, it can lead to the qualification of knowledge commons. Value is created by increasing the number of people who use the resource and join a community of users who benefit from data in various sectors, such as knowledge of space, planning of launches and space operations, and information relating to orbits, particularly with regard to the future challenges of their exploitation. Users can engage in governance, regulation, enforcement, education, or similar activities to conduct their space operations in a sustainable manner and foster mutual trust and understanding, ensuring peaceful and secure dynamics of interaction.

7

Terrestrial Environmental Data Obtained from Space

Andrea J. Harrington

7.1 INTRODUCTION AND CLARIFICATION

This chapter is about data gathered in one commons and used to manage another commons: outer space and the Earth environment, respectively. From the commencement of space activities, space data have aided humanity in managing resources, advancing science, predicting weather, mitigating disasters, and understanding human migration, among other activities (Lyall and Larsen 2024, 333–334). As the use of the term "commons" can be controversial in space context particularly "global commons" (Hertzfeld et al. 2015; Pace 2017), it is important to note that the use of the term in this chapter does not attempt to limit how states may use the outer space environment, but rather uses the term with respect to space because space is available for use by all countries and data gathering from space affects all countries. It has been asserted that

> "[g]lobal commons" is not some talismanic term that demands every utterance invoke Elinor Ostrom … Instead, it has multiple legitimate meanings, and they can apply to outer space in different ways. Outer space is a global commons in the sense of being a domain beyond national jurisdiction and with free and open access, but it is not a global commons in the sense of being commonly owned such that nations cannot assert private property interests in space resources. (Goehring 2021, 588)

It is essential to approach the use of the term "commons" in this chapter as providing opportunities rather than restrictions. Notably, the Outer Space Treaty does not use *common heritage of mankind* language, nor does it denote a special status to the physical domain of outer space (Hertzfeld et al. 2015). Instead, in Article I, it denotes space activities as the "province of all mankind." That said, the concept of a knowledge commons is far more contextually important here. A knowledge commons can be understood as "institutionalized community governance of the sharing and, in some cases, creation of information, science, knowledge, data, and other types of intellectual and cultural resources" (Dedeurwaerdere et al. 2014, 1). The institutionalization of remote sensing data about Earth gathered from space, through the United Nations (UN) and other organizations, has led to the formation of a massive knowledge commons which creates new information through continued analysis of the gathered data. The variety and volume of gathered data is enormous, and applications using differing tools and accessing multiple data sources have increased, leading to additional challenges in effectively using this data (Sudmanns et al. 2020, 833).

7.2 EXISTING LEGAL/NORMATIVE FRAMEWORKS

7.2.1 *Outer Space Treaty*

When the Treaty on Principles Governing the Activities of States in the Exploration and Use of Outer Space, including the Moon and Other Celestial Bodies (hereinafter referred to as the Outer Space Treaty) came into force in 1967,[1] it created the basic legally binding framework under which actors operate in space to this day, and hopefully far beyond. Its predecessor was a nonbinding principles document, Resolution 1962: Declaration of Legal Principles Governing the Activities of States in the Exploration and Use of Outer Space (United Nations General Assembly 1963),[2] which helped to generate the consensus needed during the height of Cold War tensions to encourage and enable human endeavors in outer space. Resolution 1962 contained similar provisions to the Outer Space Treaty and helped start the process of crystallization into custom of several key principles, including freedom of access and use and nonappropriation (Lyall and Larsen 2024, 50). While it is beyond the scope of this chapter to address all Outer Space Treaty principles, the ones with particular bearing on Earth observation (hereinafter EO) data are highlighted here.

Article I sets forth the most fundamental underlying rule in the international space law regime. It establishes, first and foremost, the freedom of exploration and use. Additionally, the *benefit principle* is derived from Article I, which requires that space activities "be carried out for the benefit and in the interests of all countries." The equal right to access space without discrimination for all states is reiterated. Additionally, provision is made to facilitate and encourage cooperation in scientific investigation of space. The obligations contained in this Article are foundational for EO activities. Data obtained from satellites in space is used for weather prediction and monitoring, disaster recovery, natural resource management, agricultural management, climate modeling, tracking human migration, and numerous other purposes (Lyall and Larsen 2024). The right of all states to conduct these activities and the obligation for states to carry them out in a nondiscriminatory way while

[1] Treaty on Principles Governing the Activities of States in the Exploration and Use of Outer Space, Including the Moon and Other Celestial Bodies, Jan. 26, 1967, 18 U.S.T. 2410, 610 U.N.T.S. 205.

[2] G.A. Res. 1962 (XVIII), Declaration of Legal Principles Governing the Activities of States in the Exploration and Use of Outer Space (Dec. 13, 1963).

respecting the interests of all are critical when it comes to this kind of data that can be obtained from space.

It is worth noting that space is not the only jurisdiction in which freedom of access and use are mandated, while appropriation is prohibited as in Article II of the Outer Space Treaty. Both the high seas and Antarctica operate under regimes that are similar from that perspective.[3] That said, outer space does operate under a state responsibility regime that is unique in international law. This specialized regime is implemented through Article VI of the Outer Space Treaty, which mandates that states take legal responsibility for their national actors, including private entities, and conduct authorization and supervision for their activities (Cheng 1972). Notwithstanding the distinct nature of this attribution rule for outer space, the application of the law of state responsibility to space activities remains, in accordance with Article III of the Outer Space Treaty that otherwise incorporates general international law.

The application of the Article I benefit principle is widely debated among space law scholars (Matte 1987, 319). Some argue that the requirement to act for the benefit of all countries has been broadly met by the improvements in daily life planetwide that have flowed from space activities, including not only the EO benefits mentioned above but also importantly precision navigation and timing, communications access, provision of telemedicine, as well as other services and spin-off technologies (Gorove 1971, 101). Others, however, argue that the often incidental benefit that has accrued does not meet the legal requirement, as the benefit principle has not been implemented with the appropriate level of intentionality.[4] Either interpretation has a reasonable basis (Lee 2012, 157–159).

Likewise, the language in Article I addressing cooperative scientific endeavors is framed for facilitating and encouraging such endeavors, rather than using language of a more binding character. That said, in the view of this author, other clear obligations exist in Article I that protect key rights for states in terms of EO and its relevant data. First, there is an unambiguous requirement to permit use of a space on a nondiscriminatory basis, regardless of technological or economic development. Second, while the benefit principle may not expressly require active engagement to provide benefit to all for each individual activity conducted, it is obvious that a state cannot act knowingly against the interests of other states while complying with their *pacta sunt servanda* obligations to undertake treaties in good faith.[5] Thus, Article I

[3] *See* Convention on the Law of the Sea, Dec. 10, 1982, 1833 U.N.T.S. 397; Antarctic Treaty Dec. 1, 1959, 12 U.S.T. 794, 402 U.N.T.S. 71.

[4] "While opinion may differ on what constitutes 'the interests of all countries' and compliance with this part of the obligation might have to rely largely on the good faith of the contracting States, the rest of the sentence is much more concrete in meaning. It strongly suggests that 'all States' have a legal right to the fruits of space exploration and use" (Cheng 1997, 15).

[5] For the codification of the customary international law principle of *pacta sunt servanda*, see Vienna Convention on the Law of Treaties, art 26, 22 May 1969, 1155 U.N.T.S. 331 [Vienna Convention].

provides a framework for nondiscriminatory use of EO data that does not knowingly contravene the interests of other states.

Article IX of the Outer Space Treaty mandates that states "shall conduct all their activities in outer space [...] with due regard to the corresponding interests of all other States Parties to the Treaty." Thus, the Treaty implements a balancing mechanism to maximize overall use of space. States' free use of space is limited to the extent that such use takes into account the corresponding interests of other states (Harrington 2023). A useful formulation of the due regard principle was provided, though in a maritime context, by the tribunal in the *Chagos* arbitration: "'due regard' calls for the [State party] to have such regard for the rights of [another state party] as is called for by the circumstances and by the nature of those rights."[6] Here, it is important to note that the consideration due is to those interests, rather than just the space activities of other states. Thus, a state carrying out an EO activity must provide reasonable regard for the interests of states that may be affected by the data collected.

Finally, Outer Space Treaty Article XI creates a legal environment that facilitates the importance of sharing of space data. The Article reads:

> In order to promote international co-operation in the peaceful exploration and use of outer space, States Parties to the Treaty conducting activities in outer space, including the moon and other celestial bodies, agree to inform the Secretary-General of the United Nations as well as the public and the international scientific community, to the greatest extent feasible and practicable, of the nature, conduct, locations and results of such activities. On receiving the said information, the Secretary-General of the United Nations should be prepared to disseminate it immediately and effectively.

While this requirement is clearly tempered by the feasibility and practicability language contained within (Keefe 1995, 351), the types of data collected by civil space agencies, at least, fall within this purview of required sharing, which has been generally respected. That said, it may not be feasible or practicable for private companies to freely share the data obtained from their space activities, and likewise with regard to sharing data that have particular pertinence to national security.

7.2.2 *Remote Sensing Principles*

The 1986 UNGA resolution *Principles Relating to Remote Sensing of the Earth from Outer Space*[7] (hereinafter Remote Sensing Principles) took fifteen years to negotiate and set the stage for enhanced data sharing within the scope of activities addressed (United Nations General Assembly 1986; Ito 2011). Part of the reason for the long

6 Chagos Marine Protected Area Arbitration (Mau. v. U.K.) ¶519 (Perm. Ct. Arb. 2015).

7 G.A. Res. 41/64, Principles Relating to Remote Sensing of the Earth from Outer Space (December 1986) [Remote Sensing Principles].

tail of time in reaching agreement on the Remote Sensing Principles is that it took that time to build consensus on the *opinio juris* that freedom to sense other states' territories from space without authorization is legally permissible (Ito 2011; Lyall and Larsen 2024, 340–342). The scope of remote sensing activities addressed by the Remote Sensing Principles is limited to "sensing of the Earth's surface from space by making use of the properties of electromagnetic waves emitted, reflected or diffracted by the sensed objects, for the purpose of improving natural resources management, land use and the protection of the environment," thereby staying away from discussion of remote sensing data obtained for other purposes, including national security.[8] For the purposes of this chapter, the remote sensing activities discussed here are also limited to those conducted to sense Earth (excluding data gathered by the remote sensing of outer space, except for those data relevant to the Earth environment), but does not necessarily limit itself to data for the specific uses articulated in the Remote Sensing Principles.

While the Remote Sensing Principles are not a treaty and are thus not legally binding in and of themselves,[9] they have contributed to both the development of customary international law and states' practice under the Outer Space Treaty (Aust 2010). While the status of each principle as customary international law and/or an interpretive tool for the Outer Space Treaty in accordance with the custom articulated in Article 31(3) of the Vienna Convention on the law of treaties is not essential to this chapter (Harrington 2017; Zannoni 2019, 155–157; Lyall and Larsen 2024, 344–345),[10] it is worth noting their status as "soft law," though the distinction between hard and soft law is actually not decisive in determining legal character.[11] Soft law is generally viewed as a method to focus consensus, legitimize desired conduct, and create a positive environment for consistency in the relevant state practice (Cheng 1997). Many of the UN Remote Sensing Principles are "merely re-affirmations of existing rules of international law or provisions of existing treaties" (International Law Commission 2004, para. 9).

At the end of the negotiating process, the only (new) substantial benefit for sensed or non-sensing states derived from the UN Remote Sensing Principles is contained in Principle XII, which grants the sensed state data access rights on a nondiscriminatory basis (Cheng 1997), in addition to such reaffirmed rights as nondiscriminatory access to space and full sovereignty over the natural resources of a state, in Principles III and IV, respectively. These are clearer formulations of requirements embedded in Article I of the Outer Space Treaty and discussed earlier. Disclosure of remote sensing programs under the Principles and a specific call to disclose matters that

8 Remote Sensing Principles, see note 7, at Principle I(a).

9 They do not fall into any of the three categories of binding international law articulated in Article 38(1) of the International Court of Justice statute. Statute of the International Court of Justice art 38(1), June 26, 1945, 15 U.S.T. 2494, 33 U.N.T.S. 993.

10 Vienna Convention, see note 5.

11 North Sea Continental Shelf (Ger/Neth;Ger/Den), Judgment, 1969 I.C.J. 3. (February 20).

may be detrimental to the Earth environment and natural disaster information are also useful to all states. Principle XIII requires consultations with a sensed state, but only upon request of the sensed state; this proposition could be tricky in cases where a state is unaware that it is being sensed. In such a case, the state would not know to make such a request (Harrington 2017). The Remote Sensing Principles and subsequent initiatives enabled by them further indicate very widespread support of data sharing for the purposes enshrined therein (Harrington 2017). In particular, Principle XI expressly sets out the protection of mankind from natural disasters as a purpose of remote sensing, and calls upon sensing states to release processed data and analyzed information to states affected by natural disasters or likely to be impacted by impending natural disasters.

One of the most important clarifications, however, found in the Remote Sensing Principles regards the status of data. Principle I(e) provides a definition of the term "remote sensing activities" as "the operation of remote sensing space systems, primary data collection and storage stations, and activities in processing, interpreting and disseminating the processed data." While the Principles themselves are non-binding, this definition provides clear evidence that they believe activities relating to collection, use, and storage of data fall within the scope of remote sensing activities, a covered space activity under the Outer Space Treaty. It may thus be argued that these data management activities are included as part of the national space activities of the state, and thus fall within states' responsibility in accordance with Article VI of the Outer Space Treaty. These activities would also likewise be captured in other relevant sections of the Outer Space Treaty, including the Article I principles as well as the obligation to act with due regard in Article IX. Of course, however, this interpretation would only hold to the extent that its results are not absurd or manifestly unreasonable.[12]

Additional definitions contained in the Remote Sensing Principles are helpful to understanding the nature of EO data in its many forms. Principle I provides definitions for each type of data within the scope of the Principles. These are primary data, processed data, and analyzed information. Primary data is the raw data collected, and though the Principles contemplate film and magnetic tape in addition to digital data transmitted through the radiofrequency spectrum, it is that digital data which is the almost exclusive form in the current day.[13] Processed data results "from the processing of the primary data, needed to make such data usable."[14] And finally analyzed information includes the interpreted data that takes into account other sources of knowledge and information, which can include information produced by human manipulation and analysis of data, information produced by running

[12] For the codification of the relevant customary international law interpretation rule, see Vienna Convention, note 5, at Art. 32(b).

[13] Remote Sensing Principles, see note 7, at Principle 1(b).

[14] Remote Sensing Principles, see note 7, at Principle 1(c).

data through existing software algorithms, and information produced by artificial intelligence analysis of data.[15] These definitions can help to conceptualize the wide variety of data that fall within the scope of this activity, some of which may involve significant human effort after the initial data collection, and some of which may be presented with the inclusion of implicit biases of human analysts and programmers.

7.2.3 *International Charter on Space and Major Disasters*

Under the *Charter on Space and Major Disasters* (hereinafter Disasters Charter), more than a dozen countries have committed space assets since 2000 to the continuing service of warning about and mitigating the effects of disasters (both natural and human-made) (The International Charter Space and Major Disasters n.d.; About the Charter n.d.). Parties to the Charter provide satellite data (processed and unprocessed) free of charge to countries (associated bodies and beneficiary bodies) affected by natural and technological disasters using a single point of contact (Lyall and Larsen 2024, 354–355). The hundreds of activations since its inception indicate a consistent state practice on the part of sensing states to deploying assets and freely share data for the stated purpose (Activation List n.d.). Though the Charter itself is not a legally binding instrument, it acts as *opinio juris*, demonstrating the obligation of states with EO capabilities (or more specifically the agencies within those states) to deploy those capabilities to manage disasters threatening humankind (Activation List n.d., Art. I; Ito 2005, 142).

7.2.4 *United Nations Platform for Space-Based Information for Disaster Management and Emergency Response (UN-SPIDER)*

Following the successful creation and implementation of the Disasters Charter, UN-SPIDER was subsequently created in January 2007, carrying out the agreement established by UN Doc. A/RES/61/110 (U.N., 2007; Lyall and Larsen 2024, 356). The mission of UN-SPIDER is to "Ensure that all countries and international and regional organizations have access to and develop the capacity to use all types of space-based information to support the full disaster management cycle" and is the first such agreement to support the full cycle of disaster management. The creation of UN-SPIDER and its continued activities provide further evidence of state practice in the area of disaster management.

7.2.5 *World Meteorological Organization Resolution 40*

With regard to meteorological data, the World Meteorological Organization (WMO), consisting of 191 member states, has established a policy of sharing of

[15] Remote Sensing Principles, see note 7, at Principle 1(d).

space-based meteorological data since 1995. Resolution 40 (*WMO Policy and Practice for the Exchange of Meteorological and Related Data and Products including Guidelines on Relationships in Commercial Meteorological Activities*) was used to foster sharing, and the WMO has further expanded this policy in a twenty-five-page document providing for the policy, practice, guidelines, and implementation of Resolution 40 (Resolution 40, n.d.).

The practices adopted by Resolution 40 are as follows:

> 1. Members shall provide on a free and unrestricted basis essential data and products which are necessary for the provision of services in support of the protection of life and property and the well-being of all nations, particularly those basic data and products, as, at a minimum, described in Annex 1 to this resolution, required to describe and forecast accurately weather and climate, and support WMO Programmes;
>
> 2. Members should also provide the additional data and products which are required to sustain WMO Programmes at the global, regional, and national levels and, further, as agreed, to assist other Members in the provision of meteorological services in their countries. While increasing the volume of data and products available to all Members by providing these additional data and products, it is understood that WMO Members may be justified in placing conditions on their re-export for commercial purposes outside of the receiving country or group of countries forming a single economic group, for reasons such as national laws or costs of production;
>
> 3. Members should provide to the research and education communities, for their non-commercial activities, free and unrestricted access to all data and products exchanged under the auspices of WMO with the understanding that their commercial activities are subject to the same conditions identified in Adopts (2) above (WMO, n.d.).

If Practice 2 is implemented in such a way that conditions on reexport for commercial purposes do not impinge the rights of sensed states, as established under the Remote Sensing Principles, then this Resolution and subsequent documentation further indicate very widespread support of data sharing for the purposes enshrined therein. Thus, another example of effective "soft law" implementation can be seen. Given the widespread membership of states in WMO, as well as the importance of weather forecasting, Resolution 40 has played an important role in creating a shared knowledge commons for EO data from space-based sources.

7.2.6 *Long-Term Sustainability Guidelines*

In 2018, the UN Committee on the Peaceful Uses of Outer Space adopted the *Guidelines for the Long-Term Sustainability of Outer Space Activities* (hereinafter LTS Guidelines) by consensus (Commission on the Peaceful Uses of Outer Space 2018). While many of these guidelines are focused on issues relating to safety of space operation and minimization of space debris, they do take into account the importance of space activities in achieving the UN Sustainable Development Goals more broadly (Commission on the Peaceful Uses of Outer Space 2018, 1; The 17 Goals, n.d.). Like the Remote Sensing Principles, the LTS Guidelines are nonbinding (Commission on the Peaceful Uses of Outer Space 2018, Section I para. 15). In fact, they contain extensive discussion on their voluntary nature, which was necessary to build consensus for them (Commission on the Peaceful Uses of Outer Space 2018, Section I paras. 16–20).

Two guidelines in particular contain subparts relevant to the governance of EO activities and remote sensing data. Guideline C.3.4 addresses sharing of data for disaster mitigation purposes.

> States and international intergovernmental organizations should also undertake efforts to make relevant space-based information and data accessible to countries affected by natural disasters or other catastrophes, guided by considerations of humanity, neutrality and impartiality, and to support capacity-building activities aimed at enabling the receiving countries to make optimal use of such data and information. These space-based data and information with appropriate spatial and temporal resolution should be freely, quickly and easily available for countries in crisis.

This language continues to reinforce the legally binding data-sharing obligation of Outer Space Treaty Article XI, as well as the benefit principle from Article I. It also reinforces concepts found in the non-legally binding Remote Sensing Principles and Disasters Charter. Though the LTS Guidelines contain specific language indicating that they are not intended to interpret or modify existing international law, they still have value in showing consistent state views on these important matters of data commons.

Within Guideline C.4, both paragraphs 1(a) and 2 likewise address relevant matters, though these are not so specifically focused on data. In paragraph 1(a), states are called upon to "[p]romote institutional and public awareness of space activities and their applications for sustainable development, environmental monitoring and assessment, disaster management and emergency response" (Commission on the Peaceful Uses of Outer Space 2018, Guideline C.4); while in paragraph 2, public awareness and education take the focus:

> States and international intergovernmental organizations should promote public awareness of space applications for sustainable development, environmental monitoring and assessment, disaster management and emergency response through information-sharing and joint efforts with public institutions and non-governmental entities, taking into account the needs of current and future generations. In designing space education programmes, States, international intergovernmental organizations and non-governmental entities should pay special attention to courses on enhancing knowledge and practice of the utilization of space applications to support sustainable development. States and international intergovernmental organizations

> should initiate the voluntary collection of information on public awareness and education tools and programmes with a view to facilitating the development and implementation of other initiatives with similar objectives. (Commission on the Peaceful Uses of Outer Space 2018, Guideline C.4.2)

Though the handling of the data themselves is certainly important, when considering the EO knowledge commons, it is necessary to engage in longer term planning to ensure public support and development of a future geospatial workforce. Importantly, paragraph 2 brings intergenerational equity into account when considering information-sharing efforts. Though not expressly mentioned in the early public international space law instruments such as the Outer Space Treaty, it has become clear that intergenerational equity is taking center stage, largely as a result of the consequences of anthropogenic climate change. Building the future workforce is another tool that can be used towards satisfaction of the benefit principle, in addition to providing substantive benefits to both sustainable development and disaster management. Though they are quite general and not highly technical, the LTS Guidelines contribute to the normative framework through which EO activities and associated data are understood.

7.2.7 *Selected United Nations Efforts Regarding Climate Change*

It is helpful to briefly mention the UN Framework Convention on Climate Change of 1992 (hereinafter Framework Convention) and associated efforts.[16] It seems remarkable that climate change garnered sufficient attention more than thirty years ago to produce the Framework Convention, but yet we are still in the relatively early stages of climate change mitigation. The Framework Convention emphasizes both intergenerational equity and the importance of acting with precaution.[17] Articles 4, 6, 7, 9, 10, and especially 12 all contain elements of information sharing. Article 4 paragraph 1(g) specifically calls for the "development of data archives related to the climate system and intended to further the understanding and to reduce or eliminate the remaining uncertainties regarding the causes, effects, magnitude and timing of climate change and the economic and social consequences of various response strategies," thus creating a specific knowledge commons. Article 5, paragraphs (a) and (b) call for support to further cooperative data sharing and collection efforts. Paragraph (b) promotes "access to, and the exchange of, data and analyses thereof obtained from areas beyond national jurisdiction." Certainly, data collected from space falls expressly within the relevant purview of the Framework Convention, and thus this instrument plays an important role in our knowledge commons.

[16] United Nations Framework Convention on Climate Change, May 9, 1992, 1771 U.N.T.S. 107.

[17] See, e.g., Art. 3.

Within this framework exists the Global Climate Observing System (GCOS) Programme, administered through the WMO (Global Climate Observing System n.d.). There are four main contributors to the satellite network of the programme, namely the Climate Change Initiative of the European Space Agency, the Copernicus Climate Change Service operated on behalf of the European Union, Climate Service EUMETSAT, and Earth Science Division of the US National Aeronautics and Space Administration (GCOS Satellite Programs n.d.). The data from these networks, along with atmospheric, terrestrial, and ocean-based sources are used to measure the Essential Climate Variables to measure climate change. Meanwhile, the Intergovernmental Panel on Climate Change is the UN body charged with assessing climate change-related science, including the data produced by the GCOS Programme (The Intergovernmental Panel on Climate Change n.d.). One only needs to glance at the UN Environment Programme (UNEP) organizational chart to obtain a sense of the scale and complexity of intergovernmental agreements, organizations, and actors within the UNEP system (United Nations n.d.).

7.3 ORGANIZATIONS WITH SPACE DATA SHARING INITIATIVES, A SAMPLING

While some organizations with space data sharing initiatives have been discussed in the context of legal and quasi-legal instruments normalizing space data commons, there are far more groups with various data sets, provided by various actors and for various purposes. This section endeavors to address some of these efforts to provide a sense for how extensive and potentially overlapping space data commons can be.

Though not entirely within the scope of the topic of this chapter, the International Asteroid Warning Network is an interesting example of a data commons using both ground-based and space-based data sources to provide information about outer space (International Asteroid Warning Network n.d.). The data in question specifically addresses naturally occurring Near Earth Objects that could pose a direct threat to Earth and Earth's environment, which is why it is mentioned here.

The UN Development Programme Geographic Information System and Satellite Imagery Team (United Nations Development Programme Pacific Office 2020) works in cooperation with the UN Satellite Centre (UNOSAT) to provide specialized applications and data to countries in need (United Nations Satellite Centre n.d.; United Nations Institute for Training and Research 2019). Within UNOSAT's primary mandate is to "support Member States with satellite imagery analysis over their respective territories and to provide training and capacity development in the use of geospatial information technologies, on the basis of voluntary contributions." Thus, UNOSAT both analyzes and provides data directly while also performing other capacity-building efforts including workforce development. UNOSAT has also partnered with NVIDIA to utilize artificial intelligence in their efforts (United Nations Institute for Training and Research 2022).

Perhaps an unexpected addition to this list, the UN Human Settlements Programme (UN-Habitat) endeavors achieve the goal of providing sustainable and adequate shelter for all people. So where does EO data fit in here (UN-Habitat n.d.)? UN-Habitat maintains the Earth Observation Toolkit for Sustainable Cities and Human Settlements, tied to UN Sustainable Development Goal (SDG) 11 (The Earth Observations Toolkit n.d.). "The primary motivation for this toolkit is to support local communities, cities and countries in understanding the value and usefulness of Earth observations for SDG 11 and the New Urban Agenda and to provide practical guidance and examples of Earth observation data, tools, and use cases in support of sustainable urbanization and resilience" (The Earth Observations Toolkit n.d.). This organization is highlighted as it offers a demonstration that EO data is aggregated, freely shared, and analyzed for purposes beyond weather/climate monitoring and disaster mitigation.

Likewise, the UN Office on Drugs and Crime plays a role in this knowledge commons as well, incorporating data obtained from remote sensing systems into their efforts to combat crime and drug trafficking (United Nations Office on Drugs and Crime n.d.). Space-based data is essential for creating a safer human society in addition to managing the relationship of humans with our natural environment here on Earth. That said, this particular use of data can (reasonably) raise heightened concerns regarding its potential misuse by governmental entities or private bad actors. Privacy concerns are legitimate with the aggregation of any big data and must be considered with regard to human rights and data protection.

The World Health Organization (WHO) Geographic Information Systems (GIS) Centre for Health uses geospatial data to aid in effective and rapid decision-making in human health policy (WHO GIS Centre for Health n.d.). "By connecting maps, apps, data and people the WHO GIS Centre is dedicated to support countries and partners to make informed public health decisions faster and to extend the reach of geospatial information across the organization." Not all countries are currently prepared to integrate GIS data into their public health system, so the services provided by the WHO GIS Centre help to equalize the health opportunities across countries of differing levels of development, a good example of space activities leading to benefit for all humankind.

UN Geospatial is made up of geospatial experts who use data, including EO data obtained from space, in support of all UN missions and mandates (United Nations Geospatial n.d.). Their objective is to improve the effectiveness, efficiency, and universality with which geospatial data is applied to these ends (United Nations Geospatial n.d.). UN Geospatial is embedded in the Office of Information and Communications Technology (United Nations Office of Information and Communications Technology n.d.), which is a key player in the implementation of the Secretary-General's Data Strategy (Secretary-General's Data Strategy n.d.). The Data Strategy seeks to build "a whole-of-UN ecosystem that unlocks our full data potential" (United Nations Secretary n.d.). Implicit in the data strategy is a recognition of the complexity of the UN data gathering, management, and analysis apparatuses, and the inherent inefficiency that can arise among such a tangled web of organizational structures. At a fundamental level, the Data Strategy can be seen as a streamlining effort. The UN Global Service Centre (UNGSC) of the Department of Operational Support also plays a significant role in GIS through the UNGSC Service for Geospatial, Information, and Telecommunications Technologies (ITT), which "provides a direct single point of contact for digital technology services and solutions" (Geospatial, Information and Telecommunications Technologies n.d.; United Nations Global Service Centre n.d.).

The Group on Earth Observations (GEO) and its Global Earth Observation System of Systems (GEOSS) play a vital role in the coordination and dissemination of the space-based environmental data commons (About GEOSS, n.d.). The participation of 152 partnering organizations, including intergovernmental, international, nongovernmental, and regional partners operating in EO and related spaces goes a long way to ensuring availability of data across these platforms and venues for sharing. The simple fact however, that there are indeed 152 of these organizations, which are inherently international groups, demonstrates the significant fragmentation of laudable efforts for sharing data. While many of the relevant groups are mentioned in this chapter for illustrative purposes, it is certainly not feasible to include description of all 152 organizations here.

UN Global Pulse, which is notably not a partner or GEOSS, identifies as itself as the innovation lab for the UN Secretary-General (United Nations Global Pulse n.d.). This office includes data and digital tools in its innovation portfolio, but its endeavors are far broader than just EO. UN Global Pulse may be an ideal place to continue to work on the problem, in cooperation with GEO, to simplify access to, tracking of, and analysis of EO data acquired from space-based sources.

7.4 OPPORTUNITIES, ISSUES, AND RECOMMENDATIONS

7.4.1 *Opportunities*

Many positive developments can be seen in the use of data obtained from space to better environmental conditions and human life on Earth. The UN SDGs, in particular, have catalyzed use of space data to achieve their goals (Commission on the Peaceful Uses of Outer Space 2018, 1; The 17 Goals n.d.). The global nature of the SDGs requires a global data collection and management strategy. There is now wide availability of commercial data, much of it offered free of charge and with additional processing or analytical services provided. While the increasing incidence of natural and human-made disasters is, of course, tragic, their escalating pace and severity has raised awareness of the importance of working together. After all, no state is isolated from the possibility of such disasters, and the state that is a provider of data and services today may be the recipient of such when it inevitably faces one or more disasters in the future. Tragedy, while unfortunate, does bring people together to work for the common good.

Numerous efforts are aimed at capacity building, and not just providing data and analysis. While the proverb "give a man a fish, and he eats today; teach a man to fish and he eats for the rest of his life" is true, perhaps the better formulation is "give a man a fish today and then teach him how to fish, so he isn't hungry today and is ready to learn the skills he needs for the rest of his life." In terms of data from space, there has been clear effort to provide the initial fish, but also the fishing skills and equipment. Such capacity-building efforts contribute positively to data compatibility, as downstream experts and users will already be trained to produce data in a format that is more universally usable.

7.4.2 *Issues*

Despite, or perhaps because of, best efforts, the complexity of the data sharing environment is dizzying. It is possible to get lost in the array of arrangements and organizations who are standing by to provide data and/or analysis for a range of problems and under a variety of circumstances. These efforts have led to a fragmentation of data sharing, wherein dozens of organizations may be implicated in any one circumstance. The end user in need of data needs to be aware of where and how to obtain what they need. Smaller countries with lower budgets may struggle to allocate personnel who are prepared to navigate these complex systems. Technical challenges abound. "Developments of sensing observations and producing information from it need to be accompanied by suitable storage, processing and retrieval systems" (Sudmanns et al. 2020, 844). The specific technical challenges regarding both hardware- and web-based systems are broadly beyond the scope of this chapter.

Though there is widespread agreement that states should help each other to mitigate disasters, forecast weather, and model climate change, geopolitical tension and security implications can and do still get in the way. Export controls are applied to satellite remote sensing technologies, making technology transfer and cooperation more difficult. Countries have a patchwork of laws governing the capture of EO data from space, limiting resolution either universally or in certain geographic areas and designating sensitive security zones for which images are often not legally available. These challenges arise even when all parties enter a situation in good faith and with the best intentions. Data just might not be available. Additionally, domestic legal systems may provide personal or institutional penalties for those who share technology or data in violation of these security rules, even if they do so unknowingly.

International competition and conflict have led to the breakdown of international cooperation. Mistrust is rampant, and states have less faith in international law to mitigate risks in the international system. Thus, political will for new treaties and even (to some extent) new soft law instruments has evaporated, allowing our international normative system to stagnate. Likewise, contentious domestic politics in many states have all but precluded the possibility of new treaty ratification, and even make the prospect of new domestic legislation difficult.

It would be unfair, however, to place all the blame on politics, governments, or intergovernmental complexity for these challenges. Proprietary commercial data can also serve as a roadblock to obtaining data that exists, but that is not available. Privatizing EO operations permits commercial control of data in general. Commercial companies do not inherently have the same incentives to share data as governments do, as owners or shareholders expect their companies to turn a profit. While making some data freely available is feasible, contributes to goodwill, and in some cases can lead to lucrative government contracts, there will always be a limit on what private companies will release for nothing, and how low their prices can be for data that is not freely given. After all, even the Remote Sensing Principles endeavor to set up a system where data are provided to sensed states on "reasonable cost terms."[18] Even weather forecasting is increasingly being carried out by private companies (Cirac-Claveras 2019).

Of course, a lack of public awareness of the role space plays in day-to-day life and the benefits space has provided, increasing quality of life around the globe. Increasingly people, especially young people, push back on the value of "space exploration" – lacking an understanding of what a domestic space budget provides (Ramani 2023). Growing governmental domestic EO capabilities, or even the capacity for budgets to purchase EO data, can become challenging when constituencies do not understand the value of funding. The problem is exacerbated when such constituencies see space as an active detractor, a contributor to climate change rather than a set of activities and technologies that can significantly improve our ability to manage climate change as a species.

7.4.3 *Recommendations*

This chapter provides three key recommendations with regard to the management of the EO environmental data commons. First, public communication strategies need to be developed and implemented specifically with a focus on the benefits of EO data provided from space. The images offered by Maxar in the news following Russia's invasion of Ukraine hinted at the usefulness of this data being available (SatNews 2022). The myriad other uses of data and imagery need to be made clear. The likelihood that the average person knows that space data can improve crop yields, map efficient routes, and contribute significantly to sustainable urban housing solutions is quite low. While maybe somewhat higher, it is likely that many people are either unaware or take for granted the extent to which weather forecasting and climate data is obtained from space. These communications campaigns can come from intergovernmental, nongovernmental, public, and private organizations, but should include a common message: Data from space are highly beneficial, especially when those data can be aggregated and shared.

[18] Remote Sensing Principles, see note 21, at Principle XII.

Such a communications strategy would not only ease the path for space-related budget allocation, but (arguably) even more importantly, would pave the way for the next generation to prepare themselves to undertake careers in systems engineering, software development, and geographic information system applications. Without a sufficiently developed workforce of tomorrow, humanity cannot expect to continue to reap the benefits of the technologies we have developed. "The sheer amount of multi-dimensional and multi-temporal data, interdisciplinary research, and the dynamics of new developments, in general, makes sharing results, algorithms and knowledge between the experts of different fields and non-expert users essential" (Sudmanns et al. 2020, 842). Thus, actual sharing of results should factor prominently in any communications campaign.

Of course, ensuring that capacity-building efforts take interoperability into account is essential, as is the continued organization and streamlining of international efforts for data sharing, primarily facilitated at the UN level and through GEOS. Capacity building efforts must likewise recognize that not all data are equal – a workforce needs to be prepared to manage raw, processed, and analyzed data, respectively. In particular, enlisting the efforts of UN Global Pulse in achieving these objectives, in line with the existing Secretary-General's Data Strategy, is likely to prove highly beneficial. While some states may challenge the status of space as a global commons, it seems more difficult and less worthwhile to challenge the idea that data about our planet constitute a knowledge commons from which all of humanity should benefit (where feasible and practicable).

PART IV

8

The Prospects for Green Patent Commons

Jorge L. Contreras

8.1 INTRODUCTION

This chapter considers whether, and under what conditions, private firms can productively combine existing patent assets to support the dissemination and use of green technology around the world.

The patenting of technologies directed to renewable energy, climate change mitigation, pollution control, and the like – green technology (Sanguir 2023a, 214–215; Iaia 2024, 310–312) – presents a paradox: On the one hand, proponents of the patent system argue that patents are necessary to incentivize innovation in these critical technological areas (Dechezleprêtre 2013; Gallari 2013; Tee et al. 2021; Sanguir 2023a), while on the other hand, critics claim that patents can impede the broad development, deployment, and usage of these technologies (Reichman et al. 2008; Sovacool 2008; Ouellette 2010; Sarnoff 2011; Chavez 2015). Given the high stakes involved and the pressing need for technological solutions to the climate crisis, a range of proposals have been made to promote more and better green technology development, deployment, and usage.

Accordingly, patent offices around the world have adopted "fast track" procedures designed to facilitate the examination of green technology patent applications and to reduce fees and procedural barriers to obtaining these patents (Dechezleprêtre 2013; Siemons 2023; Rodrigues Pinho and Oliviera 2024). These programs have seemingly succeeded in increasing the number of patents issued in these jurisdictions (Dechezleprêtre 2013; Chavez 2015; Mewburn Ellis 2021; Siemons 2023; Rodrigues Pinho and Oliviera 2024), though perhaps not at the rates expected or desired (Hilty and Batista 2024). At the same time, numerous proposals have been made to reduce the impact of such patents on relevant markets through mechanisms such as compulsory licensing (Reichman et al. 2008; Chavez 2015), the governmental march-in rights (Sarnoff 2011, 2013; Ouellette 2010), expanded exemptions from patent infringement for research and experimental use (Reynolds, Contreras, and Sarnoff 2017), legal constraints on exclusive licensing (Sarnoff 2011), and statutory patentability exclusions for some key green technologies (Parthasarathy et al. 2010), as well as for highly polluting inventions (Iaia 2024, 318–320). Finally, a growing number of scholars and commentators have concluded that patents, while important in other technology sectors, may play a limited role in incentivizing necessary green technology innovation, and that governments should focus instead on alternative incentive programs to promote the development and deployment of these key technologies (Derclaye 2010; McManis and Contreras 2014; Vandenberg 2015; Tur-Sinai 2018; Hilty and Batista 2024).

Nevertheless, patents exist and, as noted earlier, an increasing number continue to be granted in the green technology sector. Accordingly, alongside proposed changes to the scope and availability of patent protection, a range of international initiatives have emerged to promote the dissemination and sharing of green technology within the framework of existing patent systems. Bodies promoting these alternative approaches include the United Nations Framework Convention on Climate Change (UNFCCC) Conference of the Parties, the Clean Development Mechanism under the Kyoto Protocol to the UNFCCC, the Climate Technology Center and Network under the UNFCCC Technology Mechanism, the Green Climate Fund (GCF) under the UNFCCC Financial Mechanism, and the Paris Agreement Technology Framework (Xiang 2019, 13–16). While these international and intergovernmental efforts have promise, each depends on action by government agencies, legislatures, or international bodies. As such, they remain subject to political vagaries (Miller and Dills 2023) that create inherent uncertainty and risk. Moreover, given differences between the market structures, development costs, and deployment practicalities of green technologies and other patented products such as pharmaceuticals and electronics, it is not clear that governmental intervention modeled on experiences with these other market sectors can readily be translated to green technology (McManis and Contreras 2014, 127–130). This chapter considers, instead, whether nongovernmental private actors can impact climate mitigation and remediation through the voluntary formation of patent commons in the green technology sector.

Other chapters in this book have demonstrated the viability of knowledge commons to aggregate and make information relating to green technology broadly available. Patents, too, embody information, and some have proposed that greater information transparency regarding existing patent rights could facilitate the development of green technology (Cahoy and Glenna 2009). Yet patents, unlike other informational assets, also embody a bundle of legal rights that enable their holders to exclude competitors from the market. As such, the sharing of patent information alone, while sometimes useful from a technical standpoint (Seymour 2010), will not enable greater product development or usage. In order for patent rights to be shared, licensing or transfer transactions must be completed by patent holders (Cahoy and Glenna 2009; Sanguir 2023b). When multiple patents in a field are held by different parties, then effecting all transactions needed to enable desired development and distribution activity may be cumbersome, time-consuming, and costly. This reality has attracted some patent holders to the idea of patent pools or commons that offer users limited rights to practice patented technologies within an existing landscape of patent laws and large numbers of issued patents.

Patent commons have achieved significant success in other market sectors. For example, the developers of technical interoperability standards such as USB, Bluetooth, IPv6, and HTML have largely agreed not to assert their patents against parties making products that embody those standards (Contreras et al. 2023). These "royalty-free" standards are broadly deployed and form the basis for the internet and other ubiquitous technologies. Likewise, over twenty years ago, large patent holders pledged not to assert their patents against open-source software such as the Linux operating system, laying the groundwork for the broad adoption of that software around the world (Contreras 2015).

Yet while multiparty green patent sharing arrangements have been formed to advance commercial ventures and projects (Sanguir 2023b), organizers have had little success in forming publicly available, royalty-free patent commons for green technology. The limited success of green patent commons in the face of successful patent-sharing arrangements in other sectors thus presents a puzzle.

This chapter considers the unique challenges that face the organizers of private patent commons in the green technology sector. To do so, it first reviews prior efforts to form green patent commons, as well as recent commons proposals that have not yet been implemented. Next, it asks why these efforts have not been successful in achieving their respective goals. Finally, it offers suggestions for future planners seeking to promote the global dissemination and use of patented green technologies through the formation of commons structures.

8.2 PRIOR ATTEMPTS TO FORM GREEN PATENT COMMONS

Unlike commercial patent sharing arrangements in the green technology and other industry sectors, the green patent commons described in this section appear to have been formed by patent holders largely to advance "mission-oriented" goals such as corporate social responsibility, philanthropy, and employee relations (Mattioli 2012; Contreras 2015; Contreras 2018b). The implications of this not-for-profit orientation are discussed later.

8.2.1 *Eco-Patent Commons*

In 2008, IBM announced the launch of the Eco-Patent Commons, an effort that was cosponsored by Nokia, Pitney Bowes, and Sony and eventually included thirteen large firms (Contreras et al. 2019). The stated mission of EcoPatent Commons was "to manage a collection of patents pledged for unencumbered use by companies and IP rights holders around the world to make it easier and faster to innovate and implement industrial processes that improve and protect the global environment"

(Contreras et al. 2019). A total of 248 patents were pledged to the EcoPatent Commons, with the last such contribution occurring in 2011. In 2016, after an extended period of inactivity, the EcoPatent Commons was formally discontinued. Subsequent analysis of the citations of the patents contributed to the EcoPatent Commons suggests that the effort did little to increase the diffusion of the technology covered by contributed patents (Contreras et al. 2019).

8.2.2 *GreenXchange*

The GreenXchange was launched in 2010 as a web-based marketplace through which firms could notify others of patent rights that they wished to make available for licensing on a set of standardized terms. The principal backer of GreenXchange was Nike, which contributed the lion's share of patents to the platform (444 of 463 patents, or 96 percent) (Ghafele and O'Brien 2012). Despite the involvement of nine other entities, few contributed patents to the platform, and most of the contributed patents were licensed only for noncommercial use. The project appears to have wound down within two years of its launch (Xiang 2019, 40–41).

8.2.3 *Low Carbon Patent Pledge*

The Low Carbon Patent Pledge (LCPP) is a legal framework that enables patent holders to commit not to assert identified patents relating to carbon reduction against users throughout the world.[1] The project, based on the 2020 Open Covid Pledge (OCP) (Contreras 2021), was initiated by three OCP members, Hewlett-Packard Enterprise (HPE), Meta and Microsoft, and now includes a number of other contributors, including Morgan Stanley and international shipping giant Maersk. The LCPP enables the free use of contributed patents via a self-executing license. Approximately 300 patents have been contributed to LCPP (lowcarbonpatentpledge.org).

8.2.4 *Tesla Motors Pledge*

Unlike the other efforts described in this section, which involve cooperation among a number of industrial players, the CEO of Tesla Motors unilaterally announced in 2014 that Tesla would no longer assert patents against other electric vehicle manufacturers acting in "good faith." While this move was followed six months later by Toyota, which similarly pledged its patents in the area of hydrogen fuel cell technology, other car makers failed to join the effort (Contreras 2015). In 2023, Tesla asserted

[1] The author was involved in the planning and operation of the LCPP on a volunteer, uncompensated basis.

two patents relating to energy storage technology against an Australian firm that had previously sued Tesla under its own patents (Contreras 2025).

8.2.5 *WIPO Green*

WIPO Green, operated by the UN-based World Intellectual Property Organization (WIPO), is not itself a private-sector initiative or a commons, but is considered here because it is intended to facilitate private commons formation. WIPO Green is essentially a clearinghouse for green patents, know-how, and other technology that their owners wish to sell or license, usually for a fee. The online resource can be searched by technology category or field, and also enables potential users of a technology to post technical needs or requirements to which technology owners can respond. Though WIPO Green has been operational since 2013, it is not clear that a substantial number of transactions have been effected using the platform, and commentators have suggested several improvements (Xiang 2019; Sanguir 2023b, 270).

8.2.6 *Other Proposals*

In addition to the efforts described here, several other proposals have been made to aggregate green technology patents for broad dissemination and use around the world. These include the Global Technology Pool for Climate Change, proposed in 2009 by a group of developing countries, which would promote and ensure royalty-free access to patented technology and associated know-how (Xiang 2019, 38), and a cleantech patent pool proposed to be formed under the auspices of the UNFCCC GCF, which would itself develop and acquire patented technologies for use and dissemination in developing countries (Xiang 2019, 38). Maitra has made a similar proposal involving the subsidy of technology acquisition in developing countries through two international funds (Maitra 2010). None of these proposals has gained significant traction.

Likewise, a group of academics has proposed that a commons be formed around solar climate engineering (SCE) technology to facilitate responsible SCE research and development. The proposed commons would permit public and private sector research institutions to share their research data and pledge that any patents or trade secrets would be managed so as to reduce unnecessary barriers to research and development of safe and effective SCE technologies (Reynolds et al. 2017). While this proposal has not yet been put into effect, there has not yet been significant assertion of patents in the SCE research community.

8.3 CHALLENGES FOR GREEN PATENT COMMONS

As noted, the few green technology patent commons that have been launched have had limited success in terms of both inbound participation (number of patent contributions) and outbound impact (use of contributed technologies in the field). This section analyzes some of the factors that have proven most challenging for the planners of green patent commons as contrasted with more successful commons in, for example, the information and communications technology (ICT) sector.[2]

8.3.1 *Attracting Patent Contributors*

Participation in green patent commons, as defined in this chapter, will generally not result in a direct financial benefit to participants. That is, participants will not charge royalties or other amounts for the use of their patents. Yet, given that patents are potentially valuable corporate assets that require the expenditure of resources, both financial and personnel, to acquire, some justification for relinquishing patent rights is required. The benefits that private firms obtain from participation in green patent commons are largely indirect: enhancement of public image and reputation, pursuit of corporate social responsibility goals, improved employee relations, government relations, and the opportunity to collaborate with other like-minded firms (Contreras 2018b). But while these factors may enhance a firm's value, they are not likely to outweigh financial gains that might be reduced by forgoing patent-related revenue in industries that are heavily dependent on such revenue (e.g., pharmaceuticals) (Contreras 2021, 898–899).

While a patent commons need not include all patents in a given technology area, it is most useful if it contains at least a critical mass of patents such that the collective availability of these patents encourages use of the patented technology in the field. Most of the commons formation efforts described earlier originated with one or a small group of firms: EcoPatent Commons with IBM, GreenXchange with Nike, and LPCC with HPE, Microsoft, and Meta. While an early champion and convenor of every commons project is likely necessary, such projects seem to require more general industry backing in order to succeed. Both EcoPatent Commons and GreenXchange attracted around ten participating members, which seems to have been too few to be sustainable.

8.3.2 *Funding*

Adequate funding is key to any project. But as already noted, most of the green technology commons projects described in this chapter were motivated by corporate mission-oriented goals rather than commercial considerations. As a result, several of these, the EcoPatent Commons in particular, suffered from a lack of sustained financial support (Contreras et al. 2019). This lack of resources prevented

[2] It is worth noting that green technology is not the only field in which years of effort have failed to produce widely used patent commons. The same is true in the biotechnology sector for reasons that may differ somewhat from those discussed in this chapter (Contreras 2018a).

the effort from continuing to recruit new members, seeking users for its technology, and tracking usage of contributed patents. WIPO Green, on the other hand, is a relatively well-funded effort with significant staffing and backing from the UN. As such, it has engaged in various outreach efforts and has a sophisticated and comprehensive online presence. Mattioli (2012, 148–149, 155) suggests that governmental support may be necessary for patent-sharing activities to succeed, an observation that may be borne out by the apparent unwillingness of private actors to spend significant amounts in support of commons formation that is largely motivated by mission-oriented goals.

8.3.3 *Scope*

Unlike technical standards such as Bluetooth or even more general ICT fields such as broadband wireless communication, the field of green technology is intractably broad. Green technology includes technologies ranging from massive infrastructural projects such as wind turbines, nuclear power stations, underwater server farms, and water treatment plants to complex manufactured products such as solar panels, electric batteries, and smart electric meters to sustainable agricultural products, building materials, carbon capture and sequestration methods, environmentally friendly personal care products, and thousands of others.

As such, general calls for the contribution of green technology patents invariably result in a hodgepodge of different and unrelated technologies that lack any coherent connection or useful synergy. For example, patents eligible for inclusion in the EcoPatent Commons could belong to any of sixty enumerated International Patent Classification codes relating to environmental or sustainability technology and including energy conservation, pollution control, sustainable materials, water conservation, and recyclability technologies (Contreras et al. 2019). WIPO Green is similarly broad in scope. The GreenXchange, led by Nike, was slightly more focused on concerns of the consumer products industry, including packaging, recycling, adhesives, "green leather," and manufacturing efficiency (Ghafele and O'Brien 2012, 8). The most focused effort, though it has largely remained a single-company program, has been Tesla's pledge of patents in the electric vehicle industry.

8.3.4 *Usage Tracking*

The key measure of a commons' success is whether its assets are put to productive use by the target user base. Thus, whether it is a technical standard, an open source software program or a green technology, the contribution of rights covering such a technology is pointless if others do not utilize the invention. Yet because most commons do not, and cannot, track usage of their included assets, it is nearly impossible for them to assess their impact on the industry.

Contreras, Hall, and Helmers, in studying the EcoPatent Commons, found few citations of contributed patents in later patents (Contreras et al. 2019). And while counting patent citations is only a crude and indirect means for measuring the adoption and use of a technology, no other obvious indicia of usage present themselves in most of the green commons to date. Even WIPO Green, which allows users to indicate their usage of a technology licensed through the platform, offers little evidence of such usage.

The lack of usage tracking presents a critical problem for firms that wish to justify their participation in a commons program by pointing to some positive result of the program. Without this evidence of impact, commons efforts can be criticized as mere public relations stunts or "greenwashing."

8.3.5 *Technology Transfer*

In some technology sectors, obtaining patent "freedom to operate" is important to technology dissemination and a commons offering such freedom to market participants can provide significant value (e.g., in the computing sector, the royalty-free USB standard can be implemented by all manufacturers with relative ease, and the lack of patent coverage eliminates barriers toward its adoption). Yet in other areas, such as vaccine and pharmaceutical production, it has become increasingly clear that the grant of patent rights alone is insufficient to promote the dissemination and use of a technology (Price et al. 2020). Complex technologies often cannot be understood and implemented, especially by nonexperts working in the developing world, merely through patent disclosures. Instead, some form of technology assistance or transfer is necessary to enable local users to take advantage of patented technologies, or even to realize that such technologies are available and applicable to local problems. This is especially the case with complex engineering and infrastructural technologies, many of which are not patented in low-income countries, but which are still difficult to implement without significant technical expertise. Yet few of the patent commons discussed earlier made allowance of the transfer of nonpatent know-how or encouraged their participants to offer hands-on training or technical assistance to potential users.

8.3.6 *Localization*

As Xiang has pointed out, "cleantech needs to be adapted to local circumstances" (Xiang 2019, 9). It often cannot simply be ported in the form conceived in a wealthy industrialized country to a country that lacks the same infrastructure and resources. As such, contributions of patent rights to a commons may have little direct relevance to users in much of the world absent specific and careful attention to local implementation needs and capabilities.

8.4 SUMMARY

As shown in this section, private efforts at commons formation require a compelling story regarding the value that can be created through a commons approach. While private firms have proven willing to contribute valuable patent assets to commons, their willingness to do so is often conditioned on being able to discern some positive impact of that contribution down the road. Yet without formal tracking mechanisms, it is difficult to determine the use of patented technologies in the field. Moreover, take-up of patented technologies, particularly in the global south, is hindered by a lack of accompanying technical assistance and know-how transfer. For all of these reasons, the effectiveness of prior green patent commons has been limited.

8.5 RECOMMENDATIONS FOR COMMONS FORMATION

If private sector actors wish to create or contribute to green patent commons in the future, there may be ways to improve their prospects for success. A few suggestions in this regard are listed next. It is important to note at the outset, though, that many of these suggested actions can only be undertaken with adequate funding. Thus, planners should identify sources of funding, whether governmental, philanthropic, or member-based, to support these activities for at least several years.

8.5.1 *Narrow Technical Focus*

As noted, the field of green technology is dauntingly broad. As a result, green patent commons that have been open to participation by a broad range of patent holders have attracted diverse and unrelated patent assets (Contreras et al. 2019). This lack of focus has limited the value of such efforts (Mattioli 2012, 155). As a result, a new green patent commons should have a narrow technical focus limited to no more than a single, well-defined product category (e.g., electric vehicles, sustainable concrete, low-power computing centers). While a narrow focus may limit the number of participants that eventually contribute assets to the commons, it is more likely that contributed assets will represent a meaningful portion of the patents covering the technology in question, thus making the commons a valuable resource for potential users.

The initial promoters of a new green patent commons must select its technical focus. If the promoters are from a single industry (e.g., the automotive industry), then it is likely that they will gravitate toward a focus that overlays on their own patent holdings. If, however, the initial promoters are not industrial participants (e.g., academic or governmental players), then they may wish to target the technical focus based on areas of perceived need or demand. For example, if their concern is with water supply, they may wish to focus the commons on water desalination and purification technology, or perhaps low-flow plumbing fixtures or efficient irrigation technologies. In all cases, commons planners should consider the factors raised in the following section prior to finalizing their choice of the commons technology focus.

8.5.2 *Patent Landscaping*

With a proposed technical focus in mind, commons planners would be well advised to determine the level of patent protection that exists for the chosen technology. A patent landscaping exercise, which can be accomplished via one of several different commercial service providers, identifies the patent coverage for a particular technology across a range of selected jurisdictions. A landscaping exercise can help to identify (a) the number of patents relevant to the technology, (b) the geographic scope of protection, and (c) the specific entities holding these patents. Each of these types of information can be valuable at the planning stages of a commons. For example, if a particular technology such as wireless communication capabilities for smart meters is covered by a large number of patents, while a different, yet similarly valuable technology, such as smart meter tamper-proofing, is covered by only a few patents, then it may be worthwhile to focus on the technology that has lesser (or greater) patent coverage, depending on the resources that will be at the commons' disposal. Likewise, the geographic profile of patent coverage can shape commons strategy. For example, if a technology is protected largely in Western high-income countries, then an approach that seeks to disseminate that technology in the global south through knowledge transfer and technical assistance could be fruitful. Finally, knowing how many and which entities own the patents covering a technology can be extremely useful. For example, a technology covered by patents held by a small number of governmental agencies could be approached in a different manner than a technology covered by patents held by dozens of private firms. For example, in one recent study, researchers found that the vast majority of Indian patents covering smartphone technology were held by a handful of foreign firms well known for aggressively monetizing their patent portfolios (Contreras and Lakshané 2017). Pursuing a commons in this technology space and geography would likely have been fruitless.

8.5.3 *Targeted Recruitment*

As shown by the examples of the EcoPatent Commons and other green patent commons, a general solicitation for participation, unless backed by a significant and well-funded recruitment program, is not likely to result in significant growth of the commons. However, the patent landscaping exercise described in the preceding section can identify individual patent holders that can be approached regarding participation in a commons effort. Such an approach can emphasize the potential benefits that a firm can obtain from participation in the commons including, in addition to the "soft" factors discussed in "Contribution of Patents," the potential to sell related products or services (a common motivation for royalty-free patent pledges in other industries (Contreras 2015).

8.5.4 *Guaranteeing Freedom to Operate*

Both GreenXchange and WIPO Green permitted patent holders to charge users to operate under contributed patents in certain cases, such as commercial use. The possibility of such charges is likely to reduce overall uptake of patented technology. As the designers of the Open Covid Pledge concluded in 2020, the greatest uptake of a pledged or contributed technology is likely to occur when the technology is made available without charge, as this guarantees that the user will have freedom to operate, at least with respect to the contributed patents (Contreras 2021, 861–862).[3] Thus, rather than leave open the possibility of direct monetization of contributed patents, patent holders should seek compensation, direct or indirect, via the means described in the preceding section.

8.5.5 *Technology Transfer and Assistance*

As noted earlier, one of the key drawbacks of prior green patent commons was their lack of know-how transfer and technical assistance, and it is likely that assistance from patent holders would increase dissemination and use of contributed technology. However, unlike the contribution of patent rights to a commons, which is a legal action that, once effected, requires little human intervention, technical assistance is a resource-intensive activity that imposes ongoing costs on the provider. As such, such assistance is unlikely to be provided unless (a) the patent holder is willing to commit significant financial and human resources to technical assistance, potentially detracting from its own research and development efforts, (b) the patent holder is compensated for the provision of technical assistance, either by the recipient (which is unlikely) or by a third party (e.g., a foundation interested in promoting green technology dissemination), or (c) such technical assistance is provided by a third party such as the foundation noted earlier. Planners of a commons should carefully consider and seek the support necessary to provide technical assistance under one of these models if the relevant technology requires such assistance in order to be most useful in the target market(s).

[3] Even royalty-free pledges may permit the patent holder to suspend its license and assert its patents against a licensee that has itself sued or threatened the patent holder (so-called defensive suspension) (Contreras 2021, 886–887).

8.5.6 *User Outreach*

Just as targeting potential contributors to a green patent commons is important, so is the thoughtful targeting of potential users. Commons planners should identify potential users, or classes of users, when selecting the technical focus of the commons. One clear group of potential users is the holders of patents identified through the landscaping exercise suggested earlier. These are firms that have already invested in the development and protection of the technology in question and are likely to benefit from increased freedom to operate in the relevant technical field. Beyond patent holders are firms active in providing products or services in the technical field, but which rely on others to source the relevant technology. Beyond these (particularly in the developing world) are firms, governments, and nongovernmental organizations that have missions relevant to the technology field but may not yet be active in it. All of these prospective users should be identified and contacted, with an offer of technical assistance, by commons organizers or their designees.

8.5.7 *User Tracing*

As noted, a key deficiency of the EcoPatent Commons and other green patent commons has been their inability to trace the usage of contributed assets, or even to assess definitively whether such assets have been used at all. This lack of usage data has deterred firms from participating in patent commons, as they have little basis on which to assess the value of the activity. There are several ways that usage tracking can be improved. First, if know-how transfer and technical assistance are more closely linked to patent usage, then identifying potential technology users will be substantially easier, as the recipients of such assistance can be observed. But even without technical outreach, contributors can monitor the industry for evidence that patented technologies are being put to active use. Such monitoring will be made substantially easier if the technical focus of green patent commons is narrowed, per the suggestions made here, rather than broadly open-ended, as prior commons have been (i.e., it is easier to monitor developments and product introductions in a narrow field than a broad one). In all cases, commons organizers should either dedicate sufficient internal resources to user identification or contract with a reliable and dedicated third party, such as an academic or nonprofit research group, to undertake this activity over a sufficient number of years following the contribution of assets.

8.6 CONCLUSION

Private green patent commons have the potential to facilitate the broad dissemination and usage of green and clean technologies worldwide. While prior commons formation efforts in the green technology space have not been broadly successful, they offer several lessons that can be used to improve planning and execution of future commons efforts. In particular, a narrow technical focus, accompanied by patent landscaping and with targeted recruitment of patent holders has the potential to increase participation in selected technical fields, while thoughtful identification of, and outreach to, potential users of the contributed technology can improve its chances of broad dissemination and use.

9

The IPCC as Expert Knowledge Commons

Michael J. Madison

9.1 INTRODUCTION

"Knowledge commons" describes a research framework aimed at characterizing and understanding processes of governing knowledge and information shared in collective or community settings. The rhetoric of commons is often linked to the intuition that knowledge commons is, or ought to be, associated with inclusive and collaborative knowledge production and distribution. This chapter describes and builds on the opposite intuition, that knowledge commons governance may be associated with the construction of expertise and expert authority, which is to say, governance of a sort of collective epistemological exclusivity. It offers a brief review of the Intergovernmental Panel on Climate Change (IPCC), as an illustration of what the chapter refers to as expert knowledge commons.

The IPCC was established in 1988 as an intergovernmental body of the United Nations, charged with advancing scientific knowledge about climate change in order to inform public policy decision-making. As an institution and instrument of authority grounded in scientific expertise, the IPCC has come to play a critical role in advancing political, cultural, and economic awareness of the character of climate change. The IPCC has been the subject of a great deal of research, none of which has focused directly on the manner in which its authoritative status rests both formally and informally on multiple layers of shared knowledge, information, and data. Examining the IPCC as expert knowledge commons highlights the essential role that knowledge commons analysis plays in understanding intersections between knowledge governance and scientific expertise both generally and with respect to environmental policy and the applications of climate science specifically.

The chapter is organized as follows. Section 9.2 describes the Governing Knowledge Commons (GKC) research framework and earlier GKC studies connecting it to expert scientific knowledge and to expertise and authority generally. Section 9.3 describes a model of expert knowledge commons inferred from the GKC case studies summarized in Section 9.2 and links that model to key research on the character of expertise and authority. Section 9.4 illustrates the model with a brief review of the IPCC as expert knowledge commons. The GKC research framework is deployed not as a device for a full-fledged case study of the IPCC as knowledge commons but instead as a means of drawing out elements of the IPCC, and earlier research on the IPCC, that can be productively characterized in knowledge commons terms. Section 9.5 concludes with some implications and suggestions for further research.

9.2 GOVERNING KNOWLEDGE COMMONS AND THE INSTITUTIONS OF EXPERTISE

GKC research has previously addressed knowledge commons governance in the context of scientific knowledge. This section extracts key elements of that earlier research in order to direct attention to the uses of the GKC framework in understanding institutions of expertise and authority themselves.

9.2.1 *The Elements of the GKC Framework*

The GKC research framework is used to capture key elements of governance contexts involving (i) knowledge, information, and data resources that are (ii) shared within or by a community or collective, and (iii) subject to social dilemmas (Frischmann et al. 2014). "Commons" and "knowledge commons" are, in this framing, labels that attach to the governance strategies used to respond to those dilemmas rather than to the resource(s) or to the community/ies involved. Full open access, sometimes associated with the public domain in intellectual property law, is a governance strategy that partly solves social dilemmas associated with next-generation innovators needing access to earlier technological inventions. (The public domain, in short, is not "a commons.") Open source licenses for computer software are governance strategies that solve a dilemma associated with software developers to coordinate with one another in building complex computer programs. The GKC framework is described in the Introduction to this volume.

The pairing of shared knowledge resources and institutional context stands in contrast to a typical focus in the history of ideas and the progress of knowledge on individual contributions by individual thinkers, inventors, creators, and practitioners. Conventionally, where knowledge or information is treated as a pooled resource, it is often characterized in both cultural and legal senses as "open" or "public." The GKC perspective navigates between those two poles, by observing that individual actors are characteristically operating in important communal or collective contexts, and that even "open" or "public" information either poses or responds to social dilemmas.

The term "commons" offers only a modest amount of normative or categorical guidance, aside from aligning the framework with the earlier work of Elinor Ostrom describing commons governance largely with respect to natural or biophysical resources (Ostrom 2005). Instead, the key contribution of the GKC framework is its focus on the production and distribution of shared (often pooled) information and knowledge resources in their institutional settings. Whether or not a case study of knowledge commons is directed to a "commons" as opposed to "a corporation" or "a clearinghouse" or some other institutional setting is far less significant than whether the analytic framework offered by GKC research contributes significantly to understanding institutional dynamics (Madison 2024).

9.2.2 *GKC Case Studies Addressing the Origins of Expertise*

GKC research has proceeded to date largely via qualitative case studies. Four of those stand out here for their utility in illustrating how GKC-style analysis helps to frame research on expert knowledge commons.

In "The University as Constructed Cultural Commons," I, along with Frischmann and Strandburg, interpreted the evolving form of the research university through history as a story of the evolution of a multilayered or polycentric knowledge commons (Madison et al. 2009). Whether looking at the US experience, the history of higher education in Continental Europe, in the UK, or elsewhere around the world, any given model of the university and any given specific institution constitutes primarily an exercise in governing the production and distribution of specialized, shared bodies of knowledge through teaching, research, scholarship, and the composition and curation of libraries, archives, and collections. Bureaucratically, universities are organized into faculties, schools, colleges, and centers and institutes, formally marking the boundaries of communities that we know as research fields and disciplines, sometimes joining them in the pursuit of "interdisciplinary" collaboration. University administrators and faculty develop and apply rules for admitting both students and faculty colleagues to the rank of "inside" community participants of different sorts, granting them specialized training, capabilities, and control over the intellectual contours of different disciplines, practices, and professions. In many countries, especially the US, the specialized knowledge communities that define the university (and are defined by it) are marked physically by the boundaries of the university campus.

In "Commons at the Intersection of Peer Production, Citizen Science, and Big Data: Galaxy Zoo," I described a citizen science research project in astronomy (Madison 2014). A pair of junior astronomy researchers, then at Oxford University, faced a research question where the relevant data (images of galaxies) could be analyzed only by hand and eye (given the technology of the time) and therefore, using conventional "insider" faculty and student labor, only over an extended period of time. To accelerate the research, the insiders built a web-based system that shared the image data with the public and invited "ordinary" citizens to participate in the data analysis. The result was, among other things, the formation of an especially successful "citizen science" collective, known as the Galaxy Zoo for its breadth, demographic diversity, and unifying theme. Without expressing the intention to do so directly, the project's academic leaders in effect created modest "researcher identities" among many of those who contributed their time and talents, without the certification or validation that typically accompanies the pursuit of disciplinary training, and without the tight control over development and distribution of disciplinary knowledge that is often characteristic of the academic enterprise.

In "The Republic of Letters and the Origins of Scientific Knowledge Commons," I looked to the earlier practices of scientific communication in late seventeenth- and eighteenth-century Europe, the UK, and colonial America that came to be called the "Republic of Letters," after the fact that the bulk of the communications constituted letters written and delivered by individual investigators to other individual investigators (Madison 2021). What we recognize today as early forms of scientific knowledge were produced and documented in the first place by individuals who were in the process of developing versions of a scientific method in the isolation and privacy of their respective homes. Transmitting their findings to one another, and then, per customs that evolved across decades, retransmitting the letters and ultimately authorizing their publication in early scientific journals, enabled the emergence of an early community of publicly identified scientists, even if that modern label did not exist at the time. They were individually engaged in communal scientific practice, including early forms of peer review, built on the foundations of purely private, and often recreational, inquiry.

In "The Kind of Solution a Smart City Is: Knowledge Commons and Postindustrial Pittsburgh," I examined practices of technology- and data reliant urban administration in one modestly scaled American city, Pittsburgh, beginning in the early twentieth century and continuing through the contemporary "smart city" era (Madison 2023). The "smart city," I concluded, represents a synthesis of technological and administrative expertise and political and administrative power, collecting data from citizens and deploying analytics technologies with scant participation or oversight from the community, broadly considered. The shared or commons character of the phenomenon lies in the manner in which data is shared across a technocratic polycentric order, organized institutionally in public sector actors (city and county governments), private sector actors (large and small technology vendors), private philanthropies (funding much of the administrative systems necessary to build effective collaborations between the two), and the region's two major universities (sources of both technological expertise and public policy expertise).

Section 9.3 builds on these case studies, offering and illustrating a preliminary model of expertise knowledge commons that will be illustrated in Section 9.4 by the IPCC.

9.3 A MODEL OF EXPERT KNOWLEDGE COMMONS

Robin Mansell (2013), following Nelson and Sampat (2001), uses the phrase "social technology" to describe different patterns of authority and control over shared information resources. She describes versions of "constituted authority" (longer-standing, more formalized forms and procedures of authority, more likely to be useful where the relevant knowledge accumulates in durable forms over time) and "adaptive authority" (more fluid forms and procedures, more likely to be useful where information and knowledge is developed for near-term application).

Expert knowledge commons characteristically is an instance of the former: constituted authority. But that label begins the inquiry rather than closing it. The question remains: Where does expertise come from? How does the authority of expert knowledge commons arise? How does it operate, change, and perhaps expire? In what respects does looking at expert knowledge commons in terms of the conceptual syntax of commons and knowledge sharing add to or refine existing scholarship on expertise and expert communities?

A model anchored in the GKC framework gets us started on responses to those questions.

9.3.1 *Expertise: Lessons from GKC Research*

GKC researchers to date have largely avoided characterizing their research in terms of building models and instead have relied, as Ostrom often did, on the idea that GKC research builds from a common research framework. Here, I undertake preliminary steps in the direction of offering one model of knowledge commons in one domain: expertise and expert communities.

The three GKC case studies described earlier yield, preliminarily, the following attributes that are characteristic of expert knowledge commons:

[1] *New knowledge, or mechanisms for generating knowledge resources. The relevant resources may constitute a pool of "resource units" or a body of propositional knowledge or knowledge of methods, processes, (at times) associated skills, that is not necessarily decomposable into units or flows.*

The protoscientists of the Republic of Letters generated knowledge via observation and experiment, documenting their results and sharing them with one another; the citizen scientists of the Galaxy Zoo generated almost innumerable small-scale items of knowledge – observations and classifications of galaxies – that were pooled via the Zoo mechanism. University-based researchers throughout history have developed new knowledge via study, analysis, observation, and experiment. The "smart city" generates new knowledge and information via the collection of massive quantities of observational data.

The knowledge or information in question need not always be novel or inventive, as if expert communities are grounded in concepts often associated with patent law. "Expertise" often is associated with decision-making or action by others (Grundmann 2017), but as I derive the model, I assimilate that narrower reading of "expertise" to the broader category of "knowledge." Here, the substance of the resource has some specialized character, because of the costs of obtaining it or documenting it (in time, labor and skill, or money). Collecting, gathering, analyzing, organizing, or synthesizing previously developed knowledge, located metaphorically both "inside" or "outside" the community, may be a useful foundation for a body of expertise. The uses of expertise may vary from field to field and over time.

[2] *Codified knowledge, or mechanisms for embodying knowledge durably as true, factual, and/or authoritative within the community or collective.*

The Republic of Letters produced an actual body of letters, many of which later found their way into printed scholarly publications. The data collected via the Galaxy Zoo were gathered in a massive database, which was the basis for a number of scholarly publications. (The citizen "scientists" were included as "authors" of some of those works, to the extent that scholarly publishers permitted that.) Academic researchers working in university settings produce journal articles, monographs, datasets, and other "scholarly" works. Smart city practitioners collect and house data in massive databases and construct computer interfaces for accessing them that may be accessible to expert public sector administrators.

Knowledge not only has to be shared from person to person but also has to be documented, in text or other embodied form – scientific instruments, for example – for it to persist across a population and across time and for it to be capable of being shared more widely. The mechanisms of embodiment might include forms of human practice, particularly where "expertise" consists of methods associated with craft or trades rather than forms of knowledge production associated with educational systems or scientific research. The mechanisms may be informal and normative, as in the case of prestige economies; may be systematized, as in the case of peer review for scientific publication; and may be anchored in law, as in certain provisions of copyright law that exclude certain forms of knowledge and human creation from copyright coverage, that is, that characterize certain material as "ideas," in order to render them accessible for downstream uses.

The fact that the codified knowledge resource and its mechanisms should be "durable" does not mean that they should be inflexible, nor that they should be, in effect, permanent. Universities usually have buildings, including housing and social spaces for faculty and students (at times), libraries (traditionally), and places for teaching and researching (classrooms, laboratories). But not all do. Mechanisms of knowledge production and contribution have to interrelate productively with mechanisms of codification. The "progress of science," a phrase that appears in the US Constitution as a justification for Western intellectual property law, means, among other things, that the progress of knowledge is associated with both expansion of communities and domains of expertise and also with changes to both. Codifying expert knowledge entails mechanisms for resolving conflicts among different claims to truth.

Codified or durable forms of shared knowledge may be and often are accompanied by shared tacit knowledge, some of which may be directed to means of codification, some of which may be directed to means of transmission or distribution, and some of which may be directed to means of adaptation and evolution. Those three dimensions of tacit knowledge are, to be sure, not sharply distinct from one another.

[3] *Associated knowledge, or mechanisms for confirming the association of individuals who create or embody knowledge with a collection of "experts" recognized internally (that is, within the group) as an authoritative custodian of both the resources and the processes of codification.*

The Republic of Letters was recognized as such in its own time by members of the correspondence network. The citizens in the Galaxy Zoo seem to have bonded themselves to the collective scientific effort by adopting some of the trappings and habits of professional scientists; the bonding was ratified and documented by the leaders' practice of publicly acknowledging the citizens' "authorial" contributions to their published work. In the university setting, in modern times the terminal degree is the standard currency used to recognize a person as a member of an expert community, even if not all full-time academic researchers have earned the PhD and not all holders of PhD degrees work as academic researchers. Academic rituals, notably installations of university presidents and vice chancellors and conferral of degrees, retain the color and pomp of medieval academic ceremony. The smart city phenomenon has become brand as well as practice, meaning that those who design, implement, and supervise the operation of smart city systems are well-aware of their insider status as practitioners of the smart city.

The expert community has formal and/or informal means of determining who is an expert and who is not, which is to say, for identifying and then reproducing itself, constituting itself as a body with privileged understanding of the knowledge that constitutes the "expertise." This entails a reasonable degree of purposefulness and collective self-awareness; it seems unlikely that a group of individuals would identify itself as an expert community, or would include or exclude a member, by inadvertence or accident. These may include educational pathways and certifications, such as the PhD; may include professional associations for disciplines and professionals; licensing systems administered wholly or partly by the state; rituals of communal recognition; and informal normative systems, again, perhaps more frequently associated with amateur or hobbyist practitioners who aspire to recognition as experts.

Membership rules may be more porous or more rigid, so that the expertise in question may be formally open to anyone, but understanding and use of that expertise may require formal or informal association of individuals with the expert community. Once "in" the community of experts, membership may erode over time (for example, an expert practitioner may change the direction of their research or practice) or, at the margin, the incumbent members may eject a noncompliant or nonparticipating individual. Expert communities may wither away as the relevant body of "expertise" loses its authoritative status (for example, in the late nineteenth century, as the "practice" of "patent medicine" gave way to science-based medicine, the "community" of charlatan practitioners gave way to a new community of trained physicians) or as subgroups split off and form their own expert groups, perhaps combining with other expert communities.

[4] *Translated knowledge, or mechanisms for groups and individuals outside the expert community for recognizing its existence, its status as custodian of a relevant body of expertise, and, where and when appropriate, the privilege of the group and its individual members to speak outside the group with legitimacy and authority on matters within its subject matter domain.*

The citizens of the Republic of Letters had no voice or audience for their correspondence until some of the letters were collected and published as parts of earlier scientific journals. The citizen scientists of the Galaxy Zoo saw their work rewarded via the development of online Galaxy Zoo research products and by the spillover of the "Zoo" citizen science model into other crowdsourced data analysis projects, as one lay-group-turned-expert modeled the pathway for others to do the same. Academic researchers are tasked with the central purpose of educating and training their own disciplinary successors and also transmitting relevant portions of their expertise to nonexperts, which is to say, undergraduates and other trainees. Smart city practice depends in the first place on ongoing trusted relationships among technical experts and administrative experts, and in the second place on reliance by the broader citizenry on the expertise of those who "run" their communities.

Polycentricity is, among other things, the term that captures the concept that governance practices, including knowledge commons governance, are constituted by interactions among rules and actors operating in intersecting and overlapping institutions or informal groups (Aligica and Tarko 2012). "Translated knowledge" signifies that expert knowledge commons are characteristically polycentric. There are expert insiders and both nonexpert outsiders and other expert outsiders; the presence of boundaries and divides among them is cause for exploring patterns of porosity and influence rather than a means of isolating expertise only on one side of the proverbial line. Acknowledgment of an expert knowledge commons by other experts or by outsiders is often central to the authority and legitimacy of the group and of its efforts to share its knowledge via teaching, participation in public policy dialogues, and advocacy and decision-making of other sorts. That makes explicit the idea that legitimacy and authority are social phenomena, generated via mechanisms of transferring trust and judgments of credibility from the relevant audience to the relevant expert community, rather than phenomena associated inherently with the truth or accuracy claims of the expert knowledge commons passing from the inside to the outside.

These are, in short, recursive, feedback-driven processes. Once generated, the legitimacy and authority that build on that trust require continued credible internal expert practice. If the expertise-producing or membership-policing functions of the expert community fail or are corrupted, the broader legitimacy and authority of the expert community may be at risk. But internally consistent expert practice may not be sufficient to preserve the expert knowledge commons relative to outside audiences. The fact that expert knowledge commons always operate at the intersection of insider expert communities and various outside nonexpert or different expert communities means that legitimacy and authority may be challenged by political, economic, cultural, and social influences emanating from outside the expert knowledge commons.

9.3.2 *Antecedent and Allied Research on Experts and Expertise*

Why add a model to the GKC research framework? The framework itself offers a mechanism for aligning research on expert knowledge commons with research on other institutions that may be characterized as knowledge commons, such as data commons, open code, biobanks, and infrastructure commons. The model adds two important features. One, the model helps to make explicit the premise of GKC research that resources and institutional contexts – here, expertise and governance of expertise – are closely intertwined knowledge commons phenomena that can be, nevertheless, disentangled. The "expert community" (the institutional context) both generates and is generated by the production and transmission of expertise (the resource). Two, the model offers accessible analytic clarity ("is this institution a case of expert knowledge commons?"), prescriptive guidance ("how might this institution develop into an expert knowledge commons?"), and diagnostic utility ("what are the causes of the prosperity of the expert knowledge commons, or its fragility?"). The uses of those questions are illustrated in Section 9.4.

Intellectual continuities should be noted along with these departures. Other scholars have hinted at least briefly at the concept of the "expert commons" as a species of knowledge commons (De Moor 2011) but have not pursued the subject in any depth. Other research traditions and key earlier work wrestles with some of the themes included in the GKC approach but often not in the comparativist vein that motivates it nor consistently in attention to governance processes alongside the character of knowledge or authority as such. Inevitably, given the brevity of this chapter, the following review is incomplete.

In the history and philosophy of science, in different respects Michael Polanyi (1962), Robert Merton (1974), and Thomas Kuhn (1962) each emphasized community, community identity, and the cultivation and uses of knowledge both within structured groups or by structured groups, as fundamental to the development of knowledge, and particularly scientific knowledge, by individual researchers. Similarly, Haas (1992) consolidates research on epistemic communities, operating both within and beyond scientific research. Jasanoff (2005, 255) uses the phrase "civic epistemology" to describe institutionalized practices by which members of a given society test and deploy knowledge claims uses as a basis for making collective choices. Though much of the work organized around those contributions has focused on science, the development and codification of what we know today as the humanities similarly progressed through a series of institutional or collective forms, culminating in the refinement of universities and their schools and faculties (Wellmon 2016). Snow's division of the world of knowledge into scientific and humanistic "cultures" builds on that institutional foundation (Snow 1959).

Work on knowledge, learning, and material culture has been consistently attentive to institutional implications and to resulting implications for knowledge classification (Blair 2010), for canons of literatures (Searle 1990), and to the construction of material infrastructures, including scientific instruments (Daston and Galison 1992) and archives (Daston 2017), among other things. The concept of the "community of practice" as a model for learning apprenticeships (Wenger 2010) has long since escaped its original research and practice context and been used to model collective knowledge practices of different sorts, including copyright and creativity (Madison 2004).

Turning from scientific knowledge communities to research on expertise and disciplines, researchers in information science, sociology, and social epistemology have explored patterns of community definition (Brown and Duguid 2000; Abbott 2001) and the development of trust in expert communities in the context of formal epistemology (Goldman 2001). Histories of higher education draw attention to intersections among formal, public-facing institutions, on the one hand, and "invisible colleges" or intellectual networks (Kealey and Ricketts 2014), such as disciplines, on the other hand, where the latter may or may not be formalized via professional societies, conferences, journals, and otherwise.

Questions of trust in and reliance on expert communities bring in larger issues of institutional design and political legitimacy, recalling Hayek (Hayek 1945) as well as the different views of Walter Lippmann (for) and John Dewey (against) as to the proper role of technical experts in confronting public policy problems arising from the complexity of modern society (Lippmann 1922; Friedman 2019). Debates over the relative merits of decentralized and centralized collections of experts and expertise in public administration persist to this day (Chandler 1998; Lofthouse and Schaefer 2024).

Last but far from least, the legal system itself makes important contributions to understandings of expertise in institutional context. In *Daubert v. Merrell Dow Pharmaceuticals, Inc.*,[1] the US Supreme Court adopted an interpretation of the Federal Rules of Evidence mandating that expert testimony may be admitted into evidence in federal cases only so long as the testimony is grounded in "scientific knowledge," that is, so long as the testimony relies on knowledge generated according to scientific methods. The *Daubert* approach aims specifically to exclude from judicial proceedings so-called junk science and pseudoscience (Golan 2007).

In sum, it appears that (to date) the interrelated dynamics of bodies of expert knowledge ("expertise"), bodies of experts ("expert communities"), and governance of knowledge and information sharing within and across those communities and

[1] 509 U.S. 579 (1993).

adjacent communities have not been summed up into a model or system that permits ready comparative institutional analysis. Gustafsson (2021) comes close, blending substantive expertise, relational expertise, technical knowledge, situated knowledge, and communitarian perspectives, but not recognizing the sum of those pieces as a system of knowledge governance.

Relative to the IPCC itself, O'Reilly and coauthors, in an extensive ethnographic study of the scientific review processes operating inside the IPCC, distinguish the organization from the "traditional" epistemic community described by Haas (1992) yet draw a sharp line between the review processes undertaken by IPCC authors and governance, which seems to be what happens elsewhere, in the policy and decision-making spheres (O'Reilly et al. 2024). Miller and Edwards link expert knowledge with environmental policy (Miller and Edwards 2001), rightly steering away from a linear model by which expertise migrates from knowledge communities to decision-making communities, but without developing a single concept usable for analyses of knowledge governance generally. That is the contribution of a model of expert knowledge commons.

9.3.3 *Dealing with Drawbacks and Gaps in the Expert Knowledge Commons Model*

Models simplify. Using models presses researchers to examine conformity between the abstractions of the model and the case on the ground. Elements of the GKC research framework are subsumed in judgments associated with modeling expert knowledge commons, suggesting drawbacks and gaps. At the same time, models press researchers to examine alignment and consistency in how institutional concepts extend from one setting to another; operating manifestations of underlying structural patterns may be more important than functional details. In practice, the model and the framework should be deployed alongside one another, so that the possible absence of nuance and flexibility in the model can be recovered via the framework. Section 9.4 illustrates that rhythm in its case study of the IPCC. Section 9.3.3.1 briefly anticipates that illustration with a catalog of material that the model appears to exclude and that the framework might reintroduce.

9.3.3.1 What the Model Omits

Research using the GKC framework characteristically begins by exploring institutional history, both purposive and accidental or inadvertent. The model captures only a snapshot of institutional practice at a given moment in time.

The framework encourages attention to the character of shared "resources," including knowledge goods or items that compose a knowledge "pool," an adaptation of focus in the Ostrom tradition on shared "goods" and, by extension, on characterization of those goods in terms of the economics of property: private goods, public goods, club goods, and "common pool" resources. By contrast, even if the GKC framework were invested in that taxonomy, the model as outlined earlier may assume a body or pool of expertise that is not decomposable into units or flows of information. As a result, the GKC framework may be used to analyze knowledge-sharing practices in which shared knowledge is manifest even while the shared material does not constitute a collection of immaterial "things." Frischmann's study of "common sense" commons offers an illustration (Frischmann 2021).

The GKC framework emphasizes specific "action arenas" and specific governance strategies deployed within them often referred to as "rules in use." Those strategies may be polycentric and nested. By contrast, the model defaults to identifying unspecified "mechanisms" rather than "rules in use." Expertise may or may not have material or virtual "venues" or "locations."

Last, even though the GKC framework is in itself a means for engaging in descriptive research, it encourages researchers to develop and apply clear standards for evaluating the normative implications of knowledge governance institutions. The standard starting point is the institution's success in addressing the social dilemmas that prompted development of knowledge commons governance strategies. Looking beyond that beginning, however, evaluating commons governance effectively and consistently has proved elusive, because questions inevitably arise as to the virtues of assessing institutional performance using externally imposed criteria (such as responsiveness to social need; compliance with formal legal systems; sustainability; efficiency; or fairness) or internally imposed criteria (such as the extent of voluntary community participation; transparency; and responsiveness or accountability to community members). By contrast, the expert knowledge commons model includes no normative assessment features. That omission is salient in light of material that the model highlights, which is considered next.

9.3.3.2 What the Model Highlights

The expert knowledge commons model sharpens awareness and understanding of certain features that research using the GKC framework may otherwise obscure.

The model draws attention to the nuanced character of the purposes motivating the development of expertise. Expert knowledge commons typically have designs, even if those designs may emerge over time. GKC research has long acknowledged that "commons happen" sometimes; not all knowledge commons are purposeful responses to social dilemmas involving shared knowledge resources. The focus on purpose brings forward key questions about the development, constitution, and evolution of disciplines, fields, and professions. How do these come into being? What patterns of collaboration and leadership, on the one hand, and technological, economic, and cultural conditions, on the other hand, contribute productively to the cultivation of expertise and expert communities, both inside and outside practitioner groups? What patterns undermine the development of expertise? In the modern era, data science is an example of a new field of expertise motivated largely by technological and economic conditions. A century ago, recognition of the field of forensic science received a substantial boost in the Sherlock Holmes stories of Sir Arthur Conan Doyle.

The model draws attention to distinctions between centrally managed commons, in which mechanisms guiding the use and maintenance of resources are determined largely by actors operating outside the community, and user-managed commons, in which the opposite condition applies. Any given expert community is likely to involve a combination of the two, leading potentially to conflicts between the difference governance strategies and the actors involved in each and to attention to power dynamics within an expert community (between junior and senior experts, for example) and between expert communities and external institutions or actors (such as nonexpert community groups or political actors).

The model draws attention to the role of expertise as a vehicle for social and cultural authority. Because expertise is largely relevant to the extent that it is incorporated into governance processes or strategies of other sorts, the uses of expert knowledge commons in mediating between actors on the inside of the expert community and actors and institutions on the outside are particularly significant. The model therefore brings the politics of expertise and expert communities into focus, engaging questions of normative and descriptive legitimacy and of possible harm produced by reliance on outdated or corrupted expertise and expertise improperly equated with social status or uncritically aligned with political power, in ways that the GKC framework, as a mechanism primarily aimed at descriptive analysis, is not obviously equipped to do. The collected GKC case studies focusing on governance of urban data and "smart city" technologies illustrate the tensions between normative framings (planning experts' overreliance on technocratic solutions to urban governance dilemmas) and descriptive ones (surfacing the details of technology implementations and human oversight) (Frischmann et al. 2023).

Last, the model anticipates understanding the erosion and possible demise of authority. Much knowledge commons analysis depends conceptually on identifying conceptual and material boundaries of various sorts, along with the processes through which contests over boundaries are initiated, conducted, and resolved. Boundaries may be more or less clear, distinct, firm, fixed, fair, and accurate, or durable. Understanding how boundaries are built and managed is to take, usually, an optimistic view of governance; understanding the failure of boundaries is, usually, to look cynically or pessimistically. The changing patterns of recognized expertise over time turns the erosion of boundaries into a central theme.

9.4 THE IPCC AS EXPERT KNOWLEDGE COMMONS

This chapter originated in the instinct that the IPCC would offer a full-blown knowledge commons case study. The quantity of scholarly literature examining the

IPCC in different respects made that approach seem unproductive, in the sense that the IPCC's status as an institution synthesizing scientific knowledge for public policy decision making has been uncontroverted for a long time (Beck 2011).

The character of the IPCC's status as an expertise-based organization has long been contested, especially within the community of scholars of scientific knowledge and environmental policy (Boehmer-Christiansen 1993; Shackley and Skodvin 1995; Shackley 1997; Beck and Forsyth 2015; Grundmann 2023). That contest leads to the proposition advanced here, that the expert knowledge commons model derived earlier offers a novel and useful way to understand the IPCC both in its own settings and as an illustration of the utility of the GKC approach generally, beyond climate policy and beyond scientific expertise.

9.4.1 *What Is the IPCC?*

The following uncritical, abbreviated history of the IPCC and its operations sets the stage for using it to illustrate the expert knowledge commons model, borrowing generously from earlier research results that echo the themes of the GKC research framework.

The IPCC was established in 1988 as an intergovernmental organization initially formed by the World Meteorological Organization (WMO) and the United Nations Environment Programme and endorsed shortly thereafter by the United Nations General Assembly. The formation of the IPCC followed flurries of international activity as to climate, including convenings and syntheses of climate research by the WMO and by the International Council of Scientific Unions (Zillman 2007). Its purpose, as outlined in the corresponding United Nations Resolution,[2] has been "to prepare a comprehensive review and recommendations with respect to the state of knowledge of the science of climate change; the social and economic impact of climate change, and the potential response strategies and elements for inclusion in a possible future international convention on climate."

The IPCC has been, ever since, part of the organizational hierarchy of the UN, delivering expert knowledge to participants in negotiations under the United Nations Framework Convention on Climate Change (UNFCCC, adopted in 1992). The IPCC is governed by 195 member governments, acting through national delegations, who nominate and elect an IPCC Bureau of expert scientists (itself governed by an IPCC Executive Committee) to serve through an assessment cycle – usually six to seven years.

The IPCC Bureau supervises three Working Groups (climate science, impacts of climate change, and economic and social dimensions) and a task force, which undertake the IPCC's scientific work and produce periodic consensus-based "Assessment Reports" for use by policymakers and others. The Working Groups and

[2] UN General Assembly Resolution 43/53, December 6, 1988.

their chairs are supported internally by Technical Support Units and rely on hundreds of external contributing authors and thousands of expert reviewers. A document titled "Principles Governing IPCC Work" (which includes three appendices), approved initially in 1998 and amended periodically since then, sets out the formal principles, practices, and procedures that govern the work of the IPCC, the IPCC Bureau, and the Working Groups and Task Forces.[3]

The IPCC has produced a total of six Assessment Reports to date and a handful of supplemental reports. The length and density of the Assessment Reports means that policymakers are more likely to rely on briefer "Summaries for Policymakers" for each of the Working Groups. Following the release of the Fourth Assessment Report in 2007, the IPCC was awarded the Nobel Peace Prize, along with former US Vice President Al Gore, in connection with contributions to the state of knowledge about man-made climate change. The Fifth Assessment Report was part of the scientific foundation for the Paris Climate Accords in 2016. Nevertheless, the reputation and quality of the IPCC's work has been called into question, especially since the leak to the public in 2009 of certain internal documents that criticize the IPCC's methods for evaluating different scientific contributions and indicate various sources of bias in constituting participation in the IPCC's consensus-based processes, coming from within the organization and from external critics.

Even in this uncritical review, clear themes emerge that feed directly into using the IPCC to illustrate the expert knowledge commons model. As observers have said from the earliest days of the IPCC, the IPCC is not purely a scientific organization; it combines formal governance by political actors (hierarchically organized member governments) with both formal and informal governance by scientists, acting as twentieth- and twenty-first-century scientists typically do: in self-governing, peer-assessed scientific communities (Boehmer-Christiansen 1993). Both "wings" of that polycentric governance architecture are supported in large part by formal, technical, hierarchical bureaucracies of the sort familiar to anyone experienced in international relations but foreign, at least at the scale at which the IPCC has operated, to research science. The IPCC combines centralized bureaucratic governance and decentralized community governance in unprecedented and still unmatched ways.

The fact that the IPCC has been as successful as it has been in producing Assessment Reports, acquiring widely if not universally recognized status as an authoritative voice on matters of climate science and influencing international climate treaties is remarkable, in a way, given the fact that it addresses two noteworthy, interrelated social dilemmas (Madison et al. 2022). One, scientists working in climatology and related fields up through the mid 1980s, together with corresponding government actors, realized that the proper way to address the harms of human-made climate change was to coordinate decisions and actions by national governments. This was, in Ostromian terms, a classic "tragic commons" social

[3] All of the foregoing is both summarized and available in detail at the IPCC's website, ipcc.ch.

dilemma at a global scale. Two, addressing the governance dilemma as to global environmental policy and action required organizing a mechanism that had never before been produced successfully: a means for compiling and synthesizing scientific evidence to inform coordinated global decision-making. This was, in GKC terms, a knowledge commons social dilemma, one framed partly by the need to make sense of an abundance of diverse scientific information and data (Madison et al. 2022), including not only geophysical data but also social science data, and partly by the need to make sense of that data in a way that would be useful and persuasive to lay audiences.

9.4.2 *The IPCC as a Model Expert Knowledge Commons*

The chapter concludes by pulling together observations and research about the IPCC to support its claim that the IPCC meets the criteria of the model expert knowledge commons, both supporting and extending arguments for reform of the IPCC and also enabling comparative research that aligns analysis of the IPCC analysis not only of other organizations undertaking research on climate change but also of other expert institutions, organizations, and communities, scientific and otherwise, as forms and practices of knowledge governance.

[1] *New knowledge, or mechanisms for generating new knowledge resources.*

[2] *Codified knowledge, or mechanisms for codifying knowledge durably as true, factual, and/or authoritative within the community or collective.*

These two features of the IPCC should not be in doubt, given the summary earlier and what is widely known about the purposes, practices, and products of the IPCC. As O'Reilly and coauthors write: "While the IPCC claims to not produce new knowledge, our previous studies disagree. The IPCC process and its reports synthesize and reorganize existing knowledge, drive research agendas, and inspire new research questions" (O'Reilly et al. 2024, 8) (citations omitted).

It is an error to limit understanding of the commons-relevant elements of the IPCC to the fact that its formal and informal review processes for gathering and integrating scientific research yield synthesized and documented new knowledge produced, formally, by "consensus" among scientific researchers, IPCC authors, and IPCC reviewers. Stopping there reinscribes a misleading linear framing of expertise production and delivery to decision-makers (Beck 2011). An equivalent error treats the IPCC and related scientific organizations as intellectual and bureaucratic infrastructures, feeding higher-order decision-making systems (Edwards 2017).

[3] *Associated knowledge, or mechanisms for confirming the association of individuals with a body of "experts" recognized internally (that is, within the group) as an authoritative custodian of both the resources and the processes of codification.*

With respect to the relative "self"-awareness of the IPCC as a community of expertise, the key is understanding the IPCC itself as a collection of people who constitute expertise but who may not produce expert knowledge in themselves, located both inside IPCC processes and adjacent to it. They are reviewing, sorting, assessing, and prioritizing the results of scientific research produced elsewhere.

Because the IPCC does not itself conduct scientific research, it faces a social dilemma caused rather than solved by its design as institution intended to collect and synthesize scientific research product by others. The expertise presumptively associated with individual researchers, aligning them with their home institutions (in part) and with their respective scientific or technical disciplines (in part), needs to be shared, in some salient, legible way, with the IPCC itself.

The governance solution to this dilemma, as it so often is in the world of academic research, lies in the character of reputation and prestige as a form of professional currency. Reputation and prestige in any field are partly institutional, so that a person taking a position in that organization may benefit by the institution's prestige being shared with the individual. The relationship works in the opposite direction: Individuals acquire reputations and prestige, which may be shared with an institution as part of the individual's becoming a member. Reputation and prestige circulate recursively within the institution and its constituent members, cross-cutting with reputation and prestige effects of individuals associating with fields, disciplines, professional associations, and the like. Prestige is far from free-floating; individuals must do the work, and be known for doing the work, that generates prestige effects. Function and symbol go together, if rarely hand in glove. There is no assurance that the dynamics of prestige will foster cooperation and prosocial behavior – that is, that governing prestige as an intangible resource will solve social dilemmas productively – but some evidence suggests that prestige effects may do just that (Henrich et al. 2015).

O'Reilly and coauthors focus on precisely this phenomenon in the IPCC context. Those administering IPCC processes both borrow and confer prestige benefits in order to align individual expertise with the institutional authority of the IPCC:

> Writing reports for the Intergovernmental Panel on Climate Change (IPCC) is a sociocultural experience shared among authors. Being selected as an IPCC author is generally considered a high-status service gig, one that offers no financial compensation. To be an IPCC author is to be identified by your nation, which nominates you, and the IPCC itself, which confirms you, as a leading climate scholar. One author noted that "my university president now knows who I am," suggesting, at a minimum, reputational benefits to the role. Authors also note the serious fun of scholarly assessment, getting to know other climate experts, having the opportunity to travel, and helping to make a difference with one of the most critical issues of our time. Authors also often publish with members of their chapter team or other people they work with in the IPCC; so along with the report citation, authors may get some publications or projects – the major expectation for university researchers' jobs – or secure new positions from the effort. (O'Reilly et al. 2024, 7–8) (citation omitted)

The end point of this governing "prestige as knowledge commons," as this pattern might be known, is not simply reinforcement of the IPCC's status in itself. The IPCC acquires a sort of "prestige shell" or shield, an outer coating of authoritative status as the leading singular voice in climate science, that permits the IPCC to exercise that voice, and be accepted in decision-making processes, in intergovernmental processes and public dialogue on climate change.

In an analogous sense, in corporate law, Gindis and Cole argue that an equivalent process of knowledge governance bundles the entirety of a corporation's complex functions and identities beneath a singular "corporate mask," through which the corporation acts and should be held accountable in commerce and in law (Gindis and Cole 2025).

Likewise, the prestige and authority of the IPCC as an organization clearly depends on its sharing the prestige of the IPCC's associated scientific researchers, authors, and reviewers, along with the extended prestige associated with their collective reliance on accepted scientific methods in research and peer review. But the IPCC's prestige also stands on its own, in the sense that the shared prestige that the IPCC absorbs is also paid forward, in a way, as the IPCC's products (principally the Assessment Reports) are accepted as authoritative by the IPCC's stakeholders and audiences, or are at least intended to be accepted as such.

Finally, acceptance of and reliance on the IPCC's products by government actors and others reinforces the status and authority of the IPCC and its associated scientists and technical experts. These are recursive processes, complicated enormously by the many ways in which the state and science intersect, as Miller and Edwards (2001) noted long ago.

[4] *Translated knowledge, or mechanisms for groups and individuals outside the expert community for recognizing its existence, its status as custodian of a relevant body of expertise, and, where and when appropriate, the privilege of the group and its individual members to speak outside the group with legitimacy and authority on matters within its subject matter domain.*

The last element of the expert knowledge commons model focuses precisely on the spaces and practices where those recursive processes take place, where expert communities and audiences intersect. In this instance, it is the boundary where science and the state abut one another and overlap. Prestige is one form of shared knowledge resource in this instance; expertise itself is the general knowledge resource that spans and connects different communities. In both respects the shared character of the resource is a sort of institutional glue, holding the multiple centers of authority in a pattern that defines a coordinated whole. The dynamics of "prestige" in that pattern are described earlier. The dynamics of expertise as a resource need some additional explanation. Expertise is not a single, static thing to which experts contribute and on which others rely. Instead, what we refer to as expertise, even in its codified or documented forms, constitutes an evolving body of propositions and practices that takes on different colors and attributes in the hands of different stakeholders and their purposes. "Expertise" in this sense renders the definition of the expert knowledge commons model disappointingly unclear, at least at the edges. But it is the very fluidity of the boundary condition that permits "translated knowledge" to bind multiple communities into a single expert knowledge commons.

Boundaries imply a certain number of relatively fixed poles or nodes. In that sense the IPCC is, like expert knowledge communities generally, an example of polycentric social order. Scientific expertise is gathered, weighed, and documented, according to both scientific practices (peer review and consensus mechanisms) and hierarchical bureaucracies descended significantly external state-related constraints on the IPCC's design. Within the scientific center of order, there are multiple sources of scientific knowledge and expertise to be gathered, weighed, and documented; on the "state" side, the interests of different member states have to be identified and sorted.

Among the poles or nodes, rhetorical practices of documentation, translation, and persuasion can be collected as so-called boundary work, but here I distinguish the meaning of that term from its historical association with efforts by scientists to negotiate the separateness of their work from entanglements with market practices or with interference by the state. Examining the IPCC, Beck and Mahon (2018) usefully summarize recent research that casts the IPCC as a "boundary organization" practicing "boundary work" both in "proceduralist" terms (in which the scientific world and the policy world each retains a significant degree of autonomy around a boundary that defines their negotiating interface) and in "interpretive" terms (in which the boundary itself represents the negotiated interdependence of the two worlds. That judgment seems correct, and it helps to confirm the status of the IPCC as an expert knowledge commons within the scope of this last element of the expert knowledge commons model.

To this characterization of the "boundary" function represented and performed by the IPCC, I would add only the note that Beck and Mahon, like virtually all of the other researchers whose work they cite and discuss, spend far more time and effort disentangling the sociopolitical attributes of the IPCC as an organization and far less time disentangling the similarly multifaceted attributes of the knowledge resources that the IPCC is intended to marshal, document, and distribute. In that regard, the research of Star and Griesemer on "boundary objects," knowledge objects subject to different interpretations in the context of different, adjacent interpretive communities, is instructive (Star and Griesemer 1989). The IPCC's Assessment Reports are not quite "boundary objects" in that sense, but they perform an analogous function, enabling multiple communities of interest to coordinate their activities around common focal points. A system – an institution – results: the expert knowledge commons, oriented to a shared conceptual "map" of climate knowledge that is always simultaneously fixed, given its documentary character, and fluid, given the different intersecting ways that it may be "read" by different experts. The allusion to Schelling (1960) and research on focal points as coordination mechanisms is purposeful. Maps of knowledge create conceptual legibility; they help both researchers and practitioners see where their interests intersect, and how, and where they do not (Madison 2009). The knowledge commons literature resists reifying "commons" as a space or as a place, but on occasion the metaphor suits.

9.5 CONCLUSION: IMPLICATIONS AND FURTHER RESEARCH

This chapter has described a model of expert knowledge commons derived from research using the GKC framework, and it has illustrated the model via brief review of the IPCC. Modeling knowledge commons governance in any sector is necessarily tentative. The review here is preliminary, particularly in the sense that it takes as its subject mostly formal and stylized representations of the IPCC. The chapter relies on the premise that GKC research to date justifies taking this step in the direction of model building, and on the related premise that existing literatures on experts, expertise, and epistemology leave open space to document expert knowledge commons as the chapter proposes.

Specifying the elements of an expert knowledge commons model clarifies the implications of seeing the IPCC as an expert knowledge commons, meaning that those who would diagnose its successes, failures, and future opportunities have firmer specific grounds on which to base their assessments. Flaws, biases, gaps, and missed opportunities remain to be woven into the narrative, though the hope is that alignment of the IPCC with the model provides a guide for doing so, consistent with the model's derivation from the GKC framework. Continued exploration of the IPCC using the GKC framework gives both researchers and analysts the means to understand, in systematic ways, how the IPCC continues to evolve and adapt as an institution whose purpose is to support thoughtful policymaking. The model-based approach is necessarily comparatively static; the complementary framework-based approach is comparatively dynamic.

What difference does it make that the IPCC is viewed as an instance of expert knowledge commons, rather than as (for example) a cross-institutional scientific institution, an information clearinghouse or repository, an instrument of international relations, an instance of "civic epistemology," or something else?

The answer likely lies in the ways in which GKC analysis is used in multiple respects, but always comparatively, to draw attention to overlaps and parallels between knowledge commons institutions with related structural functions despite dissimilar outward appearances, and to overlaps and intersections among the different insider and outsider communities that participate in governance of shared knowledge and information. Future research and analysis might compare the IPCC as expert knowledge commons to other governance institutions building expertise and expert knowledge communities focused on climate science. The IPCC as an expert knowledge commons might be situated directly alongside other expert knowledge commons with recognizable (that is, legible and sometimes bureaucratized) expert knowledge commons: universities, schools, research organizations (industrial, academic, and independent), departments, degrees, certifications and licensing, disciplines, professions, and trades, each involving different blends of substantive shared knowledge, decision-making modalities, and intellectual and embodied skills.

Comparative analysis need not be limited to climate science expertise or to scientific expertise of any sort. Expert knowledge commons governance may be observed in practice in any number of domains of human activity, ranging from the general to the specific, from literary analysis to competitive sport. Literature on norm-governed creative communities, which produce original, creative material without relying on incentives offered by intellectual property law (Darling and Perzanowski 2017), may be assimilated easily to the expert knowledge commons model.

With respect to the IPCC itself and climate science generally, this case study and follow-on research can refine a general model for the role of shared expertise in environmental policy design, one that focuses not only on governance that addresses the social dilemmas associated with combining scientific research across multiple disciplines but that also addresses social dilemmas associated with documenting that body of knowledge and translating and transmitting it persuasively to nonexpert audiences. Scientific authority, like political authority, cannot and should not be taken simply as givens. Instead, scientific expertise should be examined – like any other community-based knowledge institution – for the dynamics of its construction, evolution, and effective application.

Conclusion

Environmental Knowledge Commons – An Appraisal

Michael Mattioli and Jessica Steinberg

C.1 INTRODUCTION

Climate change, the accelerating loss of plant and wildlife species, and declining natural resources are some of the central challenges of our time. Individuals working alone cannot overcome problems of this scale. Instead, society needs shared pools of ecological information accessible to all and enriched by many – what we call "environmental knowledge commons."

This book has shown how such pools take many forms – from satellite data, to stormwater management, to patents. While each of these case studies offers a wealth of insights, there are still more lessons that can come from comparing them. This chapter draws together some of the most important insights of this kind.

C.2 KEY CHARACTERISTICS OF ENVIRONMENTAL KNOWLEDGE COMMONS

Before we examine the challenges and opportunities of environmental knowledge commons, it is helpful to look at what makes them unique. This section highlights the following themes, which emerged across the chapters:

1. The high complexity and interconnectedness of the natural systems knowledge commons aim to understand and manage;
2. The diverse range of stakeholders involved, from local communities to global institutions;
3. The complex (and at times contentious) interactions between these stakeholders; and
4. The need for governance structures spanning multiple sectors and scales.

By exploring each of these themes, we can better grasp both the challenges environmental knowledge commons face and their potential to address critical environmental issues.

C.2.1 *Complexity and Interconnectedness of Environmental Systems*

Several authors remind us that natural processes connect places that are geographically distant, separated by mountains, oceans, and even continents. Draper and Sun (Chapter 3) vividly illustrate this point in its description of Iowa's nutrient runoff traveling the Mississippi and fueling blooms in the Gulf of Mexico, creating low-oxygen areas where fish cannot survive. Nordman et al. (Chapter 4) detail how city pavement, unlike soil, funnels polluted water into drains and eventually into local rivers. Harrington (Chapter 7) and Kurian et al. (Chapter 5) describe the movement of greenhouse gases, storms, floods, and droughts across borders, with farm communities in developing nations often facing the direst effects. Cesari and Sun (Chapter 6) turn the viewpoint skyward, to orbital debris and space operations, where small actions can have lasting consequences. The result is that we cannot consider any one environmental challenge in isolation – instead we must take seriously the externalities, and more concretely, the linkages between data and knowledge in different geographies, scales, and systems.

C.2.2 *Wide-Ranging Participants*

Each chapter highlights the remarkable variety of stakeholders – local, regional, and global, private and public – that can be involved with environmental knowledge commons. At the global level, organizations such as the United Nations and its specialized agencies serve as central coordinators of some international efforts. Harrington's work (Chapter 7) illuminates how bodies such as the United Nations Office for Outer Space Affairs and the World Meteorological Organization play crucial roles in space-based environmental data. These entities facilitate data sharing and establish the normative frameworks that guide our collective environmental stewardship on a planetary scale.

Madison (Chapter 9) describes a collaboration among several key players: international organizations such as the World Meteorological Organization and the United Nations Environment Programme; the United Nations General Assembly that endorsed the creation of the Intergovernmental Panel on Climate Change (IPCC); 195 member governments and their national delegations; the elected IPCC Bureau and its Executive Committee; specialized Working Groups and a Task Force; as well as Technical Support Units, hundreds of external contributing authors, and thousands of expert reviewers.

National governments and their agencies form another layer in this complex stakeholder landscape. Aagaard and Frischmann's examination of the US Forest Service (Chapter 2) offers a compelling case study of this. Here, we see a national agency managing forests for multiple, often competing uses. From timber harvesting to recreation, from conservation to economic development, the Forest Service must navigate competing interests among diverse stakeholders. This balancing act exemplifies the broader challenges in environmental governance.

Local government agencies have emerged as key players in environmental initiatives in our urbanized world. Nordman et al.'s study of Detroit's Water and Sewerage Department (Chapter 4) showcases how city-level entities are at the forefront of implementing innovative solutions such as green stormwater infrastructure. These local initiatives, though addressing specific urban issues, add valuable insights to our overall environmental practices.

The private sector, previously seen mainly as a source of environmental challenges, has become part of the solution in many cases. From commercial satellite operators revolutionizing Earth observation to companies participating in green patent initiatives, private firms bring innovative technologies and resources. However, their involvement also raises critical questions about balancing private interests with the public good.

Nongovernmental organizations (NGOs) and academic institutions often play a crucial role in linking various stakeholders. These entities contribute cutting-edge research and facilitate collaboration among diverse groups. Nordman et al.'s description of The Nature Conservancy's role in promoting green stormwater infrastructure in Detroit exemplifies how NGOs can catalyze local environmental initiatives.

Local communities and Indigenous groups bring invaluable perspectives to environmental knowledge resources. Their traditional ecological knowledge, often developed over generations of close interaction with specific environments, provides insights that can complement and enrich scientific understanding. Bloom's account of Public Lab's collaboration with Palestinian communities in Jerusalem (Chapter 1) highlights both the importance of community involvement and the delicate balance between openness and local sovereignty in knowledge sharing.

The scientific community remains the foundation of our environmental understanding. Scientists from diverse disciplines contribute to our knowledge of complex environmental systems and develop potential solutions. However, as Aagaard and Frischmann astutely point out (Chapter 2), even scientific information is not immune to stakeholder interests – for instance, research funding can influence study outcomes – underscoring the need for rigorous peer review and diverse perspectives in knowledge creation.

Policymakers and decision-makers at various levels form another crucial stakeholder group. They rely on collective environmental data to inform policy decisions and are responsible for creating frameworks that govern these shared resources. Kurian et al.'s study in Jordan (Chapter 5), involving both academic experts and policymakers, illustrates the potential for collaborative approaches to climate change adaptation.

Finally, we must recognize the role of the general public in environmental knowledge sharing. Advancements in technology have enabled citizen scientists and community members to contribute meaningfully to data collection and analysis. This trend, evident in some space data initiatives described by Cesari and Sun (Chapter 6), has the potential to radically expand our collective environmental understanding.

The varied interests and expertise of these stakeholders necessitate governance structures that are inclusive and adaptable. These structures must balance different interests, facilitate collaboration, and ensure equitable access to shared knowledge resources. Moreover, they highlight the importance of developing common languages and frameworks that can bridge the gaps between different stakeholder groups and their unique perspectives on environmental issues.

Collaborating across this diverse stakeholder landscape will be crucial. We can develop more effective and equitable approaches to environmental governance by fostering mutual understanding among these varied actors.

Identifying the stakeholders is only part of the equation; examining how they interact within the environmental knowledge commons is essential for effective collective management. If done successfully, the diversity of actors will be an asset to the development and management of environmental knowledge commons.

C.2.3 *Interactions and Relationships among Stakeholders*

In light of the wide variety of stakeholders involved, it is unsurprising that collaboration is not always smooth. Harrington (Chapter 7) describes tensions arising when government agencies become commercial data clients, risking "paywalls" around information that was once public. Aagaard and Frischmann (Chapter 2) depict conflicts among the people who hunt, hike, or log in a shared forest. Nordman et al. (Chapter 4) show how city fees and incentives can persuade property owners to adopt green measures, yet also require public education. Contreras (Chapter 8) warns that patent commons can fail if private incentives are misaligned. Draper and Sun (Chapter 3) note that investors and companies both rely on environmental, social, and governance (ESG) ratings, which can become confusing when agencies use varied standards. Kurian et al. (Chapter 5) offer a more optimistic take: In Jordan, stakeholders found common ground through data and consistent communication. Finally, Cesari and Sun (Chapter 6) note that while open data helps space sustainability, security concerns still limit access. The result is the emergence of a new set of questions about how to mitigate the trade-offs between security and environmental sustainability.

C.2.4 *Governance Across Many Levels*

The authors describe a variety of governance frameworks supporting environmental knowledge commons. These span international treaties to local ordinances. Harrington (Chapter 7) notes the importance of United Nations offices and cross-border instruments in overseeing satellite data. Aagaard and Frischmann's account of US forests (Chapter 2) reveals a single federal agency juggling everything from conservation to recreation. Nordman et al. (Chapter 4) locate ground-level projects under the umbrella of federal laws, such as the Clean Water Act. Contreras (Chapter 8) notes that organizations such as the World Intellectual Property Organization (WIPO) can facilitate patent commons globally but need sustained commitment. Draper and Sun (Chapter 3) explain how ESG oversight may come from regulators, investor communities, or even consumer pressure. Kurian et al. (Chapter 5) credit success in Jordan to sustained coordination among ministries, experts, and local communities. Cesari and Sun (Chapter 6) see how data about near-Earth orbit might come from a single nation's program but remain relevant for every country with satellites.

While most of the governance frameworks discussed emphasize flexibility and adaptability, one highlights a critical tension between the need for authoritative decision-making and inclusive collaboration. Madison's discussion of the IPCC (Chapter 9) demonstrates how central expertise can guide complex environmental strategies. Sometimes, balancing authority with collaborative inclusion is essential to ensure decisions are both scientifically robust and adequately supported.

The polycentric nature of these governance structures allows for flexibility and adaptability in addressing complex environmental issues while also recognizing the importance of coordination and integration across different decision-making centers. As we face increasingly complex environmental challenges in the future, these governance structures will likely be crucial in fostering collaboration, ensuring access to knowledge, and developing effective strategies for environmental stewardship.

C.3 GOVERNANCE CHALLENGES AND EFFECTIVE APPROACHES

C.3.1 *Openness versus Protection*

The authors grapple with the fact that leaving knowledge open can spur innovation, but can also expose trade secrets or sensitive data. Harrington (Chapter 7) notes that some governments limit data access on security grounds; Contreras (Chapter 8) shows how companies fear losing competitive advantages if patents go unrestricted; Draper and Sun (Chapter 3) focus on the tightrope companies walk between transparency and revealing too much. Some wildlife data, Harrington points out, might aid poachers if made public.

C.3.2 *Adapting to Shifting Conditions*

Many chapters underscore the need to adapt. Aagaard and Frischmann (Chapter 2) call for robust structures that change in tandem with environmental conditions. Bloom (Chapter 1) recommends clear statements of values so that people know their shared principles even when circumstances evolve. Kurian et al. (Chapter 5) demonstrate how expert panels and ongoing learning can make climate strategies more responsive. Nordman et al. (Chapter 4) look at Detroit's green infrastructure, showing that each project yields lessons that can inform future decisions.

C.3.3 *Legal and Regulatory Webs*

International treaties, national laws, and local rules intersect in these commons. Harrington (Chapter 7) references space treaties, while Nordman et al. (Chapter 4) point to the Clean Water Act, and Draper and Sun (Chapter 3) discuss emerging ESG disclosure standards. Contreras (Chapter 8) looks at patent rules that can accelerate green-tech distribution. Bloom (Chapter 1) raises ethical frameworks such as the CARE Principles that aim to protect community rights and ensure respect for local knowledge.

C.3.4 *Technology's Role*

The authors highlight that while advanced technologies hold immense potential to unify diverse environmental knowledge, inequities may arise if access and oversight remain the privilege of a select few. Harrington (Chapter 7) and Cesari and Sun (Chapter 6) describe satellites and other advanced systems that produce immense troves of data. Aagaard and Frischmann (Chapter 2) warn about bias in algorithms if oversight is lax. Contreras (Chapter 8) and Draper and Sun (Chapter 3) examine tools such as WIPO Green or blockchain that can match innovators with investors or secure data provenance. Meanwhile, Nordman et al. (Chapter 4) observe that "green infrastructure" integrates simple nature-based ideas with modern engineering. Each author acknowledges that technology can unify scattered knowledge, though it can also create inequities if only a few privileged players have access.

C.3.5 *Public Institutions as Catalysts*

Harrington (Chapter 7) lists space agencies such as NASA, while Aagaard and Frischmann (Chapter 2) show how the US Forest Service manages more than just the land – publishing research for many users. Contreras (Chapter 8) thinks government sponsorship is sometimes needed to keep patent commons afloat. Kurian et al. (Chapter 5) credit national ministries for coordinating climate adaptation. Nordman et al. (Chapter 4) see how local leadership can mobilize and inform property owners. And Cesari and Sun (Chapter 6) point out that sovereign nations remain responsible for their space activities under international law.

C.3.6 *Constraints and Building Capacity*

The authors illustrate that the very fabric of environmental knowledge commons is woven from finite resources – time, money, knowledge, and technology – which demand deliberate strategies in sustained funding, inclusive capacity building, and innovative incentives to ensure their resilience and broad participation. Aagaard and Frischmann (Chapter 2) acknowledge that complex systems require continuous funding, while Contreras (Chapter 8) notes how collective projects can fade once early enthusiasm wanes. Cesari and Sun (Chapter 6) remind us that only a handful of players can afford next-generation space sensors. Harrington (Chapter 7) stresses capacity building – technology transfer and training – to broaden who can participate. Kurian et al.'s case of partnering local communities with experts (Chapter 5) shows that bridging different skill sets can yield resourceful solutions. Nordman et al. (Chapter 4) emphasize incentives that help property owners invest in practices they might not otherwise try.

C.3.7 *Policy Implications*

The chapters in this volume offer several important policy implications for managing environmental knowledge commons:

Communication and Capacity Building: Harrington (Chapter 7) suggests a need for public communication strategies about the benefits of Earth observation data. This implies that policymakers should consider developing and implementing comprehensive outreach programs to educate the public and stakeholders about the value of environmental data. Additionally, capacity-building efforts should focus on interoperability to ensure that data can be effectively shared and utilized across different platforms and stakeholders. This may require policies that promote standardization of data formats and sharing protocols.

Governance Strategies: Aagaard and Frischmann (Chapter 2) imply that understanding the relationship between environmental commons and knowledge commons can inform better governance strategies. Policymakers should consider how these relationships manifest in specific contexts to develop more effective management approaches. This might involve creating policies that explicitly recognize and address the interdependencies between physical environmental resources and the knowledge needed to manage them.

Value-Based Governance: Bloom (Chapter 1) emphasizes the importance of developing and implementing value statements in knowledge commons governance. Policymakers should consider adopting democratic writing processes to create value statements that reflect diverse stakeholder perspectives and guide decision-making. This approach could be incorporated into policy development processes, ensuring that environmental knowledge commons are governed in ways that align with community values and priorities.

Green Technology Dissemination: Contreras (Chapter 8) provides specific recommendations for improving green patent commons, including narrowing technical focus, conducting patent landscaping, and ensuring technology transfer. These strategies could be adopted by policymakers to facilitate broader dissemination of green technologies. Policies could be developed to incentivize the formation of focused green patent commons and to support the necessary infrastructure for effective technology transfer.

ESG Valuation and Transparency: Draper and Sun (Chapter 3) suggest that policymakers should consider more flexible and transparent approaches to ESG valuation and governance. This may involve prioritizing truth, transparency, and tangible outcomes to restore trust in ESG efforts. Policies could be developed to standardize ESG reporting requirements and to create more robust verification mechanisms for environmental claims.

Integrating Expert Knowledge and Data: Kurian et al. (Chapter 5) highlight the importance of integrating expert knowledge with data-driven approaches in policymaking, particularly for climate adaptation strategies. Policymakers should consider using tools such as trade-off intensity analysis to inform decision-making in complex, nonlinear systems. This might involve developing policies that mandate the use of expert panels or similar mechanisms in environmental decision-making processes.

Balanced Incentives for Green Infrastructure: Nordman et al.'s research (Chapter 4) indicates that policymakers should consider both economic incentives and knowledge-sharing mechanisms to encourage green stormwater infrastructure adoption, as economic incentives alone may be insufficient. This suggests a need for comprehensive policy approaches that combine financial incentives with education and capacity-building initiatives.

Space Data Management: Cesari and Sun (Chapter 6) suggest that policymakers should consider frameworks for aggregating and sharing space-related data in ways that benefit all stakeholders, potentially leading to the qualification of such data as knowledge commons. This might involve developing international agreements or national policies that promote open access to space-derived environmental data while addressing security and commercial concerns.

Overall, these policy implications emphasize the need for interdisciplinary approaches, stakeholder engagement, and adaptive governance strategies in managing environmental knowledge commons. Policymakers should strive to balance open access with necessary protections, foster collaboration across sectors, and develop flexible frameworks that can adapt to the complex and evolving nature of environmental challenges.

Furthermore, policies should aim to address the resource constraints and capacity-building needs identified across the chapters. This could include developing funding mechanisms for the long-term sustainability of knowledge commons, investing in technological infrastructure to support data sharing and analysis, and creating programs to build human capital in environmental data management and interpretation.

By implementing policies that reflect these insights, decision-makers can help create more robust, equitable, and effective environmental knowledge commons that contribute to improved environmental management and sustainability efforts globally.

C.3.8 *Future Directions*

As the field of environmental knowledge commons continues to evolve, several promising avenues for future research emerge from the diverse studies presented in this volume. These directions not only address current gaps in our understanding but also anticipate the challenges and opportunities that lie ahead in managing our shared environmental resources and knowledge.

Madison (Chapter 9) provides a compelling vision for future research. He argues that by juxtaposing the IPCC's role in synthesizing and translating climate science with similarly structured institutions – ranging from universities and research organizations to norm-governed creative communities – we can reveal shared structural features and decision-making modalities that cut across different domains. This approach not only enriches our understanding of how scientific authority is socially constructed and maintained but also offers practical insights for refining models of environmental policy design. In essence, Madison's framework encourages us to explore how diverse expert knowledge communities overcome social dilemmas in collaboration and communication, ultimately informing more robust strategies for managing and transmitting complex scientific information.

C.3.8.1 Investigating Complex EC–KC Relationships

A primary direction for future research, as highlighted by Aagaard and Frischmann (Chapter 2), is to delve deeper into the relationships between environmental commons and their associated knowledge commons. This involves exploring how specific features of environmental commons influence the governance of their corresponding knowledge commons and vice versa. Such research could provide valuable insights into designing more effective and adaptive governance systems that account for the interdependencies between physical resources and the knowledge required to manage them.

C.3.8.2 Retrospective Analysis of Environmental Commons Studies

Another promising approach is to conduct a retrospective empirical project revisiting prior environmental commons studies. This would involve mapping and analyzing the often understudied or implicit knowledge common aspects within these cases. Such an endeavor could uncover valuable lessons about the role of knowledge in environmental governance and help identify patterns or principles that may have been overlooked in previous analyses.

C.3.8.3 Enhancing Patent Commons for Green Technologies

In the realm of green technology, Contreras (Chapter 8) suggests focusing future research on developing more effective usage-tracking mechanisms for patent commons. Additionally, there is a need to explore the potential of narrower, more targeted patent commons in specific technological areas. This could lead to more successful collaborations and faster innovation in critical environmental technologies.

C.3.8.4 Integrating Expert Knowledge with Data-Driven Approaches

Kurian et al. (Chapter 5) point to the potential of combining expert panels with supervised machine learning in environmental governance. Future research should explore how these approaches can be effectively integrated to design better governance systems. This integration could lead to more robust and adaptable monitoring frameworks for climate adaptation and other environmental challenges.

C.3.8.5 Standardization and Ethical Considerations in Space Data

As we extend our environmental concerns beyond Earth, Cesari and Sun (Chapter 6) highlight the need for research on standardizing space data formats. This standardization is crucial for effective global sharing and utilization of space-related environmental data. Moreover, future studies should address the ethical considerations in space resource exploitation, balancing the benefits of open data with the potential negative consequences of unrestricted access to information about space resources.

C.3.8.6 Evolving Role of Artificial Intelligence and Machine Learning

As Harrington mentions (Chapter 7), the evolving role of artificial intelligence and machine learning in data governance presents another critical area for future research. Studies should explore how these technologies can enhance our ability to collect, analyze, and share environmental data while addressing privacy, security, and equity concerns.

C.3.8.7 Cross-Disciplinary and Comparative Studies

Future research should also emphasize cross-disciplinary and comparative studies. By examining how different fields approach knowledge commons (e.g., comparing approaches in environmental sciences, digital spaces, and healthcare), we may uncover transferable insights and innovative solutions to common challenges.

C.3.8.8 Practical Applications and Policy Implications

Finally, future research should focus on translating theoretical insights into practical applications and policy recommendations. This includes developing and testing new institutional designs, governance mechanisms, and technological solutions to effectively manage environmental knowledge commons in various contexts.

The field of environmental knowledge commons offers rich opportunities for future research that can significantly impact our ability to manage shared environmental resources sustainably. By pursuing these research directions, we can develop more sophisticated, adaptable, and practical approaches to environmental governance in an increasingly complex and interconnected world. The challenges we face in managing our environment are substantial, but so are the opportunities for innovation and collaboration in knowledge commons. As we progress, it will be crucial to balance theoretical advancement and practical application, ensuring that our research continues to inform and improve real-world environmental management practices.

C.3.8.9 Conclusion

As we close this exploration of environmental knowledge commons, we are reminded of the immense potential and responsibility that lies before us. Our planet's challenges are daunting, but the collective wisdom and innovative approaches showcased in this volume offer hope and direction. Environmental knowledge commons represent more than just shared information; they embody our collective capacity to understand, protect, and sustainably manage the natural systems that sustain us all.

The diverse case studies and analyses presented here demonstrate that effective environmental governance is not just about having data or technology but fostering collaboration, building trust, and creating inclusive systems that value diverse forms of knowledge. As we move forward, it is clear that the success of our environmental efforts will depend on our ability to break down silos, bridge divides between different stakeholders, and create governance structures that are as dynamic and adaptive as the ecosystems we seek to protect. By embracing the principles of environmental knowledge commons – openness, collaboration, and shared responsibility – we can build a more resilient and sustainable future for our planet and all its inhabitants. The path ahead is challenging, but with the insights and tools provided by environmental knowledge commons, we are better equipped than ever to face these challenges head on and create positive change for generations to come.

Appendix A: Expert Panel Identifier Information

Expert name	Occupation	Affiliation	GIS coordinate point	Expertise
Ayman Suleiman	Professor	University of Jordan	Latitude: 32° 00′ 30.00″ N Longitude: 35° 52′ 13.19″ E	Agricultural water and crop modeling
Khaldoon Al-Qudah	Professor	Yarmouk University	Latitude: 32° 28′ 59.99″ N Longitude: 36° 00′ 0.00″ E	Hydrology of arid regions
Ahmed Al-ta'ani	Professor	Yarmouk University	Latitude: 32° 28′ 59.99″ N Longitude: 36° 00′ 0.00″ E	Environmental science
Osama Mohawesh	Professor / Dean	Mutah University	–	Environmental engineering, sustainable agriculture, smart agriculture, water reuse, and climate change adaptation
Jawad Al-Bakri	Professor	The University of Jordan	Latitude: 32° 00′ 30.00″ N Longitude: 35° 52′ 13.19″ E	Remote sensing and water management
Dr. Issa Al-Nsour	Director	Ministry of Planning and International Cooperation	–	Water resources and environment

Appendix B: Questionnaire Covering Tradeoff Intensity, Institutional and Planetary Domains of CILDAS Model

Climate Assessments Considering Political Economy of Losses & Damages

Overview: This questionnaire contains three sections, including the expert's background, evaluation of climate change-induced loss and damage in the soil-water-food systems, and tradeoff intensity analysis to improve the effectiveness of climate financing programs.

* Indicates required question

1. Expert name

   ____

2. Occupation

   ____

3. Affiliation

   ____

4. Expertise * (Maximum 2 sentences)

   ____

   ____

   ____

   ____

   ____

5. Gender *

Mark only one oval.

- ( ) Male
- ( ) Female
- ( ) Prefer not to say
- ( ) Other
- ( ) Other:______________________

CLIMATE CHANGE-INDUCED LOSS AND DAMAGE IN THE SOIL-WATER-FOOD SYSTEMS SECTION

6. Based on your experience, please rank regions considered at high risk of climate * change-induced loss and damage in the soil-water-food systems/agriculture sector.

Mark only one oval per row.

	Most unlikely	Most Likely
Region 1	( )	( )
Region 2	( )	( )
Region 3	( )	( )

7. Based on your experience, please rank regions considered at low risk of climate change-induced loss and damage in the soil-water-food systems/agriculture sector.

Mark only one oval per row.

	Most unlikely	Most Likely
Region 1	( )	( )
Region 2	( )	( )
Region 3	( )	( )

TRADEOFF INTENSITY ASSESSMENT FOCUSED ON SOIL-WATER-FOOD SYSTEMS

This section covers the Biophysical Conditions, Tradeoff Intensity, and Institutional Response.

SECTION 1: The Biophysical Conditions

8. Please rank regions that are experiencing increasing frequency, duration and * intensity of temperature events which are trending towards extremes?

Mark only one oval per row.

	Most unlikely	Most Likely
Region 1	◯	◯
Region 2	◯	◯
Region 3	◯	◯

9. Which regions, witnessing increasing trend of extreme rainfall * events?

Mark only one oval per row.

	Most unlikely	Most Likely
Region 1	◯	◯
Region 2	◯	◯
Region 3	◯	◯

10. Which regions are experiencing deteriorating water quality for * agricultural operations that is trending towards extremes?

Mark only one oval per row.

	Most unlikely	Most Likely
Region 1	◯	◯
Region 2	◯	◯
Region 3	◯	◯

11. Which regions experiencing deteriorating quality of energy for agricultural operations that is trending towards extremes?

Mark only one oval per row.

	Most unlikely	Most Likely
Region 1	◯	◯
Region 2	◯	◯
Region 3	◯	◯

12. Based on your experience, rank the regions that witness extreme rates of land cover change.

Mark only one oval per row.

	Most Likely	Most unlikely
Region 1	◯	◯
Region 2	◯	◯
Region 3	◯	◯

13. What regions experiencing rates of soil erosion/floods/fires going to extremes? *

Mark only one oval per row.

	Most unlikely	Most Likely
Region 1	◯	◯
Region 2	◯	◯
Region 3	◯	◯

14. How would you describe regions where natural resource use per capita trending toward extremes? *

Mark only one oval per row.

	Most unlikely	Most Likely
Region 1	⬭	⬭
Region 2	⬭	⬭
Region 3	⬭	⬭

SECTION 2: *Tradeoff Intensity (TI)*

15. Based on your experience, identify the region where the Incidence of household nutritional insecurity per capita is trending toward extremes.

Mark only one oval per row.

	Most Likely	Most unlikely
Region 1	⬭	⬭
Region 2	⬭	⬭
Region 3	⬭	⬭

16. In the past 10 years, which regions have shown the greatest variability in agriculture's contribution to GDP and employment? *

Mark only one oval per row.

	Most unlikely	Most Likely
Region 1	⬭	⬭
Region 2	⬭	⬭
Region 3	⬭	⬭

17. As an expert, Which Jordanian regions where Hydropower/water discharge rates Which regions where hydropower/water discharge rates are trending toward higher variability?

Mark only one oval per row.

	Most unlikely	Most Likely
Region 1	◯	◯
Region 2	◯	◯
Region 3	◯	◯

18. In the past 10 years, which regions have shown the greatest variability in * the labor demand and supply changes for agricultural operations?

Mark only one oval per row.

	Most unlikely	Most Likely
Region 1	◯	◯
Region 2	◯	◯
Region 3	◯	◯

19. Based on your experience, which Jordanian regions, are witnessing extreme Which regions are witnessing increasing cropping intensity rates (more than 2 cropping cycles per year)?

Mark only one oval per row.

	Most unlikely	Most Likely
Region 1	◯	◯
Region 2	◯	◯
Region 3	◯	◯

20. Based on your experience, which regions are witnessing extreme rates * of land use change?

Mark only one oval per row.

	Most unlikely	Most Likely
Region 1	◯	◯
Region 2	◯	◯
Region 3	◯	◯

21. Based on your experience, which Jordanian regions most use agricultural inputs Which regions are experiencing the most use of inorganic (fertilizers, pesticides, mechanization) in agricultural operations?

Mark only one oval per row.

	Most unlikely	Most Likely
Region 1	◯	◯
Region 2	◯	◯
Region 3	◯	◯

SECTION 3: *Institutional Response (IR)*

22. Based on your experience, which regions have shown the higher variability * in the resource allocations toward infrastructure operation and maintenance?

Mark only one oval per row.

	Most unlikely	Most Likely
Region 1	◯	◯
Region 2	◯	◯
Region 3	◯	◯

23. As an expert, which regions have poorly aligned staffing and training programs targeting climate adaptation considering projected future changes in soil, water and food systems?

    Mark only one oval per row.

	Most unlikely	Most Likely
Region 1	◯	◯
Region 2	◯	◯
Region 3	◯	◯

24. In your opinion, which regions are the criteria for disbursement of * budgeted funds- prioritizing the operation and maintenance of climate-smart agricultural infrastructure/technology is trending negatively?

    Mark only one oval per row.

	Most unlikely	Most Likely
Region 1	◯	◯
Region 2	◯	◯
Region 3	◯	◯

25. In your opinion, which regions are most affected by poorly aligned trade policy targeting climate adaptation covering soil, water, and food systems?

    Mark only one oval per row.

	Most unlikely	Most Likely
Region 1	◯	◯
Region 2	◯	◯
Region 3	◯	◯

26. Which regions' officials have less recognition of political economy concerning* data in Management Information Systems (MIS)?

Mark only one oval per row.

	Most unlikely	Most Likely
Region 1	⬭	⬭
Region 2	⬭	⬭
Region 3	⬭	⬭

27. In which regions the projected fiscal trends with implications for asset * distribution (land, machinery, credit) for the resource-poor in the agriculture sector are trending negatively?

Mark only one oval per row.

	Most unlikely	Most Likely
Region 1	⬭	⬭
Region 2	⬭	⬭
Region 3	⬭	⬭

28. Which region has experienced negative trends in agricultural terms of * trade (market prices for crops) over the past decade?

Mark only one oval per row.

	Most unlikely	Most Likely
Region 1	⬭	⬭
Region 2	⬭	⬭
Region 3	⬭	⬭

29. Summary of comments (Maximum 2–3 sentences)

____

____

____

____

____

Bibliography

Abbott, A. D. 2001. *Chaos of Disciplines*. Chicago: University of Chicago Press.

About GEOSS. n.d. Group on Earth Observations. www.earthobservations.org/geoss.php.

About the Charter. n.d. The International Charter Space and Major Disasters. www.disaster scharter.org/web/guest/about-the-charter.

Activation List. n.d. The International Charter Space and Major Disasters. https://disaster scharter.org/web/guest/charter-activations?from=01+01+2000&to=31+08+2024.

Agrawal, A., J. Erbaugh, and N. Pradhan. 2023. "The Commons." *Annual Review of Environmental Resources* 48(1). https://doi:10.1146/annurev-environ-112320-113509.

Alfano, S., D. Oltrogge, and L. Arona. 2022. "Operators' Requirements for SSA Services." *The Journal of the Astronautical Sciences* 2(69): 1447–1476. https://doi.org/10.1007/s40295-022-00346-8.

Aligica, P. D., and V. Tarko. 2012. "Polycentricity: From Polanyi to Ostrom, and Beyond." *Governance* 25(2): 237–262. https://doi.org/10.1111/j.1468-0491.2011.01550.x.

Allen, D. S. 2014. *Our Declaration: A Reading of The Declaration of Independence in Defense of Equality*. New York: Liveright Publishing Corporation.

Allied Media Projects. n.d. "Network Principles." https://alliedmedia.org/network-principles.

Alston, E., W. Law, I. Murtazashvili, and M. Weiss. 2021. "Can Permissionless Blockchains Avoid Governance and the Law?" *Notre Dame Journal on Emerging Technologies* 2: 1–32.

Alvarez, A. 2022. "Courage Over Comfort." May 13. https://tinyurl.com/4dmmrd93

Antarctic Treaty Dec. 1, 1959, 12 U.S.T. 794, 402 U.N.T.S. 71.

Arjunan, P., K. Poolla, and C. Miller. 2020. "EnergyStar++: Towards More Accurate and Explanatory Building Energy Benchmarking." *Applied Energy* 276: 115413. https://doi .org/10.1016/j.apenergy.2020.115413.

Arnold, J. E. M. 1993. "Management of Forest Resources as Common Property." *Commonwealth Forestry Review* 72: 157–161.

Atkins, P. W. B., D. Sloan Wilson, and S. Hayes. 2019. *Prosocial*. Oakland, CA: Context Press.

Aust, A. 2010. *Handbook of International Law*. 2nd ed. Cambridge: Cambridge University Press.

Bakke, D. 2013. *The Decision Maker: Unlock the Potential of Everyone in Your Organization, one Decision at a Time*. Seattle, WA: Pear Press.

Barron, J. A. 1967. "Access to the Press—A New First Amendment Right." *Harvard Law Review* 80: 1641–1678.

Baseley-Walker, B., and B. Weeden. 2010. "Verification in Space: Theories, Realities and Possibilities." In *Disarmament Forum: Arms Control Verification*, edited by K. Vignard. Geneva, Switzerland: United Nations Institute for Disarmament Research. www.ipndv.org/wp-content/uploads/2017/11/UNIDIR_pdf-art3001-2.pdf.

Bataille, M., T. Hrozensky, S. Moranta, and A. N. Campos. 2022. *Space in Support of Security Missions. An Evolving Landscape with Untapped Potential* [Report No. 31]. Vienna, Austria: European Space Policy Institute. February. www.europeansources.info/record/space-in-support-of-security-missions-an-evolving-landscape-with-untapped-potential/.

Beck, S. 2011. "Moving beyond the Linear Model of Expertise? IPCC and the Test of Adaptation." *Regional Environmental Change* 11(2): 297–306. https://doi.org/10.1007/s10113-010-0136-2.

Beck, S., and M. Mahony. 2018. "The IPCC and the New Map of Science and Politics." *WIREs Climate Change* 9(6): e547. https://doi.org/10.1002/wcc.547.

Beck, S., and T. Forsyth. 2015. "Co-Production and Democratizing Global Environmental Expertise: The IPCC and Adaptation to Climate Change." In *Science and Democracy: Making Knowledge and Making Power in the Biosciences and Beyond*, edited by S. Hilgartner, C. Miller, and R. Hagendijk, 113–132. London: Routledge.

Beckwith, R., J. Sherry, and D. Prendergast. 2019. "Data Flow in the Smart City: Open Data Versus the Commons." In *The Hackable City*, edited by M. de Lange and M. de Waal, 205–221. Singapore: Springer. https://doi.org/10.1007/978-981-13-2694-3_11.

Ben-Itzhak, S. 2022. "The Future of Space Technology and How It May Benefit Humanity [Workshop Report]." In *Challenges and Opportunities at the Dawn of the New Space Age*. Philadelphia, PA: Perry World House. https://global.upenn.edu/sites/default/files/perry-world-house/space-ben-itzhakthoughtpiece.pdf.

Blair, A. 2010. *Too Much to Know: Managing Scholarly Information before the Modern Age*. New Haven, CT: Yale University Press.

Blank, S. G., and B. Dorf. 2012. *The Startup Owner's Manual: The Step-by-Step Guide for Building a Great Company*. Palo Alto, CA: K & S Ranch, Inc.

Blount, P. J., and L. Cesari. 2023. "Coexisting in Low-Earth Orbit: Large Constellations and Cybersecurity Governance." *Air & Space Law* 48, Special Issue: 1–30.

Bodon, H., P. Bustamante, M. Gomez, P. Krishnamurthy, M. J. Madison, I. Murtazashvili, J. B. Murtazashvili, T. Mylovanov, and M. B. Weiss. 2019 "Ostrom Amongst the Machines: Blockchain as a Knowledge Commons." Working Paper, University of Pittsburgh School of Law. https://scholarship.law.pitt.edu/fac_articles/402.

Boehmer-Christiansen, S. 1993. "Scientific Consensus and Climate Change: The Codification of a Global Research Agenda." *Energy & Environment* 4(4): 362–407. https://doi.org/10.1177/0958305X9300400403.

Bongers, A., and J. L. Torres. 2024. "Low-Earth Orbit Faces a Spiraling Debris Threat." *Scientific American*, April 22. https://tinyurl.com/3bxx8kef.

Bonvino, C., and M. Giorgino. 2024. "A Valorization Framework to Strategically Manage Data for Creating Competitive Value." *International Journal of Production Economics* 269. https://doi.org/10.1016/j.ijpe.2024.109152.

Borowitz, M. 2022. "Examining the Growth of the Global Space Situational Awareness Sector: A Network Analysis Approach." *Space Policy* 59. https://doi.org/10.1016/j.spacepol.2021.101444.

Borowitz, M., B. C. Gunter, M. Birch, and R. J. Macke. 2021. An investigation into potential collision maneuver guidelines for future Space Traffic Management, Advanced Maui Optical and Space Surveillance Technologies Conference (AMOS). Technical Papers. https://amostech.com/TechnicalPapers/2021/Conjunction-RPO/Borowitz.pdf.

Bozeman, B. 2007. *Public Values and Public Interest: Counterbalancing Economic Individualism*. Washington, DC: Georgetown University Press.

Brown, J. S., and P. Duguid. 2000. *The Social Life of Information*. Boston, MA: Harvard Business School Press.

Brown, R. R. 2005. “Impediments to Integrated Urban Stormwater Management: The Need for Institutional Reform.” *Environmental Management* 36(3): 455–468. https://doi.org/10.1007/s00267-004-0217-4.

Buchs, R., M.-V. Florin, E. David, and J.-P. Kneib. 2023. “Gaps Review and Improvement Pathways in the Assessment and Management of Collision Risk in Low Earth Orbit.” *Journal of Space Safety Engineering* 10(3): 374–338.

Byrnes, R., and S. Surminski. 2019. “Addressing the Impacts of Climate Change through an Effective Warsaw International Mechanism on Loss and Damage.” *Climate Policy* 19(6): 772–783. https://doi.org/10.1080/14693062.2018.1546711.

Cahoy, D. R. and L. Glenna. 2009. “Private Ordering and Public Energy Innovation Policy.” *Florida State University Law Review* 36: 415–458.

Cambridge University Press. 2023. “The Cambridge Handbook of Law and Policy for NFTs.” CambridgeCore. https://tinyurl.com/mr2n4vjb.

Campbell, B., D. Beare, E. Bennett, J. Hall-Spencer, J. Ingram, F. Jaramillo, R. Ortiz, N. Ramankutty, J. Sayer, and D. Shindell. 2017. “Agriculture Production as a Major Driver of Earth System Exceeding Planetary Boundaries.” *Ecology and Society* 22(4): 1–22.

Carbon Credits.com. 2023. Live Carbon Prices Today. https://tinyurl.com/56bedavb.

Carlile, P. R. 2002. “A Pragmatic View of Knowledge and Boundaries: Boundary Objects in New Product Development.” *Organization Science* 13(4): 442–455.

Carmichael, C., C. Danks, and C. Vatovec. 2019. “Green Infrastructure Solutions to Health Impacts of Climate Change: Perspectives of Affected Residents in Detroit, Michigan, USA.” *Sustainability* 11(5688): 1–15.

Carroll, S. R., I. Garba, O. L. Figueroa-Rodríguez, et al. 2020. “The CARE Principles for Indigenous Data Governance.” *Data Science Journal* 19: 43. https://tinyurl.com/3uajpx5c.

Census Reporter. 2021. “Census Profile: Detroit, MI.” Census Reporter. 2021. http://censusreporter.org/profiles/16000US2622000-detroit-mi/.

Cesari, L. 2022. “One Step Closer to Space Security: The Role of Multilateral Discussions.” *Global Policy* (Digital Debates, CyFy Journal): 90–98. https://orbilu.uni.lu/handle/10993/53187.

CGIAR. 2021. “Evaluation of CGIAR Platform for Big Data in Agriculture, Report.” Rome: CGIAR Advisory Services Shared Secretariat. https://cas.cgiar.org/.

Chafee, Jr, Z. 1947. *Government and Mass Communications*. Report from the Commission on Freedom of the Press. Chicago: University of Chicago Press.

Chagos Marine Protected Area Arbitration (Mau. v. U.K.) 519 (Perm. Ct. Arb. 2015).

Chandler, J. K., ed. 1998. *Questions of Evidence: Proof, Practice and Persuasion across the Disciplines*. Chicago: University of Chicago Press.

Chandrasekhar, A. 2023. “Timeline: The 60-year History of Carbon Offsets.” Carbon Brief. September 24. https://interactive.carbonbrief.org/carbon-offsets-2023/timeline.html.

Chatters, E. P., and B. J. Crothers. 2009. *Space Surveillance Network*. US Air Command and Staff College, US Air University. www.airuniversity.af.edu/Portals/10/AUPress/Books/AU-18.PDF.

Chavez, A. E. 2015. “Exclusive Rights to Saving the Planet: The Patenting of Geoengineering Inventions.” *Northwestern Journal of Technology and Intellectual Property* 13: 1.

Cheney, T. 2024. “The Extra-Planetary Mine: Space Mining as Continuity.” *Environment and History* 30(3): 353–358. www.liverpooluniversitypress.co.uk/doi/10.3828/whp.eh.63830915903596

Cheng, B. 1972. "Article VI of the 1967 Space Treaty Revisited." *Journal of Space Law* 26: 7–32.
Cheng, B. 1997. *Studies in International Space Law*. Oxford: Oxford University Press.
Chinese Academy of Science. 2024. "Discover the Moon Like Never Before: Scientists Unveil World's First High-Definition Geologic Atlas of the Entire Moon." *SciTechDaily*. August 25. https://scitechdaily.com/discover-the-moon-like-never-before-scientists-unveil-worlds-first-high-definition-geologic-atlas-of-the-entire-moon/.
Choi, E. J. 2025. "KEPLER: Status and Plans for Space Situational Awareness in the Republic of Korea." *Presentation to the UN COPUOS Scientific and Technical Subcommittee, Sixty-second Session*. www.unoosa.org/documents/pdf/copuos/stsc/2025/ListOfTechnicalPresentations/3_%20Wednesday5th%20/5a_-_R.O.K._UN_COPUOS_STSC_Item5_ROK_EJCHOI_20250205.pdf.
Christensen, I. A., I. Lange, G. Sowers, A. Abbud-Madrid, and M. Bazilian. 2019. New Policies Needed to Advance Space Mining. *Issues in Science and Technology*. https://issues.org/new-policies-needed-to-advance-space-mining/.
Cilliers, J., K. Hadler, and J. Rasera. 2023. "Toward the Utilisation of Resources in Space: Knowledge Gaps, Open Questions, and Priorities." *NPJ Microgravity* 9. www.nature.com/articles/s41526-023-00274-3.
Cirac-Claveras, G. 2019. "Weather Satellites: Public, Private and Data Sharing. The Case of Radio Occultation Data." *Space Policy* 47: 94–106.
City of Detroit. 2020a. "Eastern Market Neighborhood Framework and Stormwater Management Network Plan." https://tinyurl.com/yp932b5m.
City of Detroit. 2020b. "Post-Construction Stormwater Ordinance." https://tinyurl.com/2p9pt4c4.
City of Detroit. n.d. "Stormwater Hub." https://tinyurl.com/yf6sv4s6.
City of Detroit Water and Sewerage Department. 2022. "Green Infrastructure Progress Report – Upper Rouge Tributary Area." https://detroitmi.gov/document/2022-dwsd-green-infrastructure-progress-report.
City of Detroit Water and Sewerage Department. 2023. "Green Stormwater Infrastructure Projects." *Green Stormwater Infrastructure Projects*. https://tinyurl.com/6ja9z6n7.
Clerc, P., Hofmann M., and Cesari L. 2025a. "Legal Instruments for the Protection of Investments and Facilities." In *Mars and the Earthlings: A Realistic View on Mars Exploration and Settlement*, edited by C. Verseux, M. Gargaud, K. Lehto, and M. Viso, 301–305. Cham: Springer.
Clerc, P., Hofmann M., and Cesari L. 2025b. "Space Resources: Exploitation, Ownership, and Governance." In *Mars and the Earthlings: A Realistic View on Mars Exploration and Settlement*, edited by C. Verseux, M. Gargaud, K. Lehto, and M. Viso, 298–301. Cham: Springer.
Coase, R. H. 1960. "The Problem of Social Cost." *Journal of Law and Economics* 3: 1–44. https://doi.org/10.1086/466560.
Coglianese, C. 2009. "The Transparency President? The Obama Administration and Open Government." *Governance* 22: 529–544. https://doi.org/10.1111/j.1468-0491.2009.01451.x.
Commission on Freedom of the Press. 1974. "A Free and Responsible Press." The University of Chicago Press. https://press.uchicago.edu/ucp/books/book/chicago/F/b027983144.html.
Commission on the Peaceful Uses of Outer Space. 2018. Guidelines for the Long-term Sustainability of Outer Space Activities. Sixty-First Session, U.N. Doc. A/AC.105/2018/CRP.20.
Committee on the Peaceful Uses of Outer Space Scientific and Technical Subcommittee. 2023. European Union joint contribution on the implementation of the Guidelines for

the Long-term Sustainability of Outer Space Activities. February 6. www.unoosa.org/res/oosadoc/data/documents/2023/aac_105c_12023crp/aac_105c_12023crp_12_0_html/AC105_C1_2023_CRP12E.pdf.

Contreras, J. L. 2015. "Patent Pledges." *Arizona State Law Journal* 47(3): 543–608.

Contreras, J. L. 2018a. "The Anticommons at Twenty: Concerns for Research Continue." *Science* 361(6400): 335.

Contreras, J. L. 2018b. "The Evolving Patent Pledge Landscape." CIGI Papers No. 166. https://papers.ssrn.com/sol3/papers.cfm?abstract_id=3157572.

Contreras, J. L. 2021. "The Open COVID Pledge: Design, Implementation and Preliminary Assessment of an Intellectual Property Commons." *Utah Law Review* 2021: 833–924.

Contreras, J. L. 2025. "Patent Pledges as Portfolio Management Tools: Benefits, Obligations and Enforcement." In *A Modern Guide to Patenting. Challenges of Patenting in the 21st Century*, edited by K. Blind and N. Thumm. Cheltenham, UK: Edward Elgar.

Contreras, J. L., and R. Lakshané. 2017. "Patents and Mobile Devices in India: An Empirical Survey." *Vanderbilt Journal of Transnational Law* 50: 1.

Contreras, J. L., B. H. Hall, and C. Helmers. 2019. "Pledging Patents for the Public Good: Rise and Fall of the Eco-Patent Commons." *The Houston Law Review* 57: 61–109.

Contreras, J. L., R. Bekkers, B. Biddle, E. Bonadio, M. A. Carrier, B. Chao, C. Duan, T. Eberhart, C. Fuchs, S. Ivanov, B. Lichtenberg, C. Mazzacano, M. O'Leary, C. Quercia, and C. de Figueiredo 2023. "Preserving the Royalty-Free Standards Ecosystem." *European Intellectual Property Review* 45(7): 371–375.

Convention on the Law of the Sea, December 10, 1982, 1833 U.N.T.S. 397.

Cornes, R., and T. Sandler. 1996. *The Theory of Externalities, Public Goods, and Club Goods*. 2nd ed. Cambridge: Cambridge University Press.

Correa, A.-D. 2023. "Brazil: Three Carbon Offset Projects Accused of Being Scams." *Le Monde*, November 20. www.lemonde.fr/en/economy/article/2023/11/20/three-carbon-offset-projects-in-brazil-accused-of-being-scams_6271470_19.html.

Council of the EU. 2023. "Space Traffic Management: Council Adopts Conclusions on The Current State of Play." European Council Council of the European Union. www.consilium.europa.eu/en/press/press-releases/2023/12/08/space-traffic-management-council-adopts-conclusions-on-the-current-state-of-play/.

Crawford, S. E. S., and E. Ostrom. 1995. "A Grammar of Institutions." *American Political Science Review* 89(3): 582–600. https://doi.org/10.2307/2082975.

Darling, K., and A. Perzanowski, eds. 2017. *Creativity without Law: Challenging the Assumptions of Intellectual Property*. New York: New York University Press.

Dasgupta, S., U. Deichmann, C. Meisner, and D. Wheeler. 2005. "Where Is the Poverty-Environment Nexus? Evidence from Cambodia, Lao PDR and Vietnam." *World Development* 33: 617–638.

Daston, L., ed. 2017. *Science in the Archives: Pasts, Presents, Futures*. Chicago: The University of Chicago Press.

Daston, L., and P. Galison. 1992. "The Image of Objectivity." *Representations* 40: 81–128. https://doi.org/10.2307/2928741.

Davidson, S., P. de Filippi, and J. Potts. 2018. "Blockchains and the Economic Institutions of Capitalism." *Journal of Institutional Economics* 14(4): 639–658. https://doi.org/10.1017/S1744137417000200.

De Moor, T. 2011. "Dossier 'Le Champ Des *Commons* En Question : Perspectives Croisées' – From Common Pastures to Global Commons: A Historical Perspective on Interdisciplinary

Approaches to Commons." *Natures Sciences Sociétés* 19(4): 422–431. https://doi.org/10.1051/nss/2011133.

Debo, T. N., and A. Reese. 2002. *Municipal Stormwater Management*. 2nd ed. Boca Raton, FL: CRC Press. https://doi.org/10.1201/9781420032260.

Dechezleprêtre, A. 2013. "Fast-Tracking Green Patent Applications: An Empirical Analysis." ICTSD Global Platform on Climate Change, Trade and Sustainable Energy, Issue Paper No. 37, February, www.files.ethz.ch/isn/161230/fast-tracking-green-patent-applications-an-empirical-analysis.pdf.

Dedeurwaerdere, T., B. Frischmann, C. Hess, D. Lametti, M. Madison, C. Schweik, and K. Strandburg. 2014. An Introduction to Knowledge Commons. https://knowledge-commons.net/downloads/Knowledge.Commons.Description.pdf.

Dekker, E., and P. Kuchař, eds. 2021. *Governing Markets as Knowledge Commons*. Cambridge: Cambridge University Press.

Derclaye, E. 2010. "Not Only Innovation But Also Collaboration, Funding, Goodwill and Commitment: Which Role For Patent Laws In Post-Copenhagen Climate Change Action." *John Marshall Review of Intellectual Property Law* 9: 657–673.

Detroit Water and Sewerage Department. 2020. "Resources." Detroit Stormwater Hub. February 26. https://detroitstormwater.org/resources.

Detroit Water and Sewerage Department. 2022. "Stormwater Management Design Manual." https://tinyurl.com/2p9pt4c4.

Deutsch, L., B. Belcher, R. Claus, and S. Hoffman. 2021. "Leading Inter and Transdisciplinary Research: Lessons from Applying Theories of Change to a Strategic Research Program." *Environmental Science and Policy* 120: 29–41.

Dorward, A., J. Kydd, J. Morrisson, and C. Poulton. 2005. "Institutions, Markets and Economic Coordination: Linking Development Policy to Theory and Practice." *Development and Change* 36: 1–25.

Draper, C. 2020. "The Tragedy of Truth." *Medium*. March 17. https://medium.com/trokt/the-tragedy-of-truth-989f3a1c9e9d.

Eat Greater Des Moines. 2023 ProPublica. https://projects.propublica.org/nonprofits/organizations/472914255.

Eaves, D., M. Mazzucato, and B. Vasconcellos. 2024. Digital Public Infrastructure and Public Value: What Is 'Public' About DPI? UCL Institute for Innovation and Public Purpose, Working Paper Series (IIPP WP 2024-05). https://tinyurl.com/3f2ucarh.

Edwards, P. N. 2017. "Knowledge Infrastructures for the Anthropocene." *The Anthropocene Review* 4(1): 34–43. https://doi.org/10.1177/2053019616679854.

Eller, D. 2018. "Iowa Nitrogen Pollution in the Water Is Getting Worse, Despite Hundreds of Millions of Dollars in Spending, Study Shows." *The Des Moines Register*, June 18, updated July 9. https://tinyurl.com/ttfrtn5e.

Equal Experts. n.d. Advice Process Playbook. https://playbooks.equalexperts.com/advice-process.

Fact sheet: First national cislunar science & technology strategy. 2022. White House. November 17. www.whitehouse.gov/ostp/news-updates/2022/11/17/fact-sheet-first-national-cislunar-science-technology-strategy/.

FAO. 2020. Environmental and Social Management Framework: Building Resilience to Cope with Climate Change in Jordan Through Improving Water Use Efficiency in the Agriculture Sector (BRCCJ). https://tinyurl.com/2jmbn26w.

Farber, S. 2004. "Market-Based Instruments, Overview." *ScienceDirect*. https://tinyurl.com/4zxyk789.

Fearon, J. D. 1997. "Signaling Foreign Policy Interests: Tying Hands versus Sinking Costs." *The Journal of Conflict Resolution* 41(1): 68–90. www.jstor.org/stable/174487.

Feeding America. 2023. Food Insecurity among the Overall Population in Iowa. https://map.feedingamerica.org/county/2020/overall/iowa.

Foust, J. 2019. "Data Sharing Seen as Critical to Future of Space Situational Awareness." SpaceNews. https://spacenews.com/data-sharing-seen-as-critical-to-future-of-space-situational-awareness/.

Fredman, A., and T. Phillips. 2022. "The CFTC Should Raise Standards and Mitigate Fraud in the Carbon Offsets Market." CAP 20. October 7. https://tinyurl.com/3a2nphrc.

Friedman, B., P. Kahn, and A. Borning. 2006. "Value Sensitive Design and Information Systems." In *Human-Computer Interaction and Management Information Systems: Foundations Advances in Management Information Systems*, edited by P. Zhang and D. Galletta, vol. 5, 348–372. Armonk, NY: M. E. Sharpe.

Friedman, J. 2019. "Lippmann and Dewey: The Unjoined Debate." In *Power without Knowledge, by Jeffrey Friedman*, 80–124. New York: Oxford University Press. https://doi.org/10.1093/oso/9780190877170.003.0003.

Frischmann, B. 2012. *Infrastructure: The Social Value of Shared Resources*. New York: Oxford University Press.

Frischmann, B. 2013. "Two Enduring Lessons from Elinor Ostrom." *Journal of Institutional Economics* 9: 387–406. https://doi.org/10.1017/S1744137413000106

Frischmann, B. 2021. "Common Sense Commons: The Case of Commonsensical Social Norms." In *Governing Markets as Knowledge Commons*, edited by P. Kuchar and E. Decker, pp. 113–132. Cambridge: Cambridge University Press. https://doi.org/10.1017/9781108692915.006.

Frischmann, B. M., M. J. Madison, and K. J. Strandburg, eds. 2014a. *Governing Knowledge Commons*. Oxford: Oxford University Press. https://doi.org/10.1093/acprof:oso/9780199972036.001.0001.

Frischmann, B. M., M. J. Madison, and K. J. Strandburg. 2014b. "Governing Knowledge Commons." In *Governing Knowledge Commons*, edited by B. M. Frischmann, M. J. Madison, and K. J. Strandburg, 1–44. New York: Oxford University Press.

Frischmann, B. M., M. J. Madison, and M. Rose Sanfilippo, eds. 2023. *Governing Smart Cities as Knowledge Commons*. Cambridge: Cambridge University Press. https://doi.org/10.1017/9781108938532.

Garino, B., and J. Gibson. n.d. "Space System Threats." In *AU-18: Space Primer, US Air Command and Staff College*, edited by Air Command and Staff College (ACSC) Schriever Space Scholars, and Air War College (AWC). Maxwell AFB, AL: Air University Press.

Gattari, P. 2013. "The Role of Patent Law in Incentivizing Green Technology." *Northwestern Journal of Technology and Intellectual Property* 11(2): 41–45.

GCOS Satellite Programs. n.d. WMO. https://gcos.wmo.int/en/networks/satellite.

Geospatial, Information and Telecommunications Technologies. n.d. U.N. Global Service Centre. www.ungsc.org/Service/GeospatialInformationTechnology.

Ghafele, R., and R. D. O'Brien. 2012. "Open Innovation for Sustainability: Lessons from the GreenXchange Experience." International Centre for Trade and Sustainable Development, Policy Brief No. 13.

Ghosh, S. 2007. "How to Build a Commons: Is Intellectual Property Constrictive, Facilitating, or Irrelevant?" In *Understanding Knowledge as a Commons: From Theory to Practice*, edited by C. Hess and E. Ostrom, 209–246. Cambridge, MA: MIT Press. https://doi.org/10.7551/mitpress/6980.003.0012.

Gillibrand, N., and C. Draper. 2023. "Per 'Hu': A Unifying Constant for Calculating Complex Environmental, Social, and Governance Impacts." https://doi.org/10.2139/ssrn.4643983. https://papers.ssrn.com/sol3/papers.cfm?abstract_id=4643983.

Gindis, D., and D. H. Cole. 2025. "Toward a Knowledge Commons Perspective on the Corporate Form." In *Governing Corporate Knowledge Commons*, ed. D. Gindis, Cambridge: Cambridge University Press.

Global Climate Observing System. n.d. WMO. https://Gcos.wmo.int.

Gnanarajah, R., and G. Shorter. 2022. "Introduction to Financial Services: Environmental, Social, and Governance (ESG) Issues." Congressional Research Service, January 13. https://tinyurl.com/2wvvnfnj.

Goehring, J. S. 2021. "Why Isn't Outer Space Global Commons?" *Journal of National Security Law & Policy* 11: 573–590. https://jnslp.com/wp-content/uploads/2021/09/Why_Isnt_Outer_Space_a_Global_Commons_2.pdf.

Golan, T. 2007. *Laws of Men and Laws of Nature: The History of Scientific Expert Testimony in England and America*. Cambridge, MA: Harvard University Press.

Goldman, A. I. 2001. "Experts: Which Ones Should You Trust?" *Philosophy and Phenomenological Research* 63(1): 85–110. https://doi.org/10.1111/j.1933-1592.2001.tb00093.x.

Gorove, S. 1971. "Freedom of Exploration and Use in the Outer Space Treaty." *Denver Journal of International Law & Policy* 1: 93–107.

GreaseTrack. 2024. "Certainty from the Source." GreaseTrack. www.greasetrack.com/.

Greater Des Moines Partnership. 2022. "DSM Fellows Capstone Panel: Food Insecurity." *DSM USA*, April 7. https://tinyurl.com/ykw2pn3b.

Greenfield, P. 2023. "Revealed: More Than 90% of Rainforest Carbon Offsets by Biggest Certifier Are Worthless, Analysis Shows." *The Guardian*, last modified January 30, 2023. https://tinyurl.com/3vp3nb25.

Gregory, R. 1997. "Political Rationality or Incrementalism?" In *The Policy Process: A Reader*, edited by M. Hill, 175–191. Hemel Hempstead, UK: Prentice Hall.

Grimmelmann, J. and A. Jason Windawi. 2023. "Blockchains as Infrastructure and Semicommons." *William & Mary Law Review* 64: 1097–1120. https://scholarship.law.wm.edu/wmlr/vol64/iss4/6.

Grundmann, R. 2017. "The Problem of Expertise in Knowledge Societies." *Minerva* 55(1): 25–48.

Grundmann, R. 2023. *Making Sense of Expertise: Cases from Law, Medicine, Journalism, Covid-19, and Climate Change*. New York: Routledge, Taylor & Francis Group. https://doi.org/10.4324/9781003320227.

Gurstein, M. 2011. "'Open'—'Necessary' but not 'Sufficient'." Gurstein's Community Informatics. July 6. https://tinyurl.com/54k6hydr.

Gustafsson, K. M. 2021. "Expert Organizations' Institutional Understanding of Expertise and Responsibility for the Creation of the Next Generation of Experts: Comparing IPCC and IPBES." *Ecosystems and People* 17(1): 47–56. https://doi.org/10.1080/26395916.2021.1891973.

Guyomarc'h, A. 2023. Préparer le droit spatial français aux nouvelles ambitions lunaires. www.anrt.asso.fr/sites/default/files/2024-01/ANRT_Droit-spatial_Note%20approfondissement%20strat%C3%A9gique%20n%C2%B01_Novembre%202023.pdf.

Haapaniemi, S., Patrick Doran, V. S., Elaine Isely, E. N., Paul Isely, C. G., Shanyn Viars, S. D., E. Giese, and L. Noye. 2023. "Making Detroit's Green Stormwater Infrastructure Count: A Report." Report to The Nature Conservancy. https://tinyurl.com/ywc78txf.

Haas, P. M. 1992. "Introduction: Epistemic Communities and International Policy Coordination." *International Organization* 46(1): 1–35.

Hardin, G. 1968. "The Tragedy of the Commons." *Science* 162(3859): 1243–1248.

Harriden, K. 2021. "Small-Scale Interventions and Indigenous Water Knowledge – Moving Stormwater into the Next Decade." Paper presented at Stormwater 2021 National Conference, Brisbane, Queensland, Australia. https://tinyurl.com/mr3x7zrr.

Harrington, A. J. 2017. "The Relationship between the Remote Sensing Principles and Customary International Law." In *Proceedings of the 59th (2016) Colloquium on the Law of Outer Space. Eleven Journals*, 329–340.

Harrington, A. J. 2023."Due Regard as the Prime Directive for Responsible Behavior in Space." *Loyola University Chicago International Law Review* 20: 57–86.

Harris, J, J. Hunter, and C. Lewis. 1995. *The New Institutional Economics and Third World Development*. London: Routledge.

Hayek, F. 1945. "The Use of Knowledge in Society." *American Economic Review* 35(4): 519–530.

Hazell, P. 2017. "Global Trends in Urbanization, Agriculture and Smallholder Farming." In *Agri-food Systems into 2050: Threats and Opportunities*, edited by P. Pingali and R. Serraj. Rome: World Scientific.

Heller, M. 2013. "The Tragedy of the Anticommons: A Concise Introduction and Lexicon." *The Modern Law Review* 76(6): 6–25. https://doi.org/10.1111/1468-2230.12000.

Heller, M. A. 1998. "The Tragedy of the Anticommons: Property in the Transition from Marx to Market." *Harvard Law Review* 111(3): 621–688.

Heller, M. A., and R. S. Eisenberg. 1998. "Can Patents Deter Innovation? The Anticommons in Biomedical Research." *Science* 280(5364): 698–701.

Henrich, J., M. Chudek, and R. Boyd. 2015. "The Big Man Mechanism: How Prestige Fosters Cooperation and Creates Prosocial Leaders." *Philosophical Transactions of the Royal Society B: Biological Sciences* 370(1683): 20150013. https://doi.org/10.1098/rstb.2015.0013.

Hertzfeld, H. R. 2021. "Unsolved Issues of Compliance with the Registration Convention." *Journal of Space Safety Engineering* 8(3): 238–244.

Hertzfeld, H., B. Weeden, and C. D. Johnson. 2015. *How Simple Terms Mislead Us: The Pitfalls of Thinking about Outer Space as a Commons*. Secure World Foundation. https://swfound-preprod.azurewebsites.net/media/205390/how-simple-terms-mislead-us-hertzfeld-johnson-weeden-iac-2015.pdf.

Hess, C., and E. Ostrom, eds. 2007a. *Understanding Knowledge as a Commons: From Theory to Practice*, edited by C. Hess and E. Ostrom. Cambridge, MA: MIT Press.

Hess, C., and E. Ostrom, eds. 2007b. "A Framework for Analyzing the Knowledge Commons." In *Understanding Knowledge as a Commons: From Theory to Practice*, edited by C. Hess and E. Ostrom, 41–82. Cambridge, MA: MIT Press.

Hilty, R. M. and D. B. Pedro Henrique. 2023. "Potential and Limits of Patent Law to Address Climate Change." *GRUR International* 72(9): 821–839.

Holmes, Jr., O. W. 1897. "The Path of the Law." *Harvard Law Review* 10(457). https://moglen.law.columbia.edu/LCS/palaw.pdf.

Hsu, C. C., and B. A. Sandford. 2007. "The Delphi Technique: Making Sense of Consensus." *Practical Assessment, Research Evaluation* 12. http://pareonline.net/getvn.asp?v=12&n=10.

Hughes, S. 2020. "Principles, Drivers, and Policy Tools for Just Climate Change Adaptation in Legacy Cities." *Environmental Science & Policy* 111: 35–41. https://doi.org/10.1016/j.envsci.2020.05.007.

Iaia, V. 2024. "Eco-Patents at the Crossroads between Technological Neutrality and Environmental Sensitivity." *GRUR International* 73(4): 308–322.

IFRI. 1997. *International Forestry Resources and Institutions Research Project, Data Collection Protocols, Version 1.3*. Bloomington, IN: Ostrom Workshop in Political Theory and Policy Analysis.

In, S. Y., and K. Schumacher. 2021. "Carbonwashing: A New Type of Carbon Data-related ESG Greenwashing." Sustainable Finance Initiative, July. https://tinyurl.com/2f8wj985.

Independent Evaluation Unit. 2022. "Report of the Synthesis Study: An IEU Deliverable Contributing to the Second Performance Review of the Green Climate Fund. (March)." Songdo, South Korea: Independent Evaluation Unit, Green Climate Fund.

Ingber, S. 1984. "The Marketplace of Ideas: A Legitimizing Myth." *Duke Law Journal* 33: 1–91.

Innovation News Network. 2023. "Challenges of Space-based Space Situational Awareness." Innovation News Network. October 3. www.innovationnewsnetwork.com/challenges-of-space-based-space-situational-awareness/34979/.

International Asteroid Warning Network. n.d. International Asteroid Warning Network. https://iawn.net.

International Emissions Trading Association. 2023 "About." IETA. www.ieta.org/about/.

International Law Commission. 2004. *Rep. of the Study Group on Fragmentation of International Law*. U.N. Doc A/CN4/L663/Rev1.

International Telecommunication Union (ITU). n.d. ITU Radio Regulations, Appendices 30, 30A and 30B: Space Plan Assignments Recorded in the Master Register. International Telecommunication Union.

International Telecommunication Union (ITU). n.d. ITU Radio Regulatory Framework for Space Services.

IPCC. 2022. *Climate Change 2022: Impacts, Adaptation, and Vulnerability. Contribution of Working Group II to the Sixth Assessment Report of the Intergovernmental Panel on Climate Change*. Edited by H. O. Pörtner, D. C. Roberts, M. Tignor, E. S. Poloczanska, K. Mintenbeck, A. Alegría, M. Craig, S. Langsdorf, S. Löschke, V. Möller, A. Okem, and B. Rama. Cambridge: Cambridge University Press.

IPCC. n.d. "IPCC Principles and Procedures." https://archive.ipcc.ch/organization/organization_procedures.shtml.

Isely, E., S. Viars, E. Nordman, et al. 2022. "Modeling the Business Case for Green Stormwater Infrastructure in Detroit, Michigan." Report to The Nature Conservancy.

Ito, A. 2005. "Issues in the Implementation of the International Charter on Space and Major Disasters." *Space Policy* 21: 141–149.

Ito, A. 2011. *Legal Aspects of Satellite Remote Sensing*. Leiden: Brill Nijhoff.

JafariNaimi, N., L. Nathan, and I. Hargraves. 2015. "Values as Hypotheses: Design, Inquiry, and the Service of Values." *DesignIssues* 31(4): 91–104.

Jaramillo, F., and G. Destouni. 2015. "Comment on 'Planetary Boundaries Guiding Human Development on a Changing Planet.'" *Science* 348(6240): 1217.

Jasanoff, S. 2005. *Designs on Nature: Science and Democracy in Europe and the United States*. Princeton, NJ: Princeton University Press.

Johns, C. M. 2019. "Understanding Barriers to Green Infrastructure Policy and Stormwater Management in the City of Toronto: A Shift from Grey to Green or Policy Layering and Conversion?" *Journal of Environmental Planning and Management* 62(8): 1377–1401. https://doi.org/10.1080/09640568.2018.1496072.

Jordan, E. 2022. "Black Farmers in Iowa Plowing Different Path." *The Gazette*, February 21, updated April 19. https://tinyurl.com/3pbd4uum.

Kealey, T., and M. Ricketts. 2014. "Modelling Science as a Contribution Good." *Research Policy* 43(6): 1014–1024. https://doi.org/10.1016/j.respol.2014.01.009.

Keefe, H. 1995. "Making the Final Frontier Feasible: A Critical Look at the Current Body of Outer Space Law." *Santa Clara High Technology Law Journal* 11: 345–371.

Kellerer, W., P. Kalmbach, A. Blenk, A. Basta, M. Reisslein, and S. Schmid. 2019. "Adaptable and Data-Driven Softwarized Networks: Review, Opportunities, and Challenges." *Proceedings of the IEEE* 107(4). https://doi.org/10.1109/JPROC.2019.2895553.

Kim, J., V. Y. Ivanov, and S. Fatichi. 2016. "Climate Change and Uncertainty Assessment over a Hydroclimatic Transect of Michigan." *Stochastic Environmental Research and Risk Assessment* 30(3): 923–944. https://doi.org/10.1007/s00477-015-1097-2.

Kostopoulos, L. 2019. "The Role of Data in Algorithmic Decision-Making, A Primer." UNIDIR. https://unidir.org/files/publication/pdfs/the-role-of-data-in-algorithmic-decision-making-en-815.pdf.

Kourtis, I. M., and V. A. Tsihrintzis. 2021. "Adaptation of Urban Drainage Networks to Climate Change: A Review." *Science of The Total Environment* 771: 145431. https://doi.org/10.1016/j.scitotenv.2021.145431.

Kuchar, P., D. Cole, and D. Gindis. forthcoming. "Toward a Knowledge Commons Perspective on the Corporate Form." In *Governing Corporate Knowledge Commons*, edited by D. Gindis and P. Kuchar. Cambridge: Cambridge University Press.

Kuhn, T. S. 1962. *The Structure of Scientific Revolutions*. Chicago: University of Chicago Press.

Kurian, M. A., and R. Ardakanian. 2015. *Governing the Nexus: Water, Soil and Waste Resources Considering Global Change*. Cham: Springer.

Kurian, M., and Y. Kojima. 2021. *Boundary Science: Re-imagining water-energy-food interactions in the Context of a Data Light Approach to Monitoring the Environment-Development Debate*. Amsterdam: Elsevier.

Lal, B., A. Balakrishnan, B. M. Caldwell, R. S. Buenconsejo, and S. A. Carioscia. 2018. "Global Trends in Space Situational Awareness (SSA) and Space Traffic Management (STM)." Institute for Defense Analyses Science and Technology Policy Institute. www.ida.org/-/media/feature/publications/g/gl/global-trends-in-space-situational-awareness-ssa-and-space-traffic-management-stm/d-9074.ashx.

Lee, R. J. 2012. *Law and Regulation of Commercial Mining of Minerals in Outer Space*. Cham: Springer.

Lessig, L. 1999. *Code and Other Laws of Cyberspace*. New York: Basic Books.

Levin, P., and R. Beckwith. 2015. "Datasheds and the Remaking of Agricultural Practices: How the Internet of Things Is Changing Agriculture." In *Society for Economic Anthropology Conference*, Lexington, KY.

Lippmann, W. 1922. *Public Opinion*. New York: Harcourt, Brace & Co.

Live Carbon Prices Today. 2023. Carbon Credits. https://carboncredits.com/carbon-prices-today/?gclid=CjwKCAjwz42xBhB9EiwA48pT7ywka7NNNtuCcYxqAcc4EVCx_1ijUQIS4_a-OzSRS4x9ELvewh24FRoCi1cQAvD_BwE.

Lofthouse, J. K., and A. Schaefer. 2024. "Expert Knowledge and the Administrative State." Public Choice, November. https://doi.org/10.1007/s11127-024-01228-3.

Lunar and Planetary Institute. n.d. "Lunar Map Catalog." LPI. www.lpi.usra.edu/resources/mapcatalog/.

Lyall, F., and P. B. Larsen. 2024. *Space Law: A Treatise*. 3rd ed. London: Routledge.

Madison, M. J. 2004. "A Pattern-Oriented Approach to Fair Use." *William and Mary Law Review* 45(4): 1525–1690.

Madison, M. J. 2009. "Notes on a Geography of Knowledge." *Fordham Law Review* 77(5): 2039–2085.

Madison, M. J. 2014. "Commons at the Intersection of Peer Production, Citizen Science, and Big Data: Galaxy Zoo." In *Governing Knowledge Commons*, edited by M. F. Brett, J. M. Michael, and J. S. Katherine, 209–254. New York: Oxford University Press.

Madison, M. J. 2021. "The Republic of Letters and the Origins of Scientific Knowledge Commons." In *Governing Privacy in Knowledge Commons*, edited by M. R. Sanfilippo, B. M. Frischmann, and K. J. Strandburg, 151–184. Cambridge: Cambridge University Press. https://doi.org/10.1017/9781108749978.007.

Madison, M. J. 2023. "The Kind of Solution a Smart City Is: Knowledge Commons and Postindustrial Pittsburgh." In *Governing Smart Cities as Knowledge Commons*, edited by M. F. Brett, J. M. Michael, and J. S. Katherine and M. R. Sanfilippo, 157–220. Cambridge: Cambridge University Press. https://doi.org/10.1017/9781108938532.009.

Madison, M. J. 2024. "Knowledge Commons Past, Present, and Future." *Lewis & Clark Law Review* 28(2): 303–331. https://doi.org/10.2139/ssrn.4876589. University of Pittsburgh Legal Studies Research Paper No. 2024-17. https://ssrn.com/abstract=4876589.

Madison, M. J., B. M. Frischmann, and K. J. Strandburg. 2009. "The University as Constructed Cultural Commons." *Washington University Journal of Law and Policy* 30: 365–403.

Madison, M. J., B. M. Frischmann, and K. J. Strandburg. 2010. "Constructing Commons in the Cultural Environment." *Cornell Law Review* 95(657). https://scholarship.law.cornell.edu/clr/vol95/iss4/10.

Madison, M. J., B. M. Frischmann, M. R. Sanfilippo, and K. J. Strandburg. 2022. "Too Much of a Good Thing? A Governing Knowledge Commons Review of Abundance in Context." *Frontiers in Research Metrics and Analytics* 7: 959505. https://doi.org/10.3389/frma.2022.959505.

Maitra, N. 2010. "Access to Environmentally Sound Technology in the Developing World: A Proposed Alternative to Compulsory Licensing." *Columbia Journal of Environmental Law* 35(2): 407–446.

Malloy, A. D., K. Mohan, D. Straub, and A. Tiwana. 2003. "Copyright Laws." In *Encyclopedia of Information Systems*, edited by H. Bidgoli, 307–317. Amsterdam: Elsevier. https://doi.org/10.1016/B0-12-227240-4/00020-4.

Mansell, R. 2013. "Employing Digital Crowdsourced Information Resources: Managing the Emerging Information Commons." *International Journal of the Commons* 7(2): 255. https://doi.org/10.18352/ijc.395.

Manyika, J., M. Chui, D. Farrell, S. Kuiken, P. Groves, and E. Doshi. 2013. Open Data: Unlocking Innovation and Performance with Liquid Information. https://tinyurl.com/2xmcxa8v.

Masson-Zwaan, T., P. Martinez, F. Letizia, et al. 2024. "The Need to Improve Registration Practices in The Context of Space Traffic Management." *Acta Astronautica* 223: 242–248. https://doi.org/10.1016/j.actaastro.2024.06.052.

Matte, N. M. 1987. "The Common Heritage of Mankind and Outer Space: Toward a New International Order for Survival." *Annuals of Air & Space Law* 12: 313–318.

Mattioli, M. 2012. "Communities of Innovation." *The Northwestern University Law Review* 106(1): 103–155.

McGinnis, M. D. 2011a. "Networks of Adjacent Action Situations in Polycentric Governance." *Policy Studies Journal* 39: 51–78. https://doi.org/10.1111/j.1541-0072.2010.00396.x.

McGinnis, M. D. 2011b. "An Introduction to IAD and the Language of the Ostrom Workshop: A Simple Guide to a Complex Framework." *The Policy Studies Journal* 39(1): 169–183.

McKean, M. A. 1986. Management of Traditional Common Lands (Iriaichi) in Japan. In *Proceedings of the Conference on Common Property Resource Management*, National Research Council, pp. 533–589. Washington, DC: National Academy Press.

McKean, M. A. 1992. "Success on the Commons: A Comparative Examination of Institutions for Common Property Resource Management." *Journal of Theoretical Politics* 4: 247–281. https://doi.org/10.1177/0951692892004003002.

McKenzie, J. 2017. "LoveLand's Labor's Lost: Detroit's Dubious Civic Tech Champions." *Civicist*. https://web.archive.org/web/20210512150307/https://civichall.org/civicist/lovelands-labors-lost-detroits-dubious-civic-tech-champions/.

McKnight, D. 2019. "A Practical Perspective on Space Traffic Management." *Journal of Space Safety Engineering* 6(2): 101–107. https://doi.org/10.1016/j.jsse.2019.03.001.

McManis, C. R., and J. L. Contreras. 2014. "Compulsory Licensing of Intellectual Property: A Viable Policy Lever for Promoting Access to Critical Technologies?" In *TRIPS and Developing Countries – Towards a New IP World Order?* edited by G. Ghidini, R. J. R. Peritz, and M. Ricolfi, 109–131. Cheltenham, UK: Edward Elgar.

Meidh Technologies. 2023a. "'Hu' Is the Common Language for ESG Impact." Hu Valuation Summit. www.hu2024dsm.com/about-the-hu.

Meidh Technologies. 2023b. "Know Instantly." trokt. www.trokt.com/.

Mekala, G. D., and D. H. MacDonald. 2018. "Lost in Transactions: Analysing the Institutional Arrangements Underpinning Urban Green Infrastructure." *Ecological Economics* 147: 399–409. https://doi.org/10.1016/j.ecolecon.2018.01.028.

Merton, R. K. 1974. *The Sociology of Science: Theoretical and Empirical Investigations.* Chicago: University of Chicago Press.

Mewburn Ellis. 2021. Green IP *Report* 2021.

Michigan Department of Environment, Great Lakes, and Energy. 2019. "Authorization to Discharge under the National Pollution Discharge Elimination System – City of Detroit Water and Sewerage Department and Great Lakes Water Authority."

Mill, J. S. 1986. *On Liberty (Great Books in Philosophy)*. New York: Prometheus Books.

Miller, C. A., and P. N. Edwards. 2001. "Introduction: The Globalization of Climate Science and Climate Politics." In *Changing the Atmosphere: Expert Knowledge and Environmental Governance*, edited by C. A. Miller and P. N. Edwards, 1–30. Cambridge, MA: MIT Press. https://doi.org/10.7551/mitpress/1789.003.0004.

Miller, D. J. and M. Dills. 2023. Green Tech and IP from Obama Through Biden: What's Next? Law360, December 7. www.law360.com/articles/1774122/print?section=compliance.

Mills-Novoa, M. 2023. "What Happens After Climate Change Adaptation Projects End? A Community-Based Approach to Ex-post Assessment of Adaptation Projects." *Global Environmental Change* 80: 102655.

Mindel, V., L. Mathiassen, and A. Rai. 2018. "The Sustainability of Polycentric Information Commons." *MIS Quarterly* 42(2): 607–631.

Ministry of Environment. 2021. "The National Climate Change Adaptation Plan of Jordan 2021." https://tinyurl.com/5b3as74h.

Ministry of Planning and International Cooperation (MOPIC). 2017. "Jordan Response Plan 2018–2020 for the Syria Crisis." https://tinyurl.com/4c7jhpf9.

MITRE Corporation, and Aspen Institute. 2022. The Space Imperative: A Whole-of-Nation Approach to a Sustainable, Secure, and Resilient Space Domain. November 21. www.aspeninstitute.org/publications/the-space-imperative-a-whole-of-nation-approach-to-a-sustainable-secure-and-resilient-space-domain/.

Monteiro, E., and E. Parmiggiani. 2019. "Synthetic Knowing: The Politics of the Internet of Things." *MIS Quarterly* 43(1): 167–184.

Moranta, S., T. Hrozensky, and M. Dvoracek. 2020. ESPI Report 71 – Towards a European Approach to Space Traffic Management – Full Report. European Space Policy Institute. January. www.espi.or.at/wp-content/uploads/2022/06/ESPI-Public-Report-71-Towards-a-European-Approach-to-Space-Traffic-Management-Full-Report.pdf.

Muelhaupt, T. J., M. E. Sorge, J. Morin, and R. S. Wilson. 2019. "Space Traffic Management in the New Space Era." *Journal of Space Safety Engineering* 6(2): 80–87.

Murtazashvili, I., J. B. Murtazashvili, M. B. H. Weiss, and M. J. Madison. 2022. "Blockchain Networks as Knowledge Commons." *International Journal of the Commons* 16(1): 108–119. https://doi.org/10.5334/ijc.1146.

National Research Council. 2009. *Urban Stormwater Management in the United States.* Washington, DC: National Academies Press. https://doi.org/10.17226/12465.

National Space Law. n.d. UNOOSA. www.unoosa.org/.

National Weather Service. n.d. "United States Flood Loss Report – Water Year 2014." www.weather.gov/media/water/WY14%20Flood%20Loss%20Summary.pdf.

ND-GAIN. 2020. Notre Dame Global Adaptation Initiative, Country Readiness Index. University of Notre Dame. https://gain-new.crc.nd.edu/ranking/readiness.

Nelson, R. R., and B. N. Sampat. 2001. "Making Sense of Institutions as a Factor Shaping Economic Performance." *Journal of Economic Behavior & Organization* 44(1): 31–54. https://doi.org/10.1016/S0167-2681(00)00152-9.

Nordman, E. E., E. Isely, P. Isely, and R. Denning. 2018. "Benefit-Cost Analysis of Stormwater Green Infrastructure Practices for Grand Rapids, Michigan, USA." *Journal of Cleaner Production* 200: 501–510. https://doi.org/10.1016/j.jclepro.2018.07.152.

North Sea Continental Shelf (Ger/Neth;Ger/Den), Judgment, 1969 I.C.J. 3. (February 20).

O'Reilly, J. L., M. Vardy, K. De Pryck, and M. D. S. Feital Benedetti. 2024. *Inside the IPCC: How Assessment Practices Shape Climate Knowledge*. 1st ed. Cambridge: Cambridge University Press. https://doi.org/10.1017/9781009559843.

OECD. 2008. *Handbook of Constructing Composite Indicators-Methodology and User Guide*. Paris: OECD.

Oltrogge, D., and E. Kerr. 2024. "Space Traffic Management: Data Fusion." *Acta Astronautica*. https://doi.org/10.1016/j.actaastro.2024.08.056.

Oltrogge, D. L., and I. A. Christensen. 2020. "Space Governance in the New Space Era." *Journal of Space Safety Engineering* 7(3): 432–438. https://doi.org/10.1016/j.jsse.2020.06.003.

Oltrogge, D., J. Chan, J. Cornelius, A. D'Uva, and R. Hall. 2024. "Deep Operator and SSA Collaboration for Space Sustainability." *Journal of Space Safety Engineering* 11(2): 342–361. https://doi.org/10.1016/j.jsse.2024.03.007.

Organisation for Economic Co-operation and Development (OECD). 2024. Space Economy Investment Trends: OECD Insights for Attracting High-Quality Funding [OECD Science, Technology and Industry Policy Papers No. 166]. OECD. April.

Ortega, A. A., L. Cesari, and J. Revill. 2023a. "Constant Vigilance? Verification and Monitoring for Space Security (Space Dossier 8)." UNDIR. https://tinyurl.com/3z95efwa.

Ortega, A. A., L. Cesari, and J. Revill. 2023b. *Space Dossier 8 – Constant Vigilance? Verification and Monitoring for Space Security*. United Nations Institute for Disarmament Research.

Ostrom, E. 1990. *Governing the Commons: The Evolution of Institutions for Collective Action*. Cambridge: Cambridge University Press. https://doi.org/10.1017/CBO9781316423936.

Ostrom, E. 1991. "Rational Choice Theory and Institutional Analysis: Toward Complementarity." *The American Political Science Review* 85(1): 237–243.

Ostrom, E. 1998. "A Behavioral Approach to the Rational Choice Theory of Collective Action: Presidential Address, American Political Science Association, 1997." *The American Political Science Review* 92(1): 1–22.

Ostrom, E. 1999. "Coping with Tragedies of the Commons." *Annual Review of Political Science* 2: 493. https://doi.org/10.1146/annurev.polisci.2.1.493.

Ostrom, E. 2000. "Collective Action and the Evolution of Social Norms." *Journal of Economic Perspectives* 14(3): 137–158. https://doi.org/10.1257/jep.14.3.137.

Ostrom, E. 2005. *Understanding Institutional Diversity*. Princeton, NJ: Princeton University Press. https://tinyurl.com/ycx6xj76.

Ostrom, E. 2007. "A Diagnostic Approach for Going Beyond Panaceas." *Proceedings of the National Academies of Science* 104: 15181.

Ostrom, E. 2009a. "A General Framework for Analyzing Sustainability of Socio-ecological Systems." *Science* 325(5939): 419–422.

Ostrom, E. 2009b. *Understanding Institutional Diversity*. Princeton, NJ: Princeton University Press.

Ostrom, E. 2010. "Beyond Markets and States: Polycentric Governance of Complex Economic Systems." *American Economic Review* 100(3): 641–672.

Ostrom, E., and C. Hess. 2006. "A Framework for Analyzing the Knowledge Commons." In *Understanding Knowledge as a Commons: From Theory to Practice*, edited by C. Hess and E. Ostrom, 41–82. Cambridge: Cambridge University Press.

Ostrom, E., G. Gardner, and J. Walker. 2006. *Rules, Games & Common-Pool Resources*. Ann Arbor, MI: University of Michigan Press.

Ostrom Workshop. n.d. "Governing the Management or Production of Knowledge Commons." https://tinyurl.com/5d26kx3m.

Ouellette, L. L. 2010. "Addressing the Green Patent Global Deadlock Through Bayh-Dole Reform." *The Yale Law Journal* 119: 1727–1738.

Outer Space Treaty, Article IX. 1967. UNOOSA. www.unoosa.org/oosa/en/ourwork/spacelaw/treaties/outerspacetreaty.html.

Outer Space Treaty, Article VII. 1967. UNOOSA. www.unoosa.org/oosa/en/ourwork/spacelaw/treaties/outerspacetreaty.html.

Pace, S. 2017. "Space Development, Law, and Values." IISL Galloway Space Law Symposium Lunch Keynote. December 13. https://spacepolicyonline.com/wp-content/uploads/2017/12/Scott-Pace-to-Galloway-FINAL.pdf?utm_content=buffer66778&utm_medium=social&utm_source=twitter.com&utm_campaign=buffer.

Parmiggiani, E., and M. Grisot. 2020. "Data Curation as Governance Practice." *Scandinavian Journal of Information Systems* 32(1): 1.

Parthasarathy, S., C. Avery, N. Hedberg, J. Mannisto, and M. Maguire. 2010. "A Public Good? Geoengineering and Intellectual Property." STPP Working Paper 10-1, June 2010.

Patriarca, R., F. Costantino, and G. D. Gravio. 2019. "Risk, Safety, Reliability and Satellites. Chronicles of a Fragmented Research Field." *Journal of Space Safety Engineering* 6(3): 201–211. https://doi.org/10.1016/j.jsse.2019.08.002.

Pearce, F. 2021. "Is the 'Legacy' Carbon Credit Market a Climate Plus or Just Hype?" YaleEnvironment360. March 9. https://tinyurl.com/e8bceeus.

Polanyi, M. 1962. "The Republic of Science: Its Political and Economic Theory." *Minerva* 1(1): 54–73.

Porras, D. 2019. *Eyes on the Sky: Rethinking Verification in Space*. Geneva: United Nations Institute for Disarmament Research.

Poteete, A., M. Jannsen, and E. Ostrom. 2010. *Working Together: Collective Action, the Commons and Multiple Methods in Practice*. Princeton, NJ: Princeton University Press.

Prairie Meadows. 2022. "2022 Community Betterment Grant Recipients." https://tinyurl.com/3jb3d4jx.

Price II, W. N., A. K. Rai, and T. Minssen. 2020. "Knowledge Transfer for Large-Scale Vaccine Manufacturing." *Science* 369(6506): 912.

Pultarova, T. 2024. "Starlink Close Encounters Decrease Despite Ever-Growing Number of Satellites." *Space.com*. January 15. www.space.com/spacex-starlink-collision-avoidance-maneuver-growth-stalls.

Rahal, S., and J. Grzelewski. 2021. "Whitmer Declares State of Emergency for Wayne County; Detroit Seeks Federal Assistance after Major Flooding." *The Detroit News*, June 26. https://tinyurl.com/5n8wc93y.

Ramani, A. 2023. "Stop Spending Money on Space Exploration." *The Perennial*, November 15. https://theperennial.org/2763/opinion/stop-spending-money-on-space-exploration/.

Rambaldi, G., R. Chambers, and J. Fox. 2006. Practical ethics for PGIS practitioners, facilitators, technology intermediaries and researchers (PLA 54). www.iied.org/g02957.

Reed, H., N. Dailey, R. Stilwell, and B. Weeden. 2022. "Decentralized Space Information Sharing as a Key Enabler of Trust and The Preservation of Space." AMOS Technical Papers. https://amostech.com/TechnicalPapers/2021/Poster/Reed.pdf.

Reichman, J. H., A. K. Rai, R. G. Newell, and J. B. Weiner. 2008. "Intellectual Property and Alternatives: Strategies for Green Innovation." Chatham House – Energy, Environment and Development Programme Paper: 08/03.

Renault, C., P. Charon, and F. Laurençon. 2022. "Renseigner Autrement? Trajectoires de l'Osint Dans les Services de Renseignement." *Hérodote* 186(3): 19–30. https://doi.org/10.3917/her.186.0019.

Resolution 40. n.d. WMO. https://community.wmo.int/en/resolution-40.

Reynolds, J. L., J. L. Contreras, and J. D. Sarnoff. 2017. "Solar Climate Engineering and Intellectual Property: Toward a Research Commons." *The Minnesota Journal of Law, Science & Technology* 18(1): 1–110.

Rodrigues Pinho, R. and R. Oliviera. 2024. "Green Patents: encouraging sustainable innovation in Brazil." Kluwer Patent Blog, April 15, https://patentblog.kluweriplaw.com/2024/04/15/green-patents-encouraging-sustainable-innovation-in-brazil/.

Rose, G. 1997. "Situating Knowledges: Positionality, Reflexivities, and Other Tactics." *Progress in Human Geography* 21(3): 305–320.

Rozas, D., A. Tenorio-Fornés, S. Díaz-Molina and S. Hassan. 2021. "When Ostrom Meets Blockchain: Exploring the Potentials of Blockchain for Commons Governance." *SAGE Open* 11: 1.

Rozenberg, J., and M. Fay. 2019. *Beyond the Gap: How Countries Can Afford the Infrastructure They Need While Protecting the Planet.* Washington, DC: World Bank Publications.

Runyon, N. 2022. "Are Allegations of Greenwashing Part of ESG Fraud? It Depends on Whom You Ask." Thomson Reuters. September 12. https://tinyurl.com/4f6a5yk2.

Russell, A. L. 2006. "'Rough Consensus and Running Code' and the Internet-OSI Standards War." *IEEE Annals of the History of Computing* 28(3): 48–61. https://doi.org/10.1109/MAHC.2006.42.

Sampson, N., J. White-Newsome, C. Gronlund, E. Leaphart, C. Miller, J. Steis Thorsby, P. Larson, M. Jackson, R. Ackerman, R. Washington, and L. Thompson. 2021. "Household Flooding in Detroit: A Snapshot of Citywide Experiences, Implications for Public Health, and Potential Solutions." https://drive.google.com/file/d/1TRtT29Hvq8kOz_pPhlEWLPtzGaHhFGZB/view.

Sampson, N. R., C. E. Price, J. Kassem, J. Doan, and J. Hussein. 2019. "'We're Just Sitting Ducks': Recurrent Household Flooding as An Underreported Environmental Health Threat in Detroit's Changing Climate." *International Journal of Environmental Research and Public Health* 16(1): 6. https://doi.org/10.3390/ijerph16010006.

Sanfilippo, M. R., and B. M. Frischmann. 2023. "A Proposal for Principled Decision-Making: Beyond Design Principles." In *Governing Smart Cities as Knowledge Commons*, edited by B. M. Frischmann, M. J. Madison, and M. R. Sanfilippo, 295–308. Cambridge: Cambridge University Press. https://tinyurl.com/zwxsd4er.

Sanguir, A. M. 2023a. "Public and Private Initiatives to Accelerate The Development And Diffusion Of Green Tech – Part I." *Les Nouvelles* 58(3): 212–225.

Sanguir, A. M. 2023b. "Public and Private Initiatives To Accelerate The Development And Diffusion Of Green Tech – Part II." *Les Nouvelles* 58(4): 266–272.

Sankar, S., C. Dohrman, and M. Zimmerman. 2024. "The Military's Insistence on Owning Commercial Intellectual Property is Limiting Innovation." War on the Rocks.

January 4. https://warontherocks.com/2024/01/the-militarys-insistence-on-owning-commercial-intellectual-property-is-limiting-innovation/.

Sarnoff, J. D. 2011. "The Patent System and Climate Change." *The Virginia Journal of Law and Technology* 16(2): 301.

Sarnoff, J. D. 2013. "Government Choices in Innovation Funding (With Reference to Climate Change)." *Emory Law Journal* 62: 1087–1157.

SatNews. 2022. "Maxar Continues to Capture Satellite Imagery of The Russian-Ukraine Invasion." March 21. https://news.satnews.com/2022/03/21/maxars-satellite-imagery-captures-continue-of-the-russian-ukraine-invasion/.

Sato, K., Y. Yoshimura, T. Hanada, T. Izumiyama, and R. Shinohara. 2021. "The Collision Avoidance Strategy for Geostationary Satellites Considering Orbit Maintenance." *ScienceDirect* 4: 331–338. https://doi.org/10.1016/j.jsse.2021.08.004.

Scassa, T. 2020. "Designing Data Governance for Data Sharing: Lessons from Sidewalk Toronto." Technology & Regulation (Special Issue: Governing Data as a Resource), 44–56. https://tinyurl.com/3xa55hfb.

Schelling, T. C. 1960. *The Strategy of Conflict*. Cambridge, MA: Harvard University Press.

Schmalensee, R., and R. N. Stavins. 2015. "Lessons Learned from Three Decades of Experience with Cap-and-Trade." Resources for the Future, RFF DP 15-51, November. https://media.rff.org/archive/files/document/file/RFF-DP-15-51.pdf.

Searle, J. R. 1990. "The Storm over the University." *The New York Review of Books* 37(19): 34.

Secretary-General's Data Strategy. n.d. UN Secretary-General. www.un.org/en/content/datastrategy/.

Seeds, M. 2024. "The Balance of Protecting IP and Data Rights." *National Defense Magazine*. October 4. www.nationaldefensemagazine.org/articles/2024/10/4/policy-points-the-balance-of-protecting-ip-and-data-rights.

Seymour, S. B. 2010. "The Teaching Function of Patents." *Notre Dame Law Review* 85(2): 621–669.

Shackley, S. 1997. "The Intergovernmental Panel on Climate Change: Consensual Knowledge and Global Politics." *Global Environmental Change* 7(1): 77–79. https://doi.org/10.1016/S0959-3780(96)00035-0.

Shackley, S., and T. Skodvin. 1995. "IPCC Gazing and the Interpretative Social Sciences." *Global Environmental Change* 5(3): 175–180. https://doi.org/10.1016/0959-3780(95)00021-F.

Sharmina, M., D. Ghanem, A. Browne, S. Hall, J. Mylan, S. Petrova, and R. Wood. 2019. "Envisioning Surprises: How Social Sciences Could Help Models Represent 'Deep Uncertainty' in Future Energy and Water Demand." *Energy Research & Social Science* 50: 18–28.

Shoup, J. A. 2007. *Culture and Customs of Jordan*. Westport, CT: Greenwood Press.

Siemons, J. 2023. "Climate Mitigation Patent Program Boosts Green Tech Financing." Bloomberg Law, August 8, https://news.bloomberglaw.com/ip-law/climate-mitigation-patent-program-boosts-green-tech-financing.

Silverstein, B. 2023. "Promoting International Cooperation to Avoid Collisions between Satellites." Carnegie Endowment for International Peace. https://carnegieendowment.org/research/2023/09/promoting-international-cooperation-to-avoid-collisions-between-satellites?lang=en

Smolla, R. A. 1992. *Free Speech in an Open Society*. New York: Knopf.

Snow, C. P. 1959. *The Two Cultures and the Scientific Revolution*. London: Cambridge University Press. https://doi.org/10.1017/CBO9781139196949.

Sovacool, B. K. 2008. "Placing a Glove on the Invisible Hand: How Intellectual Property Rights May Impede Innovation in Energy Research and Development (R&D)." *The Albany Law Journal of Science and Technology* 18(2): 381–440.

Space Data Association. 2024. "Data Sharing: Risk vs Reward for Space Sustainability." Blog. www.space-data.org/sda/blog/data-risk/.

Star, S. L., and J. R. Griesemer. 1989. "Institutional Ecology, 'Translations' and Boundary Objects: Amateurs and Professionals in Berkeley's Museum of Vertebrate Zoology, 1907–39." *Social Studies of Science* 19(3): 387–420. www.jstor.org/stable/285080.

Statute of the International Court of Justice art 38(1), June 26, 1945, 15 U.S.T. 2494, 33 U.N.T.S. 993.

Stauch, J., T. Bessel, M. Rutten, J. Baldwin, M. Jah, and K. Holl. 2016. "Mutual Application of Joint Probabilistic Data Association, Filtering, and Smoothing Techniques for Robust Multiple Space Object Tracking." *AIAA Journal of Guidance, Control, and Dynamics* (Special Issue on Space Domain Awareness). https://arc.aiaa.org/doi/10.2514/6.2014-4365.

Stavins, R. N. 1988. Project 88 – Harnessing Market Forces to Protect Our Environment: Initiatives for the New President. Sponsored by Senator Timothy E. Wirth, Colorado, and Senator John Heinz, Pennsylvania. Washington, DC.

Stern, P. C. 2011. "Design Principles for Global Commons: Natural Resources and Emerging Technologies." *International Journal of the Commons* 5(2): 213–232. www.thecommons journal.org/articles/10.18352/ijc.305/.

Stevenson, J., and P. Vlek. 2018. Assessing the Adoption and Diffusion of Natural Resource Management Practices: Synthesis of a New Set of Empirical Studies. CGIAR Standing Panel on Impact Assessment Synthesis Report.

Stewart, J. 2020. "Prairie Meadows Gives Back with $2,000,000 in Community Support Contributions in 2020." *DSM USA*, December 17. https://tinyurl.com/39rshtnr.

Stickings, A. 2019. *The Future of EU-US Cooperation in Space Traffic Management and Space Situational Awareness*. www.chathamhouse.org/2019/08/future-eu-us-cooperation-space-traffic-management-and-space-situational-awareness.

Stoker, G., and M. Evans. 2016. *Evidence-based Policy Making in the Social Sciences: Methods That Matter*. Bristol: Policy Press.

Strandburg, K. J., B. M. Frischmann, and M. J. Madison. 2017. "The Knowledge Commons Framework." In *Governing Medical Knowledge Commons* edited by K. J. Strandburg, B. M. Frischmann, & M. J. Madison, 9–18. Cambridge: Cambridge University Press.

Sudmanns, M., D. Tiede, S. Lang, H. Bergstedt, G. Trost, H. Augustin, A. Baraldi and T. Blaschke. 2020. "Big Earth Data: Disruptive Changes in Earth Observation Data Management and Analysis?" *International Journal of Digital Earth* 13: 832–850.

Ta, L. 2022. "Des Moines Food Rescue Group Says United Way Unfairly Pulled $50k in Funding." AXIOS Des Moines. July 21. https://tinyurl.com/4nfvry8y.

Tarko, Vlad. 2016. *Elinor Ostrom: An Intellectual Biography*. Lanham, MD: Rowman & Littlefield International.

Te Hiku Media. n.d. "Data Sovereignty and the Kaitiakitanga License." https://tinyurl.com/mszzrewn.

Te Mana Raraunga. n.d. Our Data, Our Sovereignty, Our Future. www.temanararaunga .maori.nz/.

Tee, W.-S., L. Chin, and A. S. Abdul-Rahim. 2021. "Determinants of Renewable Energy Production: Do Intellectual Property Rights Matter?" *Energies* 14(5707): 1–15.

Temple, K., and J. D. Caytas, eds. 2003. *The Cambridge Handbook of Law and Policy for NFTs*. Cambridge: Cambridge University Press. https://tinyurl.com/mr2n4vjb.

The 17 Goals. n.d. U.N. https://sdgs.un.org/goals.

The Earth Observations Toolkit for Sustainable Cities and Human Settlements. n.d. UN-HABITAT. https://eotoolkit.unhabitat.org.

The Hashemite Fund for Development of Jordan Badia. 2023. "Jordan Badia." www .badiafund.gov.jo/en/node/317.

The Intergovernmental Panel on Climate Change. n.d. The Intergovernmental Panel on Climate Change. www.ipcc.ch.

The International Charter Space and Major Disasters. n.d. The International Charter Space and Major Disasters. https://disasterscharter.org/web/guest/home.

The World Bank. 2022. *Country Climate and Development Report: Jordan*. Washington, DC: World Bank. https://tinyurl.com/yc88rs2r.

Thiel, A., W. Blomquist, and D. Garrick, eds. 2019. *Governing Complexity*. New York: Cambridge University Press. chapter 1, 21–44.

Thorsby, J. S., C. J. Miller, and L. Treemore-Spears. 2020. "The Role of Green Stormwater Infrastructure in Flood Mitigation (Detroit, MI USA) – Case Study." *Urban Water Journal* 17(9): 838–846. https://doi.org/10.1080/1573062X.2020.1823429.

Treaty on Principles Governing the Activities of States in the Exploration and Use of Outer Space, Including the Moon and Other Celestial Bodies, January 26, 1967, 18 U.S.T. 2410, 610 U.N.T.S. 205.

Tur-Sinai, O. 2018. "Patents and Climate Change: A Skeptic's View." *Environmental Law* 48: 211–261.

Turral, H., and M. Kurian. 2010. "Information's Role in Adaptive Groundwater Management." In *Peri-urban Water and Sanitation Services: Policy, Planning and Method*, edited by Kurian and McCarney, 171–192. Dordrecht: Springer.

United Nations. 1975. Convention on Registration of Objects Launched into Outer Space (Registration Convention), General Assembly Resolution 3235 (XXIX), opened for signature January 14, 1975, entered into force September 15, 1976. United Nations Treaty Series.

United Nations. 2007. "What Is UN-SPIDER." January 15. G.A. Res 61/110. www.un-spider.org/about/what-is-un-spider.

United Nations. March 2023. Concept Paper on Interactive Dialogue 3: Water for Climate, Resilience and Environment. United Nations Conference on the Midterm Comprehensive Review of the Implementation of the Objectives of the International Decade of Action. "Water for Sustainable Development," 22–24. New York, 2018–2023.

United Nations. n.d. United Nations Environment Programme Organizational Chart. https://wedocs.unep.org/bitstream/handle/20.500.11822/35352/UNEPOrg.pdf?sequence=4&isAllowed=y.

United Nations Committee on the Peaceful Uses of Outer Space (UN COPUOS). 2019. *Guidelines for the Long-Term Sustainability of Outer Space Activities of the Committee on the Peaceful Uses of Outer Space* [Report No. A/74/20, Annex II]. United Nations, August 20.

United Nations Committee on the Peaceful Uses of Outer Space (UN COPUOS). 2021. *Proposal on the Mandate, Terms of Reference and Method of Work of the Working Group on Potential Legal Models for Space Resource Activities* [Working Paper No. A/AC.105/L.326]. United Nations, August 18.

United Nations Development Programme (UNDP) Pacific Office. 2020. "Using Satellite Imagery to Support Civil and Electoral Registries Validation." October 21. www.undp.org/pacific/press-releases/using-satellite-imagery-support-civil-and-electoral-registries-validation.

United Nations Framework Convention on Climate Change (UNFCC). 2021. *First Report on the Determination of Needs of Developing Country Parties Related to the Implementation of the Paris Agreement*. Bonn: Standing Committee on Finance, United Nations Framework Convention on Climate Change.

United Nations Framework Convention on Climate Change, May 9, 1992, 1771 U.N.T.S. 107.

United Nations Geospatial. n.d. UN Geospatial. www.un.org/geospatial/about.

United Nations General Assembly. 1963. *Declaration of Legal Principles Governing the Activities of States in the Exploration and Use of Outer Space*. G.A. Res. 1962 (XVIII). December 13.

United Nations General Assembly. 1986. *Principles Relating to Remote Sensing of the Earth from Outer Space*. G.A. Res. 41/64. December. [Remote Sensing Principles].

United Nations Global Pulse. n.d. UN Global Pulse. www.unglobalpulse.org.

United Nations Global Service Centre. n.d. United Nations Global Service Centre. www.ungsc.org/home.

United Nations Institute for Disarmament Research (UNIDIR). 2022. Threats to the security of space activities and systems. https://documents.unoda.org/wp-content/uploads/2022/08/20220817_A_AC294_2022_WP16_E_UNIDIR.pdf.

United Nations Institute for Training and Research (UNITAR). 2019. "How UNOSAT Rapid Mapping Service Contributed to Humanitarian Response to Natural Disasters in 2018." March. www.unitar.org/about/news-stories/news/how-unosat-rapid-mapping-service-contributed-humanitarian-response-naturaldisasters-2018.

United Nations Institute for Training and Research (UNITAR). 2022. "UNOSAT Collaborates with Nvidia on AI for SDGs Mapping." June 16. https://unitar.org/about/news-stories/news/unosat-collaborates-nvidia-ai-sdgs-mapping.

United Nations Office for Outer Space Affairs (UNOOSA). 2024. Registration submissions update, United Nations register of objects launched into outer space. www.unoosa.org/oosa/en/spaceobjectregister/index.html.

United Nations Office on Drugs and Crime. n.d. United Nations Office on Drugs and Crime. www.unodc.org.

United Nations Office of Information and Communications Technology. n.d. About OICT. https://unite.un.org/about.

United Nations Satellite Centre. n.d. UN Satellite Centre. https://unosat.org.

United Nations Secretary. n.d. *Data Strategy Overview*. www.un.org/en/content/datastrategy/images/pdf/UN_SG_Data-Strategy-one-pager.pdf.

United States Environmental Protection Agency. 2015a. "Basic Information about Nonpoint Source (NPS) Pollution." Overviews and Factsheets. September 15. www.epa.gov/nps/basic-information-about-nonpoint-source-nps-pollution.

United States Environmental Protection Agency. 2015b. "Soak Up the Rain." Collections and Lists. May 26. www.epa.gov/soakuptherain.

United States Environmental Protection Agency. 2019. "Detroit River AOC." Collections and Lists. New York, Great Lakes. August 27. www.epa.gov/great-lakes-aocs/detroit-river-aoc.

United States Environmental Protection Agency. 2020. "NPDES State Program Authority." Overviews and Factsheets. July 31. www.epa.gov/npdes/npdes-state-program-authority.

United Way of Central Iowa. 2023. "LIVE UNITED 2023." YouTube, May 10. https://youtu.be/x02m2WQQDyo?si=yuWKnJd32mYp2eYs&t=605.

US Energy Information Administration. 2024. "Carbon Dioxide Emissions Coefficients." U.S. Energy Information Administration. September 18. www.eia.gov/environment/emissions/co2_vol_mass.php.

US Environmental Protection Agency. 2020. "Is there uncertainty associated with the ENERGY STAR score?" Energy Star. September 15. https://energystar.my.site.com/PortfolioManager/s/article/Is-there-uncertainty-associated-with-the-ENERGY-STAR-score-1600088552462.

US Environmental Protection Agency. 2023a. "ENERGY STAR Impacts." Energy Star. www.energystar.gov/about/impacts#:~:text=Over%2520840%2520utilities%252C%2520plus%2520state,of%2520ENERGY%2520STAR%2520certified%2520products.

US Environmental Protection Agency. 2023b. "Facts and Stats." Energy Star. www.energystar.gov/buildings/about-us/facts-and-stats.

US Environmental Protection Agency. 2023c. "Nitrogen and Phosphorus Loads in Large Rivers." United States Environmental Protection Agency. https://cfpub.epa.gov/roe/indicator.cfm?i=33#1.

USEPA. August 2021. *Development of a Cumulative Resilience Screening Index for Natural Hazards: An Assessment of Resilience to Acute Meteorological Events and Selected Natural Hazards*. Florida: United States Environmental Protection Agency, Office of Research and Development, Centre for Environmental Measurement and Modelling.

US Securities and Exchange Commission. 2024a. "SEC Adopts Rules to Enhance and Standardize Climate-Related Disclosures for Investors." U.S. Securities and Exchange Commission. March 6. www.sec.gov/news/press-release/2024-31.

US Securities and Exchange Commission. 2024b. Enhancement and Standardization of Climate-Related Disclosures for Investors. Final Rule, Release No. 33-11275; File No. S7-12-22, effective March 28, 2024. www.sec.gov/files/rules/final/2024/33-11275.pdf.

Van House, N. A., M. H. Butler, and L. R. Schiff. 1998. "Cooperative Knowledge Work and Practices of Trust: Sharing Environmental Planning Data Sets." In *Proceedings of the 1998 ACM Conference on CSCW*, Seattle, WA, USA, November 14–18, 335–343. New York: ACM. https://dl.acm.org/doi/pdf/10.1145/289444.289508.

Vandenberg, J. 2015. "Using Patents to Curtail Climate Change: A Proposal." *Law360*, February 23.

Vienna Convention on the Law of Treaties, May 22, 1969, 1155 U.N.T.S. 331.

Vinsel, L. "How to Be a Better Reactionary: Time and Knowledge in Technology Regulation." *STS News, Medium*. Oct 17, 2023 https://sts-news.medium.com/how-to-be-a-better-reactionary-1630b5098fbc

Voida, A., L. Dombrowski, G. Hayes, and M. Mazmanian. 2014. "Shared Values/Conflicting Logics: Working Around E-Government Systems." In *Proceedings of the SIGCHI Conference on Human Factors in Computing Systems*, Toronto, Ontario, Canada, April 26–May 1, 3583–3592. Toronto, ON: CHI. http://doi.org/10.1145/2556288.2556971.

Wang, B., S. Li, J. Mu, X. Hao, W. Zhu, and J. Hu. 2022. "Research Advancements in Key Technologies for Space-Based Situational Awareness." *Space: Science & Technology*. https://doi.org/10.34133/2022/9802793.

Waters, D., W. E. Watt, J. Marsalek, and B. C. Anderson. 2003. "Adaptation of a Storm Drainage System to Accommodate Increased Rainfall Resulting from Climate Change." *Journal of Environmental Planning and Management* 46(5): 755–770. https://doi.org/10.1080/0964056032000138472.

Webber, J. L., T. D. Fletcher, L. Cunningham, G. Fu, D. Butler, and M. J. Burns. 2020. "Is Green Infrastructure a Viable Strategy for Managing Urban Surface Water Flooding?" *Urban Water Journal* 17(7): 598–608. https://doi.org/10.1080/1573062X.2019.1700286.

Weeden, B., P. Cefola, and J. Sankaran. 2010. "Global Space Situational Awareness Sensors." Advanced Maui Optical and Space Surveillance Technologies Conference (AMOS), Technical Papers.

Wellington, H. H. 1979. "On Freedom of Expression." *Yale Law Journal* 88: 1105–1142.

Wellmon, C. 2016. *Organizing Enlightenment: Information Overload and the Invention of the Modern Research University*. Baltimore, MD: Johns Hopkins University Press.

Wenger, E. 2010. "Communities of Practice and Social Learning Systems: The Career of a Concept." In *Social Learning Systems and Communities of Practice*, edited by C. Blackmore, 179–198. London: Springer. https://doi.org/10.1007/978-1-84996-133-2_11.

West, J. 2023. "Missed Opportunity to Curb Security Threats in Space Leaves All More Vulnerable." Centre for International Governance Innovation. September 29. www.cigionline.org/articles/missed-opportunity-to-curb-security-threats-in-space-leaves-all-more-vulnerable/.

White House. 2022. Fact sheet: First National Cislunar Science & Technology Strategy, November 17. https://tinyurl.com/yvr7y7vw.

WHO GIS Centre for Health. n.d. WHO. www.who.int/data/GIS.

Wilkinson, M., M. Dumontier, I. J. Aalbersberg, et al. 2016. "The FAIR Guiding Principles for Scientific Data Management and Stewardship." *Scientific Data* 3: 160018. https://doi.org/10.1038/sdata.2016.18.

WMO. n.d. *Exchanging Meteorological Data: Guidelines on Relationships in Commercial Meteorological Activities WMO Policy and Practice No. 837*. https://library.wmo.int/viewer/55151/download?file=wmo_837_en.pdf&type=pdf&navigator=1.

Wolff, R. P., B. Moore, Jr., and H. Marcuse. 1969. "Repressive Tolerance (full text)." Herbert Marcuse Publications. www.marcuse.org/herbert/publications/1960s/1965-repressive-tolerance-fulltext.html.

World Bank. 2022. *Country Climate and Development Report: Jordan*. Washington, DC: World Bank. https://tinyurl.com/yc88rs2r.

World Bank Group. 2016, March 22. *Transforming Jordan's Badia Deserts into "Ecosystems of Opportunity."* Washington, DC: World Bank. https://tinyurl.com/yy6uwjuc.

World Economic Forum. 2021. "Space Junk: What It Is and Why Cleaning It Up Matters." Emerging Technologies. May 20. www.weforum.org/stories/2021/05/space-junk-clean-satellite/.

World Resources Institute. 1992. The AES Corporation (B). http://pdf.wri.org/bell/case_1-56973-123-3_full_version_b_english.pdf.

Xiang, J. Y. 2019. "IPR Management in International Cleantech Cooperation." *Georgetown Environmental Law Review* 32: 1.

Zannoni, D. 2019. *Disaster Management and International Space Law*. Leiden: Brill Nijhoff.

Zillman, J. W. 2007. "Some Observations on the IPCC Assessment Process 1988–2007." *Energy & Environment* 18(7/8): 869–891.

Zimmerman, K. 2022. "Meals from the Heartland Announces another Successful Hunger Fight." DSM USA, September 27. https://tinyurl.com/bdd43bp9.

Index

Page numbers followed "n" denote footnotes. Page numbers in italics refers to figures/tables.